When Children
Love to Learn

When Children Love to Learn

A PRACTICAL APPLICATION OF

Charlotte Mason's Philosophy for Today

ELAINE COOPER

GENERAL EDITOR

CROSSWAY BOOKS

A DIVISION OF
GOOD NEWS PUBLISHERS
WHEATON, ILLINOIS

72381775

When Children Love to Learn

Copyright © 2004 by Child Light Educational Trust

Published by Crossway Books
             a division of Good News Publishers
             1300 Crescent Street
             Wheaton, Illinois 60187

Cover design: David LaPlaca

Cover photo: Getty Images

First printing 2004

Printed in the United States of America

Unless otherwise designated, Scripture verses are taken from the King James Version of the Bible.

Library of Congress Cataloging-in-Publication Data
When children love to learn : a practical application of Charlotte Mason's philosophy for today / Elaine Cooper, general editor.
    p. cm.
  Includes bibliographical references.
  ISBN 1-58134-259-4 (trade pbk. : alk. paper)
    1. Mason, Charlotte M. (Charlotte Maria), 1842-1923. 2. Education—Philosophy. 3. Education—Curricula. I. Cooper, Elaine, 1947-
LB775.M362W44   2004
370'.1—dc22   2003022313

BP		14	13	12	11	10	09	08	07	06	05	04
15	14	13	12	11	10	9	8	7	6	5	4	3	2	1

Contents

The Contributors

Susan Schaeffer Macaulay grew up in Switzerland at L'Abri Fellowship, which was founded by her parents, Francis and Edith Schaeffer. She and her husband, Ranald, have led the work of L'Abri in England over the years and are vitally involved with educational issues.

Jack Beckman (M. Ed., M.Phil., Ph.D.) has recently completed his doctorate in education at Cambridge University, England, where he concentrated on Charlotte Mason's educational principles and practice. He is particularly interested in her work as applied in the preparation of teachers and is currently a member of the education faculty at Covenant College, Lookout Mountain, Georgia. He is also on the board of Charlotte Mason Schools International.

Maryellen St. Cyr (M. Ed.) has many years of experience as a classroom teacher in both primary and middle schools. She has worked as a curriculum director and a principal of elementary schools. Currently she is Director of Charlotte Mason Schools International (CMSI), a nonprofit organization established to help teachers, parents, and schools develop a Charlotte Mason education.

Bobby Scott (M. Ed. in School Administration and M. Ed. in Counseling) is experienced in teaching both high and middle schools. He is at present principal of Perimeter Christian School, a large private school in Atlanta. He has been pivotal in bringing Charlotte Mason's ideas into the American educational scene and has helped start schools. Mr. Scott established the Charlotte Mason Institute which, now under CMSI, serves an increasing network of schools interested in the ideas and application of Charlotte Mason's educational philosophy.

Elaine Cooper runs Child Light Educational Trust in England together with Susan Macaulay. Mrs. Cooper is married, with three teenage children, and is involved in education as a concerned layperson.

Foreword

Following the success and ever widening readership of Susan Schaeffer Macaulay's book *For the Children's Sake*, the number of requests for help and guidance has increased from parents and teachers seeking a deeper understanding of educator Charlotte Mason's philosophy and teaching methods.

It is so encouraging to know that many good teachers will be helping to take this philosophy on into this century, therefore enabling many children to have the wonderful start in life of a good Christian education, with a broad curriculum, adapting it to modern needs but not forgetting the lasting values in life—appreciation of good literature and the arts, awareness of the environment, and love for God's world.

Realizing the need to train and help students understand her philosophy and teaching methods, Charlotte Mason (1842–1923) set up a "House of Education" (later named Charlotte Mason College). I was fortunate enough to spend three years at the college, albeit nearly thirty years after the death of Charlotte Mason, but we were given a thorough understanding of the philosophy by reading (and narrating) her educational books. The spirit of Charlotte Mason lived on in her college. It was always a small college where each individual was an important person. Many of the lecturers had been trained at the college, and there were still people around who had known Charlotte Mason.

It is sad that in England the many small PNEU schools (Parents' National Education Union schools started by Miss Mason) have disappeared, but Charlotte Mason was forward thinking and would have wanted us to advance thoughtfully with our times. I am sure she would have been glad that our national curriculum advocates the reading of good literature, including Shakespeare, the study of great artists and musicians, and developing an awareness of the environment. So although teachers are not necessarily aware of Charlotte Mason, her influence continues in many good schools in England.

In many ways during the last few years I have been the link between the past and the future in Charlotte Mason circles. My connections with Miss Mason started when I was five years old and my parents sent me to a small PNEU school within walking distance of home. I spent three years at this school, and a very happy time it was, learning so many things that have remained with me for life. I learned basic reading, writing, and mathematics in a painless and enjoyable way, but more important to me were the lovely afternoon nature walks with the Head Teacher or her assistant, both of whom had been students of Charlotte Mason. My other great joy was the careful study of the pictures of a different artist each term. Of course education must be shared between home *and* school; so equally memorable are the visits to London with my mother to seek out the original pictures of the artist that I had been studying. These pictures have remained lasting "friends" to me when I visit the National Gallery or other galleries. Equally important were the weekend trips into the country, my father and I sharing an interest in butterflies, caterpillars, and wildflowers. My Nature Note Book, which I still keep, brings back many special memories.

When I left school, I wanted to become a teacher; so at eighteen I started my three-year training at Charlotte Mason College. When I finished my course, I taught in three different PNEU schools, gaining valuable experience. Then in 1963 I was asked to apply for the job of Head Teacher of a PNEU school near Windsor. I remained in that position for twenty-eight years, a wonderfully rewarding and challenging time, seeing the school grow and develop. I always regarded the school as my "family," and I am still in touch with many of my former students and teachers.

Many of the PNEU schools started in a very small way, being almost a home schoolroom. Eton End was just one of these. My predecessor (also a Charlotte Mason teacher) had been asked in 1936 to start a school for the children of the teachers at Eton College. During the first two years the school was in a room of the vicarage in Eton. Then Miss Johnstone (the Head Teacher) and her mother were able to buy a Victorian house just a mile away. This was their home as well as their school. The school is still on this site, buildings have been added, and an adjoining field has been bought; so there is still plenty of space for all forms of games as well as wild space for nature walks.

When Miss Johnstone retired in 1963, I followed her as Head Teacher. I always employed good, well-qualified teachers (Charlotte Mason trained teachers were not available), but when I confronted them with the curriculum, they were amazed at the amount that the children would be learning and the breadth of the subjects. They were afraid they would not be able to cope, but they soon saw the "feast" laid before the children and themselves and were grateful for the stimulation of so many interesting subjects.

In 1991 I retired from Eton End myself, but I still visit the school regularly, by invitation. Recently at the end of school year assembly, I was pleased to hear my successor in her words of advice to the graduating girls use the words of the school motto, the motto that Charlotte Mason gave to all PNEU schools: "I am, I can, I ought, I will."

During my last term at Eton End, I had a visitor to the school—Mrs. Rosemary Moore from South Carolina. She was in England visiting schools, having read Charlotte Mason's books. When she realized I was retiring, she asked if I would visit the United States, as she was hoping to set up a Charlotte Mason school, and perhaps I could help and advise her. This was a very busy time for me, and I agreed with her suggestion without giving it much thought. But Rosemary persevered, and in October 1992 I visited America for the first time. I spent three weeks there, and it was exciting to be involved in the birth of a new school. I had thought my teaching career was over, little realizing what my American trip would lead to! My annual trips have been exciting and rewarding times, visiting a number of schools that are basing their work on Charlotte Mason's ideas, spending about a week in each, mainly giving demonstration lessons and talking with teachers and parents. But my main role is to give help and encouragement.

I can talk with experience and confidence, making people realize that Charlotte Mason's philosophy really is right for the present time and for the future. I have had so many children passing through my classrooms. I continue to hear news of many of them, all leading interesting and worthwhile lives. They are all so grateful for the broad education they received—within a caring atmosphere where each child was respected as an interesting individual. I did not just educate the elite or gifted; we had a wide range of ability, but *all* students achieved and felt good at their own level. I have met many parents and teachers who have made a brave decision to opt out of public education, having the conviction that this is right for the children. I can assure you that it will be rewarding.

I am sure that this book will be a help and encouragement to many teachers and parents who are seeking further guidance. It is Charlotte Mason's deep Christian convictions and her real understanding of children that make her philosophy so right for the twenty-first century as well as for her own times. This is not a rigid form of education but one conveying enduring values and knowledge.

EVE E. ANDERSON, *former Headmistress*
Eton End, Old Windsor, England, 1998

Preface

By Elaine Cooper, General Editor

At first glance, the reader may feel somewhat overwhelmed at the task of foraging through this tome. We prefer to think we have been thorough in our treatment of the subject at hand. Some or many of the ideas in this philosophy of education may be new to you. It is our purpose to present a fresh way of thinking about the parent and child, the home and school, the learner and the teacher. Many who read Susan Schaeffer Macaulay's book *For the Children's Sake* were moved to write asking for ways of implementing the vigorous ideas presented in that little classic. Their main questions were:

"What does a Charlotte Mason education look like in *this* century?"

"What in the world was the PNEU?"[1]

"How can I be sure my child is *really* learning when there is such an emphasis on reading 'living books'?"

"And in any case, what *are* 'living books'?"

"What about the three R's?"

Several of us have come together to try to offer some answers to these questions. Three of the major contributors bring years of experience in the classroom. All three have been principals of schools. As a result the guide will reflect their particular perspectives on their calling as educators. We offer *no technique*, but rather the simple proposition that children are best educated through careful relationships on the part of the adults—the parents and teachers—who are themselves in a lifelong process of learning and subject to the same duties and freedoms within a Christian worldview. Beyond that, each parent, teacher, or school needs to make thoughtful application of the many ideas presented in the following pages to the specific concerns and goals particular to their situations. In this guide are many practical suggestions and resources from which to choose.

We would like to draw attention to several historical observations that shape the context of this book. The first is that great educators of the past have often made strikingly similar observations about children, the way they behave and learn. So any current and serious approach to education falls within a long tradition of prior thinking, questioning, and practice. We also know, however, that the great ancient, literate civilizations of the past, both Western and Eastern, educated only a small elite of their populations to function as priests/scribes, tax collectors, and lawyers—that is, those who would communicate and perpetuate the religions, cultures, and economies within which they lived.

Secondly, as we look back to the classical period, we notice that while the Greeks and Romans contributed vital insights and asked profound questions regarding the nature of man,[2] the purpose of education and law, the best organization of society, and the role of aesthetics in personal and civic life, teachers were not conferred with any social status, and their character or reputation was of no great consequence in the education of Greek children. The Romans, however, were distinct in their emphasis on virtue in both private and public behavior. They strongly emphasized the importance of nurturing virtue within family life. However, both societies also cultivated many unhelpful concepts about what confers worth and value to the individual. Their notions of heroism and *paideia* (the upbringing of children) never addressed, for example, the fact that they functioned essentially as slave societies.

Lastly, we are struck by an entirely different view of man presented in the Bible in ancient Israel—namely that men and women are made in the image of God. The significance and ramifications of being human rested simply on this premise and was in stark and striking contrast to the surrounding cultures of the time. These cultures viewed only a few select kings, pharaohs, and other rulers as possibly made in a god's image. (For example, Alexander the Great declared himself a god, and later some Roman caesars and emperors did too.)

This biblical revelation of human origin and identity was further defined by the great commandments revealing God's character and man's right relationship to the one true and living God. Consequently, every person in ancient Israel was responsible to *know* the law and to *act* upon it. This law (later perfectly embodied and lived out in Jesus Christ) was to be treasured within the hearts and minds of *all* age-groups, through teaching, reading, memorization, festival, and ritual—to be passed on faithfully from generation to generation (Deut. 6).

The child was part and parcel of this reality. Children enjoyed a special place in the learning and commemoration of God's dealings with the nation. The Hebrew child's right to life, unlike in many other cultures, was protected by law. This heritage of a living culture and sacred view of the person formed the backbone of much of Western society until more recent times. It is the bedrock of any thinking about Christian education.

The Hebrew perception of the person and of human behavior was radically different from that of surrounding nations (then and now). Other peoples believe, for example, that a person's worth is primarily achieved through being either an honorable soldier, highly educated, athletically superior, gifted in speech or looks, vastly wealthy, or, best of all, all of the above. Thus most children remained insignificant, ignorant, small, and powerless and could be treated or shaped in a variety of ways, depending on the ends to be achieved. They enjoyed no inherent status.

While *When Children Love to Learn* affirms the value of good and great achievements in a wide variety of fields, this book soundly rejects the view that a child's ultimate worth lies in either intelligence, material circumstances, what he or she *might* become through grooming or talent, or anything else except in this remarkable fact—that he or she has been made in the image of a personal and infinite God and is especially confirmed by Jesus: ". . . of such is the kingdom of heaven" (Matt. 19:14). "Who is the greatest in the kingdom of heaven? And Jesus called a little child unto him, and set him in the midst of them, and said, . . . Except ye be converted, and become as little children, ye shall not enter into the kingdom of heaven" (Matt. 18:1-3).

Charlotte Mason was unequivocal on the most crucial starting point of education—that the child is born a *person*. This pillar of her thought is balanced by another: "We allow no separation to grow up between the intellectual and 'spiritual' life of children, but teach them that the Divine Spirit has constant access to their spirits, and is their continual Helper in all the interests, duties and joys of life."

Miss Mason was profoundly Christian, rooted in Scripture and immensely practical. This is what gives her philosophy and practice its unique combination of "form and freedom" (a phrase Dr. Francis Schaeffer used to describe the proper tension between the reality of moral law on the one hand and individual freedoms and creativity on the other). She drew her view of human beings and especially of children from Holy Writ: "And first let us consider where and what the little being is, who is entrusted to the care of human parents. A tablet to be written upon? A twig to be bent? Wax to be moulded? Very likely; but he is much more—the Bible shows the deepest insight into what is peculiar to the children in their nature and estate. . . ."[3]

She studied widely and wisely. She was able to harness many truthful observations and practices written by previous thinkers on education and accept them as part of the common grace given to all people. She was sharp in rejecting the false ideas of child-centered "freedoms" popularized by Rousseau and followers of the Romantic movement and was not sentimental or idealistic about children. Her attitude was realistic but patiently loving. She was equally clear in her exposure of adults who lord it over children merely on the grounds of a child's dependence and ignorance. She maintained that people need to be careful not to use children to fulfill adult agendas.

Miss Mason herself did not leave many personal notes or diaries. Her written legacy is contained primarily in the six volumes of her educational philosophy and practice, and also in her six volumes written as a meditation on the Gospel of St. John entitled *The Saviour of the World*. She opposed any adulation of herself, but focused attention instead on the body of work she felt she had been given to do "for the children's sake." This was her unbending goal. She wanted all children to know about their heritage of being made in God's image—sinful obviously, but nevertheless able to enjoy to their own best ability in a fallen world and in many diverse life circumstances, the life-giving relationship with God through the Savior and the Spirit, and also relationships with others, nature, art, and music.

This guide attempts to follow a tradition of giving serious thought to what Christian education *today* means for *all* children everywhere, to enable them to be learning for life and everlasting life. This is education for a purpose and not as a status symbol. Of course it means having skills to earn a living, but it also means glorifying God and enjoying Him forever (The Shorter Catechism, 1647).

Neither is this book offered as a monument to an exceptional person but rather as a continuing record of life-giving education flowing from the source of biblical Christianity. We hopefully share with our readers, along with all the practical aims implicit in this guide, the belief that we are in trust to do our utmost in providing the best education for all.

> Our crying need today is less for a better method of education than for an adequate conception of children—children merely as human beings, whether brilliant or dull, precocious or backward. Exceptional qualities take care of themselves and so does the "wanting" intelligence, and both of these share with the rest in all that is claimed for them in the following chapters. Our business is to find out how great a mystery a person is *qua* person.[4]

PART
ONE

I

The Value of Charlotte Mason's Work for Today

By Susan Schaeffer Macaulay

Until a few years ago, the name of Charlotte Mason was largely forgotten. It almost seemed as if the vast educational network that had grown out of her ideas had disappeared like an English early morning mist when the sun rises. If she was mentioned, educators and parents would look blank.

This unfamiliarity seemed curious to me. But as I reflected on recent trends in education, I saw why her innovative philosophy, based on Christian values and faith, had declined. In English teacher training colleges over the last decades, A. S. Neil was read assiduously, and his one school, Summerhill,[1] was held up as an example. "Progressive" education became the vogue. It was seen as liberating the child from the past constraints of a sure framework of knowledge and moral behavior. It was a sustained attack on the whole system of Western education. This ideology began to capture the minds *not* of the elementary school teachers, who were far too busy teaching classes of sixty or more, but rather of the educational establishment—teacher training colleges and the school inspectors. "Progressive" education developed in the wake of a change in teacher training from the apprentice-in-the-classroom model to a lecture-based course in colleges. Many of the new liberal ideas became the educational gospel that spread into primary schools in both Britain and the United States. The effect of these ideas has been cumulative; as we begin the twenty-first century, we see widespread results.

I was a young parent in London when the walls came down figuratively and actually in the 1960s and 1970s. At that time primary school teachers (for ages five to eleven) were discouraged from using any structured teaching at all. Textbooks were out; so were quiet "lessons." Teaching phonics or multiplication tables was definitely frowned on as being as passé as a dunce's hat or children working in rows on slates. Tables were pushed together with little groups sitting around them working on worksheets or projects, either as a group or individually. A hubbub of unfettered chatter made listening or concentration difficult for all except the most naturally "schoolish" child. This confusion was exacerbated as new schools ceased putting in classroom walls. The "open plan" was the liberated design.

In the various schools I visited, chaos reigned. As classes were large (between thirty-five and forty-two children), it was not surprising that parents were concerned. One of my friends was teaching five-year-olds who were meant to learn to read. She followed the liberating ideas that were *de rigueur*[2] but felt guilty that no one in her class was learning the rudiments of reading by osmosis as the theorists had promised. She sat her class around her on the floor and started teaching them sounds and words as she had been taught as a child. These little sessions lasted fifteen minutes, and the children enjoyed them. They liked learning, they appreciated having the code cracked, and they did not seem to mind the order and discipline of sitting listening together. All went well until the headmaster walked by and caught her at the shameful act. She was soon called into his study to be strongly told: "I never want to see you with all the children listening to you again at the same time. They should not be taught any particular sequence of skills."

At that time one of my friends, a professional woman, became concerned that her two bright, eager girls, twins, had reached the age of eight without any literacy or numeracy rubbing off on them in spite of long days at school. She visited the teacher of their class, who paused trying to remember the children in question. "Mary? Rachel? I'm not sure that I know which of the children they are. This class is so noisy that I don't know the children, and it really is too confused to teach them specifics. They'll be able to learn when they move up next year."

In this context my husband, Ranald, and I began a search for an educational philosophy. Surely one existed that did not crush or brainwash children and yet would actually teach them certain things they needed to know step by step. Was it not possible that they could enjoy knowledge, books, and discovery? We didn't know it, but we were looking for Charlotte Mason and the historical PNEU schools that grew out of her philosophy of life and education.

When we did discover her, the ideas and the school did not seem extraordinary. For us, encountering the PNEU was like finding and recognizing a friend. Many others since have had the same experience. When they read about Charlotte Mason's ideas, they find that she has articulated many of their own thoughts and given form to their experiences and their children's. This has been as true for parents as for professional educators and others intimately concerned with children's lives.

People are often amazed at the apparent simplicity and yet clarity of this educational approach and think, *Why, yes, of course.* Elsie Kitching (1870-1955)[3] put this quality of Miss Mason's philosophy into words for me. She talks of the Wise Men finding Jesus in "a most unroyal place" as an example of finding the truth in an unexpected place:

> [W]hen they had arrived they had no doubt. They recognized the truth when they found it.
>
> When we meet the truth, we notice I think, three things. First, that like a jigsaw, the pieces fit into place unexpectedly. Lesser truths dawn, and are seen to be connected; it all ties up. Then, we shrink in size as we see ourselves and our problems from a different and strange angle and like those algebraical numbers with recurring indices, more and more dawns on us. This might be a depressing process but it is not so because truth is always bigger than man and independent of self.
>
> Yet—and this is what strikes me most—although alien in this sense, strange and surprising, truth is always a friend; the stranger is recognized, the surprise is joyful. An old acquaintance!"[4]

This quote emphasizes a key point in what was happening in the "freed-up" education of the 1960s and 1970s. Our culture has abandoned the framework that had undergirded our shared view of the human being and life. Our Christian-based heritage gave us a worldview in which people acknowledged certain truths. They did not *hope* that there was a reasonable pattern to life; they knew it.

This framework meant an assured infrastructure for educational thought and practice. Certain facts were true. To understand reality, children and students needed to know these facts. Students were equipped to pursue various fields of knowledge by acquiring the three R's first of all. In European educational history, this meant knowing Latin and possibly Greek so as to have access to the heritage and culture shared by all European scholars. Latin was the *lingua franca*, much as English is becoming today.

In the past, academics were a small number of the total population. Most children were not considered academically inclined. Responsible growth into adulthood resulted from living with adults who taught them the code of behavior and accomplishments in different areas of a civilized society. For most children this process took place in the home and then the village or town—a rich enough tapestry of life. They developed discipline, skills, and self-esteem as they were handed a small area of knowledge and/or expertise to master. Usually their learning had a direct bearing on what they would do as their work for the rest of their lives. Everyone agreed that there was one true moral code that could be known for sure. They all agreed that it is wrong to take life, to steal, and to commit adultery. Even nonreligious people felt guilt, shame, and possibly remorse. Things were right or wrong, true or false, a duty or a waste of time. It was accepted that God existed in truth, not as a personal projection or hopeful fantasy. This clear outline gave a map for life.

Children were loved dearly or cruelly treated—as they are today. Human beings have always been much the same. Some are good and love and serve the children in their care; others are indifferent, harsh, dictatorial, and hand out unfeeling punishments. In all centuries some people have treated children as things rather than as unique persons—adults seek to make use of them.

Most of the progressive schools wanted really good things for children. But it is impossible to achieve such aims without the realism of the truth, at least to a certain extent, as a framework. Ideals cannot be reached by wishful thinking alone. Again and again in history hopes have been disappointed because people have not faced reality.

For instance, you cannot give people of any age the license to do whatever they feel like doing, even though it is right and good for them to make free choices. The constraints of what a person ought to do and should do may not be removed. Also knowledge fits into a hierarchy according to what is most worthwhile to know. It is reckless to destroy the distinction between the worthwhile and the trivial, to lose what is of enduring quality. As the century progressed, doubt prompted an exodus from the infrastructures, the core, that held our society together.

For quite a long time educators and theorists naively assumed that the fruits of a "decent society" would continue to grow on a tree whose roots had been cut away. This is romanticism. How can fruit be produced without roots, a trunk, branches? As the infrastructure becomes an increasingly dimly remembered idea, lawlessness and antisocial behavior have resulted. These problems in turn trigger the demand for stronger and stronger measures of control from governments and any in authority. We are trading in freedoms for controls that threaten to bring on the nightmare envisioned by George Orwell: "Big brother is watching you."

We have all seen how the promise of law and order will gain votes. As predicted, precious freedoms are being exchanged for surveillance and control that try to promise a certain safety.

This trend has also been evolving in schools. Without a framework—an inner skeleton of truth, knowledge, and moral "bones"—and a clear aim, society is trying to rescue the younger generation by slapping on an exoskeleton. Through rapidly increasing iron-fisted rules, regulations, and proscribed behavior requirements, some people think we can resolve the difficulties.

As we have passed the millennium mark, we exhibit a confusion of educational ideas perhaps never before seen in history. Who is the child? *A person in a life and reality created by God*—or an accident in a cosmic, computer-like machine that itself developed entirely due to random chance?

What are the aspirations that still beat in the human heart? Are these mechanical and an illusion as so much of the twentieth-century literature suggested? Can we know anything for sure? Does anything matter? Is there anything worth living for? These are the questions most people have no answers for. The general atmosphere weakens even those who do think they know.

Education must have an aim, a focus, a *raison d'être*. Many now seem to have settled on education for utilitarian reasons only—that is, when you get to the bottom line, how much money will the student be able to earn later, what status will he or she be able to achieve? Below that, for society's underclass, we simply would like to condition them to law-abiding lives.

Complicating the educational picture are several problems. The decrease of family stability (another fruit of that societal tree), disappearing communities with strong neighborhood relationships, and fears about safety hinder children's healthy development. Then families who aren't secure tend to either overregulate children or to lack clear boundaries at all. This situation has brought confusion and pressure to bear on schools and teachers. They used to be able to begin with a few hours of teaching the three R's. Cultural extras were thrown like lettuce and tomato into this sandwich. This method worked because the family and community actually directed and nurtured its children.

The situation has now changed right across the socioeconomic spectrum. Children arrive at school without breakfast, sometimes pulled out of bed before they are awake. It is not unusual for parents to go to work before the school bus comes. Rarely do children enjoy the comfortable ease of a short walk to school in their own neighborhood.

Children arrive at school lacking more than a good breakfast and a warm send-off hug. They may never have been consistently taught how to live according to a "root-trunk" system of morality. As we now say, "values" differ. A teacher of five-year-olds is typically confronted with children who have not learned to listen or concentrate. No one has treated them with much respect, and they don't respect each other. It is typical to find them at war with any authority at all, with no idea of cooperation or obedience. They may be glassy-eyed because they've emerged from hours and hours parked in front of a TV set.

And there are other difficulties. As marital stability declines, in the average group of children a high proportion suffer emotional turmoil, pain, and confusion. This state of mind obviously affects the quality of their lives and hinders their education.

We don't have the space here to consider all the problems teachers face. More and more children come to school whose parents did not read to them regularly. Many are no longer part of a family that even has a routine of eating daily meals together. When both parents work, stressful schedules may exclude the leisurely conversations so dear to a little child's heart and so necessary for their thoughts and language development. Older children often never experience a discussion of ideas. These things are a great loss. Children emerge all too often undernourished both emotionally and mentally. They have not been given the basic tools of education: language, self-expression, questioning and answers, exploration and discovery, stories and imaginative development. They aren't used to listening to others or having anyone listen to them. Often they've also been deprived of free play in the beautiful out of doors. Their eyes are closed to the wonder of the world around them, and they have missed the joy of being drawn into a lifelong love affair with nature. They may lack exploratory curiosity and initiative. Such children are hard to teach. Some professionals feel depressed about it all. There is such a gap between the romanticism and ideals in some teacher training colleges and the reality teachers face every day in the classroom.

These are some of the reasons I believe we need Charlotte Mason's educational insights more than ever before. Those of us who have discovered her, and then seen fruits in actual children's lives, experience the "ah-ha" moments of enlightenment. And then the "of course, that makes sense. Yes. This is right." I would add, "This is truth." These are insights about who the child actually is, how he or she learns, why and what is worth learning, and the purpose of it all. Like a tree with sound roots in rich, watered soil, here is an educational theory and practice that has a clear, strong infrastructure and that allows for individuality, creativity, cultural differences, technological advance, and historical development.

Miss Mason's educational philosophy is not about what someone thought as a Victorian; it is not tied into the past, as if trying to hark back to a golden age. (That is why it is inappropriate to illustrate materials about Charlotte Mason with exclusively Victorian pictures.) These ideas, being true ones, have an unchangeable underlying pattern (form) and yet give freedom for individual life and practice. When the Christian worldview gives this form, there is much stability and also freedom for appropriate adaptation. That is what makes this way of educating children so exciting.

Charlotte Mason, and those like Elsie Kitching who worked with her and carried on after her death, used the canon of Western cultural heritage with an English perspective as the core of educational content. That was appropriate, for they were educating mainly British children from nations that were part of this stream of history.

However, even while Charlotte Mason was still living, other peoples recognized that they could use the core ideas while developing their own educational applications. Japanese aristocratic families sent a gifted teacher to Ambleside to study at Miss Mason's college. The principles then and now remain adaptable. Some Jewish students used many of the educational insights. Charlotte Mason's books were translated into German.

The Ambleside books by her on education were sent out to India to Amy Carmichael, who founded the Dohnavur Fellowship. She too recognized in the writings the "roots and trunk" she was looking for as she cared for and educated Indian children. Amy Carmichael was ahead of her time in that she tried not to impose British culture on the community. She respected India and wanted the children to be Indian. She quite rightly saw that as long as the "roots and trunk" were in place (which one cannot, must not change), then she could adapt the detail, the "foliage," so that it was truly Indian. For instance, instead of using English nursery rhymes or tales, she wrote amusing poems in Tamil about local subjects such as insects ("bugs") and flowers.

In England itself at that time, educational practice was almost as socially stratified as the Indian caste system that Amy Carmichael rejected. The British upper class educated its younger children and girls mostly at home. Boys went off (and still do) to fee-based boarding schools at about thirteen years of age. These "public schools" had been developed and influenced by great educators and produced strong leaders, but the schools were far from perfect.

The subject of educating the working class was a troubling one. Christians started Sunday schools to teach the rudiments of reading, writing, and math to children who worked during the week. There were some creative educators who did great work establishing farm and/or craft-based schools and better primary schools for ordinary working-class children. A few people even thought these children could appreciate folk dancing, stories, and art plus nature study (these children were persons too, not clods).

However, most of the ruling class wanted the working class to be kept firmly in its place. The upper classes feared that workers would get ideas "above their station." This fear led to strong feelings that split educators into factions. Some wanted to keep an ossified status quo. Others believed that all people should have access to their cultural heritage and be enabled to develop skills. Still others were starting to believe in broader opportunities related to one's ability. Such pioneers were unhappy with a mechanistic control of individuals and society as "it should be."

Things are entirely different now, but there are new reasons to fear that a person may be treated like a cog in the machine of society. As we go into the third millennium, new and horrifying social controls abound: genetic manipulation, the extermination of "undesirable elements" in society through selective abortion, and chemicals to control the mind and personality. Our forebears' eyes would widen in horror at all the tyrannies scientific technology has made possible. We cannot look back at their prejudices and practices with one crumb of complacency.

From the 1880s to the 1930s, when Charlotte Mason was in her zenith, there was a general educational ferment, resulting in controversies over different methods and goals. Many tried to pigeonhole girls' education into a prescribed "slot." Working-class girls, like boys, were expected to roll up their sleeves and get on with the business of life. (Many working-class girls had a robust preparation for a satisfying life.) The working young often gained much of their mental nurture in Christian church services or open air preaching meetings. They usually had the Bible to read and *The Pilgrim's Progress*, with maybe one or two other books.

Aristocratic boys received a traditional classical education. The girls often languished in home schoolrooms with a limited and weak curriculum along with feeble expectations and stringent social protocols. Although we admire their embroidery, life must have seemed a pretty tiresome business for many a bright young woman. There were notable exceptions—for instance the Oxford and Cambridge families often gave their daughters a substantial education with discipline; there was plenty of interesting conversation and a wide range of books to read. In fact, before the women's colleges burst on the scene, they existed in embryo on cleared-off breakfast tables in academic homes. Here daughters could be educated and develop their mental ability.

Charlotte Mason was not a product of any privileged minority. She represents one of the fortunate men and women whose good minds were educated mainly at home, in ordinary conditions, as interested parents read through a rich range of books with their children.

However, she did live just at the time that women were generally beginning to seek an education. The great innovators of girls' education, Frances Buss and Dorothea Beale, were active in that same period:

> Let a girl's education be as serious as a boy's. You bring up your girls
> as if they were meant for sideboard ornaments, and then complain of
> their frivolity. Give them the same advantages that you gave their
> brothers. Teach *them* also, that courage and truth are the pillars of
> their being. There is hardly a girls' school in this Christian Kingdom
> where the children's courage and sincerity would be thought of half so
> much importance as their way of coming in at a door. And give them,
> lastly, not only noble teachings, but noble teachers.[5]

A new wind was stirring. It seemed suddenly that girls should not be merely prepared to be genteel adornments but vigorous human beings in their own right. It was a flowering of the New Testament teaching that men, women, slaves, free, Jews, and Gentiles are all on one plane as persons: "there is no difference." To Charlotte Mason this meant that *all children* had wonderful minds that should be fed and developed, just as all children needed wholesome food for their bodies, sleep, and loving care. In other words, we are all more similar as persons than different. She believed in a generously rich curriculum for all.

She knew the great shining truths of Christian belief and teaching. One of the features of her work is that for her these truths were an infrastructure, an underpinning, a solid framework of unchangeable reality that each successive generation could build on. But these truths were not a cage, and that is a huge difference from those who would legalistically impose truths on others.

Many educational theories and prescriptions confine education and childcare practice to a closed box. "It has to be like this or that," depending on the theory espoused. One theory holds that the child must learn by memorization for so and so many years—all facts. *Then* students read essays and debate them. Other educators thought that students should sit at desks facing a chalkboard. Still others explain that the "best education" conveys American or British culture. Nowadays some educators try to turn the clock back to a fictitious rosy bygone age. They believe that all will come right as long as we don't use computers, do use Victorian readers, and have students chant times tables. "Let's not do this or that . . . and then we'll get it right" is the mentality.

Charlotte Mason's ideas are remarkable because all people in all times *are alike in certain ways.* The reality is that we all share the inner framework of truth. No race is "more human" than another. No gender is higher than another. No culture is superior in itself. (For instance, whether we sit at a table to eat or around a fire on the floor does not matter much.)

If we look at this exceptional woman's ideas, we see that we can use "living books" that are American, English, Australian, German, Swedish, Russian, Senegalese, Malian, Ugandan, Indian, Chinese, Korean, Brazilian, Guatemalan, or Cuban, and so on. If the "roots" and "trunk" of Christianity are our firm infrastructure, we can use a plurality of cultural literature and histories to "leaf out" what is learned. (All children who live in countries with a link to Europe and the United Kingdom need to know this historical, literary, and religious background as well as more local content.)

All of us need to examine pagan mythological origins of our culture's literature and decide what to use (or not use). The facts that go into a child's education can thus be indigenous and related to the surrounding culture. However, with a Christian understanding of truth, all of us share the knowledge and light based on the biblical explanation of reality and who we are. So there will be a profound unity, just as all trees are trees, not ever confused with jellyfish. But at the same time, just as there are palm trees, oaks, and birches, so there can be a wonderful variety too. In philosophy this reality/necessity is expressed in the phrase "unity and diversity."

Culturally and educationally, this phrase has definite implications. All believing Christians can enhance their cultural identity. If the biblical world-view is indeed reality, we can be self-confident as men and as women, whether we are Anglo-Saxon or Asian, African or Native American. We can also fit in with our historical period—no need to try to make a school or home turn back the clock. It would be a disservice to children to bring them up as Victorians with a misty idea that they'll live in a rose-covered cottage in a friendly, safe village, for instance.

We were told to be "in the world, but not of the world."[6] Charlotte Mason thought that schools and educational programs had a duty to keep up with the thinking of their times.[7] No use fighting battles fifty years old! What do these children face today? What will they face tomorrow?

Some educational theories depend on one curriculum for all—and for all time. Charlotte Mason would disagree. It was intrinsic to her philosophy that a curriculum would stay relevant to a child's background and up to date while not ditching old treasures.

She was broadminded in a good sense. While never wavering on the infrastructure of truth—our relationship with God through Jesus as set forth in His Word—she was not narrow in vision. She was magnanimous and cultured. To her the mind of a miner's child was just as hungry for the best educational nourishment as a child of the royal family. In the same way, she did not differentiate between the minds or persons of boys and girls. All were to be given the tools of literacy so they could be nourished at the fountain of the greatest minds—right across all disciplines. Not for her the nonsense of girls being deprived of the classical world, literature, history, the great art, music, scientific thought, or languages. In her view of childhood, girls climbed trees, learned to swim, and ice-skated just as boys did. Girls were to enjoy unfettered freedoms and challenges in the great outdoors. All were to notice and appreciate nature.

God's Word had the central place, not namby-pamby sentimental or moralistic talks or booklets. It was typical of her open search for the best ideas to develop a full life that she pounced on Baden-Powell's Scout Handbook[8] designed to train soldiers. I doubt that any other Victorian educator saw the potential in that book even for boys, let alone for the demure little girls with their governesses.

Charlotte Mason not only saw potential in it, but she immediately purchased quantities of the handbooks and included them in the PUS (Parents' Union School)[9] curriculum. These she sent to aristocratic homes for the Charlotte Mason-trained governesses to use, to the PNEU schools, and to home schools taught by mothers. Thus while other children were kept indoors to have endless facts crammed into them, these fortunate children had every afternoon outside. One afternoon a week was for "scouting": tracking, noticing wind direction, learning to set up camp, and enjoying a truly hands-on education that thrilled and energized them. These children took part in the beginnings of the great scouting movement! It led to much good in the lives of boys and girls around the globe. Very few people realize the impetus given to the movement at Scale How, the building where Charlotte Mason had her House of Education for training teachers.

People like Charlotte Mason are rare and vital. They contribute both stability and continuity as they maintain the clear infrastructure of truth in their work; yet life bubbles up in them with freshness. Their response to actual life and persons creates a relevance and newness to their work without sacrificing the roots. This approach contrasts with a more usual trend toward a deadening legalism that squeezes out new ideas.

She pointed out the limitations of a set curriculum plan as well as its value. Every year new books are published, and they need to be considered. Children in various countries benefit by some of the same books and yet need others that relate to their own culture and prepare them for life in it. However, many treasures are common to us all. All of us share in the knowledge of truth set forth in God's Word. In every era and culture, children are persons; they should be served with respect. They are not parts in a machine. Not only does each have a name, but each is different from another; each has strengths and weaknesses; each will appreciate and relate to the richness of life in individual ways.

In Tokyo, Moscow, Chicago, Toronto, Mombassa, Calcutta, and Beijing, huge areas of life are the same for all persons. All of us are under the same Creator God's authority. All of us fall short of His perfection. All of us have an inner hunger for love, justice, and life. Everywhere babies smile and make sounds in response to the caring people around them. All parents experience glee as a child develops; everyone feels proud as the toddler staggers off on two feet for the first time.

All healthy little children learn to speak.[10] Children everywhere enjoy songs and stories. All explore their surroundings and ask questions. All will pet furry animals with delight unless the harsh example of cruelty and indifference has contaminated their tender hearts.

Children in all cultures enjoy imaginative play. All count and can learn to read. All have a spiritual hunger; they think metaphysically as well as factually. All appreciate loveliness; beauty speaks to all.

All respond to goodness, to fairness. Children are profoundly moral and literal. They have a lot of common sense, and it is hard to put over fanciful theories on them. They are like the little boy who saw that the emperor had no clothes on; they will often see through pretense or ideas contrary to reality. They ask down-to-earth questions. They think up new ideas.

Children love running, climbing, and swimming. They play, using their own fertile imaginations. The world over, they fight and need adults to teach them how to make and have peace in their lives.

All children enter into relationships with people. They smile back, shyly show you a treasure, imitate other people's actions and personalities, and have great curiosity. Differences are not a barrier for children; they will follow a warm, full-of-fun person who doesn't speak their language, comes from another culture, or is from an older generation. They try to communicate— copy sounds and point to objects, saying the word in their language. What they are sensitive to are harsh attitudes and people who don't appreciate them or enjoy relationships with them. Children recoil from cold, judgmental legalism that is only interested in crushing out their vitality with rules and regulations. Pride and arrogance will send them running out of the room or retreating into an inner remoteness, as does sarcasm that humiliates or ridicules them. These attitudes are terribly wrong and do much harm to children.

A damaging form of abuse to children is expecting them to be something they are not. For instance, a school system or a parent penalizes a child for not being academically oriented. (Or in reverse, the systems or parents that have nonacademic goals for a child penalize the intellectually gifted child.) We read of gifted musicians who were under a father's wrath and disapproval for wanting to play and study music. Different cultures and generations have imposed a variety of expectations or limitations that were wrong for particular children or for children in general.

Sometimes I'm asked what I think Christian education is. I think it is education that has due regard for the individual child. Children's differences in makeup are tenderly taken into account. No children should be kept in, sitting on a chair, anywhere in God's world because someone has decreed that they, even though not developmentally ready, have reached "the age" when they *should* learn how to read. However good a curriculum is, however much it has the "roots" and "trunk" of life, however worthy and living are the books, however rich the spread of subjects, children are abused if their developmental stages and abilities are not taken into consideration. The child is, after all, a whole person.

As an example, consider the PNEU program devised at Scale How by Elsie Kitching in cooperation with Charlotte Mason. Say it suggested the reading of a particular book in literature or history to children of a particular age. Imagine a teacher or school using the educational plan for a group of children new to it all. Perhaps they've never been read to aloud, certainly not out of literary books. They shift uneasily in their seats. They have poor attention, limited vocabulary. The teacher should be looking at the entire program to choose something to read that will grab their attention and interest.

On the other hand, a class of children has been using these programs from the time they started school at six years of age. By nine they *are* ready for the Shakespeare play or a substantial chunk of a narrative history. A key idea for Charlotte Mason was that the source material should be enjoyable. Thus, in using the plan, it is important for children to enter at a level they can understand and enjoy. It is better to start with smaller, easier chunks and let a child progress from there.

To jump in at the deep end may end in disaster or could surprise and delight the class. Teaching is an art—and we learn through mistakes. When students are not "latching on," sooner or later we cast around for a different choice or arrangement. Perhaps it is only that we are attempting too much of a good thing. Maybe we need to cut back on the quantity of educational offerings.

We'd never think of buying the same size of shoes for all six-year-olds! No, we take a child to have his feet measured and see what fits. In the same way, we try to fit the program to where the child is developmentally and experientially within the limits inherent in different teaching situations.

I've known teachers who apply Charlotte Mason's methods with children and teenagers in some of today's toughest schools. If these teachers are careful *to choose books that catch the children's interest and imagination,* they and the class are well into accomplishing their goals. Slavishly following a set curriculum if it doesn't fit a class, situation, or child is legalistic folly. Get "shining eyes" *first*, and the coveted question, "Can't you read more?" will come. This question shows that what you are doing is succeeding. As children become interested, chapter by chapter, they will form new habits. It won't seem like work at all! They like listening, imagining, thinking. These activities are satisfying.

If children are given a diet of dry facts, and information is read to them from books they cannot understand, if they are overworked and stressed, they will simply switch off. They may become discouraged ("I'm dumb") or decide "It's boring," or just be tired and lose interest and motivation.

One of the beauties of a curriculum based on "living books" is that nothing is twaddle. Living books have literary power; they have "soul." The writers have put their hearts into these books. As vital thought touches our minds, our ideas are vitalized, and out of our ideas comes our conduct of life. These must be books that children enjoy. The ideas they hold must make that sudden, delightful impact upon children's minds, must cause that intellectual stir that marks the beginning of an idea. These books induce in children thoughts about the world, nature, people, music, art, and the God who created it all.

In Charlotte Mason schools lessons end for younger children at lunchtime, and they are raring to go the next morning. They are neither underfed or overfed educationally. Older children naturally can do more, but still they are not under stress. They have a broad, interesting "diet" for their minds in the mornings, with afternoons a contrast including play, picture study, acting, or nature walks. Charlotte Mason did not want homework given out either. Life itself is too important to crowd out with busywork.

Contrast that with a school that has a schedule of work set in concrete for every child, whatever his or her learning style. One little boy never has to learn correct spelling. As he reads, it sticks in his memory. As he writes, he simply asks how a word is spelled and usually never has to ask again. Another child, a girl of the same age, just cannot remember the spelling words. She may concentrate so hard that sweat rolls off her furrowed brow (literally). After a day in her impersonal school (and sadly all too often), she may be found tearful and tired at suppertime, still being "helped" by a despairing mother or father. Is this "Christian" or "education"? Neither—in my mind. We should not expect the same from different children. It would make as much sense as grading two-year-olds for language skills! (Can't you see it? Johnny gets a D for a vocabulary of forty basic words. Susie has an A because she uses a large vocabulary and speaks in sentences!)

Now a proper response to these realities is to adapt a learning plan to different children. The little boy who doesn't need to learn spelling is listening to the same interesting books being read, but perhaps he starts writing his narration while the girl tells it to a scribe. She then draws a picture of the same story. At another time she has simple dictations at her own level. She writes little bits creatively too. But in discussion she is far ahead! With flaming eyes she vividly retells the story that was read. She may ask the most interesting questions of all!

In a PNEU classroom, many activities are shared by all. Everyone listens together as the Bible selection is read. Literature is read aloud to all the children, as is history and poetry. They occasionally listen to each other's narrations, or each draws a picture of the same story. However, many children move at their *own speed* through math, spelling/writing skills, and some language work. In other words, they do not compete against each other but enjoy steady personal progress. This way all the children's minds are nourished together while the differences in children are recognized and helped appropriately. A combination of the benefit of individual work and the stimulation and enthusiasm of a group works well.

The one-size-fits-all method of teaching children is not the only danger in educational practice today. Frequently children are not treated with respect, as friends. They may be shouted at, driven to tears, or bored stiff. Their minds, eager for interesting matter that stirs the imagination, may be fed the dry sawdust of irrelevant facts. Of course, they choke on it. To add insult to injury, they may be in a system that requires them to be constantly tested on how much information has been stored. They don't need teachers who are casual pals, although they do like friendly adults who lead clearly and with assurance. Children can be turned into students who are eager to listen, glad to tell back the narration as they remember it, stressing what mattered to them.

Together teacher and child are under a higher authority. The child should not be asked to be good to please a parent or teacher. Children and the adults both must choose to obey God. Both are learning how to be better people, and both children and adults are interested and learning from books, nature, art, music. Ideas are discussed. Thought is important. Children have amazing ideas! They grow in proper self-esteem as they are listened to and allowed to be themselves.

Too many of us treat education as a competition, with some idea of success as the objective. This approach is bad for the "winners" and bad for the "losers," who only see themselves more or less as failures. Such a narrow focus ignores children's strong points, their gifts. For instance, taking a rather extreme example, a child has Down's syndrome, and yet her personality shines with love and loyalty. What family, group, or community can do without these valuable qualities as an example for others? We have turned into fools when it comes to appreciating what is really worthwhile in life—proud fools with no understanding of what God treasures. We live in a worldly generation that encourages a blind pride.

What would happen if everybody planned for their children to be business executives, lawyers, scientists, or academics? Where would we be without the honored homemakers, craftsmen, artists, and musicians? Where are those who are good at pastoral care? Who will care for community needs—tend the sick, plow the fields, and, yes, collect the garbage? (Garbage collection, water purification, home construction, and similar activities are arguably more valuable to our human community than the work of many of our CEOs and star entertainers. Salary and educational attainments mean nothing in themselves.)

Charlotte Mason's educational ideal was not to remove us from the ordinary but *to enrich us, each one, with the best possible relationships*—relationships with God, with people in our family and community, with others through their books, art, or music, and with God's creation.

So one great educational mistake is the aim of "success." It seems to mean that everybody is expected to be able to climb an academic ladder of some sort or another. In Asian cities it is all too usual for such pressure to result in youth suicides or adults ashamed of their "failure" and letting down the family. There after-school "cram classes" use up the few moments left after homework is done.

Before we in the West feel complacent, consider a familiar scene. There are plenty of children who shed tears over being expected to master something that is beyond them in their "excellent" school. Perhaps they'd be fully stretched mastering English reading and writing, but this school and pushy parents expect Latin too (like C. S. Lewis's education). Another child is penalized for not possessing a photographic memory. Such children are too often left to wither without any interesting educational stimulation, creativity, or vitality. In such cases their minds atrophy, their spirits wilt, and they lose self-confidence. A common way of describing their plight is to say that they are like square pegs in round holes.

Children do perk up, like watered plants after a too-hot day, when they are interested! They forget fidgeting; their minds are stirred.

One "sin" today is a failure to lead children into full-length living books. There is something about reading one chapter, the next, and then the next that grounds a person's thinking and builds a pattern that holds together.

Sometimes children learn a bit of this, and a bit of that, and there is no continuity. Fragments of knowledge float around with nothing to connect them. Charlotte Mason would have detested "literature" classes that read a few chapters here or there or used workbooks. She would not call that education. Fragments seem meaningless and don't make an impression. What happens as a result of such dry and fragmented teaching is described by some as cultural illiteracy. Some children of fourteen in England cannot identify Paris or even France on an unlabeled map. Some children in the United States don't know Canada's location. No, we cannot rest on our laurels. Children who can't tell who Abraham was—his story—are typical. Others don't know what crossing the Rubicon refers to or what a flying buttress is and much, much else.

And so the pendulum swings wildly too far in the opposite direction. If a little learning is good, then let's cram every moment full. Surely that will be even better.

This attitude is a chief danger, and it increases by the year. Children are in danger of being force-fed (or overfed) with a very real possibility that they will reject everything—vomit up all their education, so to speak. (Beware. There is far too much information around.)

For some reason or other, Americans bear the dubious reputation of overkill if they are aiming too narrowly at an excellent education. First of all, the educational vision is too frequently factual information alone, rather than ideas or a big general picture. Look at tests from third grade to postgraduate education. *Facts. Facts. Facts.* And so teachers and children cram, cram, cram (and forget, forget, forget). Too often children discover that they learn merely to pass a test, get a grade, and then no one cares.

This approach is a profound contrast to Charlotte Mason's. In PNEU schools the learning—real learning—happened when a child was interested in the material (and interesting material was made available). It stirred their imaginations. They told what they learned back in their own words. They drew pictures too—putting in details from the stories. Yes, they learned the all-important skills—fifteen minutes of structured reading a day at six; times tables practice at seven when ready, along with French vocabulary or Latin—but all in short, focused lessons. Nothing wearied a child. That way they could give real attention and become used to not having their thoughts wandering or their little bodies fidgeting because they needed to move and play. A truly child-friendly schedule includes afternoons free to play outside, enjoy walks, or develop skills in crafts.

People today are making a colossal pedagogical error. They are rather like an uneducated person who thinks that if one spoon of medicine will do good, then ten are even better! Many children are being given far too many hours of instruction per day—sometimes in schools, sometimes in home schools. No one can do everything that would be worthwhile. The best of curriculum guides must be guides, not absolute directives. What you choose from should be the very best available and "living." And that is why the time, experience, and effort that go into using a well-chosen curriculum guide are so valuable. Teachers and individual schools do not have the time to spend hours reading history or literature books, for instance.

The schools and classes that used the old PNEU programs used to await the yearly program with interest and enthusiasm. Old favorites and classic books from our heritage are included from year to year. But then a Baden-Powell writes a scouting book, and that opens new avenues. A new book on planets, engines, or medieval castles arrives and is chosen. The curriculum guide in this book attempts to offer a similar service today.

Not everybody using this book can or should do everything suggested in it. One child or class has quite enough to keep busy and fed with "skills education" such as twenty minutes of math, twenty minutes of reading aloud, then a story to listen to out of history or legends—followed by a good long time to play, sing, and experience life-giving activities such as art, picture study, or dressing up and acting out plays or spontaneous ideas. Then there are crafts—weaving, sewing, crocheting, knitting, embroidery, woodworking, wire/metal work, puppet-making, creative productions from clay to cardboard and papier-mâché. PNEU schools typically required children to bring waterproof boots and coats to school, and the children had ample time for outdoor play whatever the weather. They'd use their imaginations for hours.

Overcrowding children's schedules deprives them of time to make their own choices for play, being alone quietly or mixing with friends, helping with chores, reading books they enjoy, or pursuing hobbies. This is a serious life-long loss. *Without such times, their inner selves are stunted; they don't develop from the inside first.* If a school's first objective is to produce a star pupil, this idea should be seriously challenged! Wisdom would know that over-filling the daytime hours with prescribed work quenches the bright spark of enthusiasm. It is as if each child is a little plant, and the sunshine, air, and rain have been kept away. The plant dies or becomes limp and languid. Then adults complain that there is a "lack of motivation" or "poor concentration" or that the child "does not try hard enough."

If we want our children to stay hungry for knowledge, remain interested and questioning, enjoy the wonder of discovery, then we must leave them some clutter-free hours for friendship, the great out-of-doors, the rich world of imagination, and the satisfaction of the skilled use of art supplies, music, dance, wood, and clay.

Charlotte Mason tells us rightly that we should see that this is the birthright of a child, just as a plant should have soil, sun, and water. We must not quench the joy of living. Furthermore, a child bonds through relationships.

Here is another Christian principle. The child is a person, not a computer program to be written. It matters not a bit if he or she remembers ninety-nine facts about the country's history or twenty-five. The child is not a machine but a lovely person.

Let children live life to the full until they are six or so. If they do not or cannot enjoy an appropriate secure, stable home where members have fun together, some substitute should be provided. They need to develop naturally at their own pace. Within relationships that matter to them, they'll soak up a great deal before "lessons" start. They love to have all sorts of conversations, ask questions, and listen to stories read again and again. They draw, sing, and help grownups. They should not be without schedules, and this is the time for them to form the habit of fitting within boundaries. That is, they are taught to freely accept what they may and may not do, to listen to what is said to them, and to cheerfully cooperate.

These children are not constantly hounded into too-early academic or sedentary routines. Some five-year-olds really are ready for reading and writing. They will enjoy twenty minutes or so of personal instruction, perhaps as a game is played. That can be fun, and when the first shadow of inattention flickers across their faces, the "work" is put away. At all times, children's abilities and maturity levels are accepted. They are enabled to feel pleased about their progress as related to "the grain of their wood."

A benefit of the PNEU approach was that although children were allowed to work in a peaceful, individual way as they learned the three R's, when they put down their pencils and notebooks, no one was held up by the level of achievement in these technicalities. A child who struggled with her own reading could relax and become absorbed in a history story such as this one:

> One day Elizabeth [Queen Elizabeth I] was passing along the street, and the people as usual came crowding to see her. Among them was Sir Walter Raleigh. The Queen stepped from her coach and, followed by her ladies, was about to cross the road. But in those days the streets were very badly kept and Elizabeth stopped before a puddle of mud. She was grandly dressed and how to cross the muddy road, without soiling her dainty shoes and skirts, she did not know. As she paused Sir Walter sprang forward. He too, was finely dressed and he was wearing a beautiful new cloak. . . .[11]

The children are listening with rapt attention to the vivid word pictures. This is what thrills them; they are seeing the story, interested in the action. They want it read right through to the end of the chapter. In the big history storybook of 547 pages are stories of British history from pre-Roman days to the end of the World War I. The children are not tied up mentally, hoping they will remember the date for a test or quiz. (In the first paragraph of the chapter it has been mentioned, 1598.) Rather, they are drawn into the story, just as C. S. Lewis managed to weave a spell of atmosphere and narrative in Narnia. They will remember far more details for a longer time as these are woven into a pattern/story that they remember as a whole.

These stories are the tales the six-year-old children and their older companions will retell with gusto. In the telling back they are not limited by their still stumbling writing skills. They can draw pictures of the tale.

With wise planning, their week is so uncluttered that the few good readings they've listened to still stand out in their memories. I have beside me a tiny sheet of paper in my secondhand copy of *Our Island Story* out of which I've quoted. On it in pencil are the page numbers the six-year-olds were to cover in a term's work—and I am struck by the modest amount planned. In the spring term (three months) of 1953, they were to listen to pages 64-93. That is only ten pages a month! The rule is to give interesting material but slowly enough so that it is absorbed, possessed, not forgotten in the overflow of "too much."

These PNEU children had so much to interest them. They *enjoyed* what they were doing. And they had fresh enthusiasm left to turn to their books for interesting relationships of other kinds.

Let's return to the question of why Charlotte Mason and the respected PNEU schools disappeared and became virtually unknown. Her educational philosophy is based on a Christian view of reality. We saw that as the century progressed, this view was widely abandoned. Furthermore, the idea that we probably will never know a real truth has become widely accepted. Belief is spoken of as almost a personal preference or experience rather than a serious proposition of truth about reality around us, seen and unseen.

Flowing from the loss of objective truth is a devaluation of an objective sense of morality. In today's parlance, Christian values have evaporated.

Lastly, these new views devalue the innate worth of each person. There is no meaning to life in general or in a particular life. It has become permissible to discard unwanted or blemished infants. The only way to see children's education with these views is that they are to be prepared to be cogs in the smoothly running wheels of society. Children's thoughts, ideas, and creativity may well hinder the operation of the machine unless someone controls it all. The choices the planners make are a kind of random selection. There is no ultimate meaning, no right and wrong, no better or worse apart from function.

Not only that, with these views we are unable to assess the relative value of learning one thing as against another. This difficulty has contributed to the cultural illiteracy our children demonstrate. (A cheap, sensational romance or action story will do as well as Charlotte Bronte.)

Then there is an economic factor. Educational publishing really is Big Business. People must be kept buying. Expensive changes and new theories make money. Thus treasured, well-written books are discarded, whatever their value. New books must be purchased. Being "relevant" is a new absolute—though what one is attempting to be relevant to is not discussed. People must be made uneasy about the relatively simple provision of basic skills books and good "living" classics that can be used for years, with only a few new purchases necessary.

Charlotte Mason's educational methods offer a firm pathway out of our postmodern educational dilemma. Her philosophy is based on a clear view of God, reality, life, and the person. Some things are certain: "We are all under authority." She valued the family, relationships, and life. Her practices are real, workable—yes, and like a friend, the truth. Children educated by her methods thrive happily and carry rich memories into their future lives.

Charlotte Mason had a broad view of education. She believed that if the materials were wisely chosen, children would eagerly listen, thus drinking at the fountain. She knew there were gifted men and women whose works could be that fountain—books, noble deeds, poetry, paintings, music. She knew another, *the* other source: God who spoke in His Word. Charlotte Mason observed how adults got between the child and the Author, the source—whether it was God, His handiwork (nature), or writers from Plato to Shakespeare to contemporary works. She called the refusal to get between the child and the source "masterly inactivity," allowing the child direct contact with and individual response to original works.

Another of her insights shows genius. We all remember a time when, as children, we listened with rapt attention to a story being read. It interested and fascinated us, and then in a "teacher voice" a little moral lesson was tacked on for the children's good. Probably we've been in both shoes, listening as children and teaching as adults. Children stop listening, eyes wander, and they think about a snack. They fidget. The lesson becomes tiresome. The joy and interest evaporates.

Charlotte Mason saw something else. If you read this interesting story and leave it as it finished, the child continues thinking about it. We do all children a massive disservice when we "chew" over the material and "spit the pulp" out for them. People reject the secondhand results of someone else's efforts. No, Charlotte Mason discovered, let the children remember because they took it in themselves. Let them think their own thoughts about it. Let them respond (in narration, with questions, ideas).

A good example of how easily we get all this wrong is picture study. In talking with people from eight to eighty who have had a proper PNEU education, I have found that for them all the love of art is a lifelong joy. They remember picture study with warm enthusiasm. I see the same thing happening in my own family. Children seem to know so much! One of our little granddaughters, five years of age, has picture study times at home with her PNEU-educated mother. When taken into the Fitzwilliam Museum in Cambridge, she came in with the anticipation and expectancy of a connoisseur. No one said anything. Suddenly she cried out with joy, "Oh, look at the Degas!" Her eleven-year-old cousin, visiting the same museum at another time, could not leave the Monet exhibit. She moved up to examine brush strokes. She stepped back to get the general effect. My youngest daughter, when she was ten (and in a PNEU school), took me around the National Gallery in London. After an enjoyable hour she galvanized into action: "We must go see the Dutch works. De Hooch—don't you *love* the way he paints the light?"

What do we see going on? Especially gifted children? No, persons who have responded to great artists without a lecture course getting in between them and the source to spoil it all.

Some well-meaning persons read about Charlotte Mason and decided it was a "good thing to study art"—to make it part of the curriculum. Beautiful art reproductions were made available. These are wonderful, but the course that goes with them gets in the way. The living, wonderful gift of art is spoiled by making it into one more lesson, textbook fashion. The children and teenagers who take this course may pass a test, but rarely will a love affair grow between the child and the art. They must learn more facts, more lists, and never fall in love (as it were) with the pictures that speak strongly to them.

The PNEU-educated children I know love art all their lives. They certainly do become expert in much—in different ways. To some it all means much, others less. Some are interested in the history angle. Others rejoice in the colors, the brush strokes. But all have had their imaginations and hearts stirred.

Some children educated in the PNEU will choose an area of interest to specialize in, either for university or further personal study. This enthusiasm sparks more interest, and these people are likely to remain eager about learning, enjoying the best, for their entire lives.

As in art, so in other areas of study (actually, areas of enticement). In English and American literature books become loved and known friends. Because children love and enjoy their books, they learn more. The habit of reading becomes rooted in them. They are becoming educated persons. I know several historians whose love for and fascination with the adventures of history began with books such as the storylike *Our Island Story*, which was read to them (or equally Hillyer's *A Child's History of the World*). They were entranced, captivated as children, and that never changed. Unlike Narnia, history is real. Readers can visit the places and read other books that can tell them more.

For Christians, the Bible is God's precious Word, but Bible-reading can easily be "killed stone dead" for children if it is turned into a tiresome continuous churning out of moralistic facts or sentimental pap. And this subject *really* matters. The Bible is so robust! There is plenty of room, of course, for good children's Bible storybooks. Two suggestions: (for five- to six-year-olds) *The Children's Bible* by Anne de Vries;[12] for older children (seven to eight years upwards) *The Children's Story Bible* by Catherine Vos.[13] The latter is a thorough and accurate telling of biblical history in fairly detailed and interesting chronological order. The child needs to be old enough for sustained listening, and even adults who are confused about historical details will find the book useful. Also, deeper aspects of the story and characters emerge. There must be many other good Bible storybooks, but the gem is the Bible itself. It contains stories, poetry, and amazing thoughts, best used by keeping sessions short, pithy, and to the point. A little truth with children listening is better than huge amounts that they tune out.

One of our mistakes is to include *too much* Christian teaching. A child will get indigestion and react, thinking, *I know all this*. I think that it is better to have the PNEU model of a short time for worship, a hymn or two, prayer, and a reading. Then go on to an interesting day of learning that is wholesome, worthwhile, and makes one think.

It will be genuineness of belief and life, along with this simplicity, that impacts children. When they ask a question as they are eating their lunches with their teacher, the answer includes the Christian viewpoint, preferably put in a few thoughtful words. The response should be casual, because if we get too intense and long-winded, we'll see their eyes glaze over. The same kind of lively discussion will be generated in the class after reading a book or while returning from a nature walk. I always sympathized with the little girl who was asked if she'd enjoyed the book about penguins. "Ye-e-s," came the uncertain reply, "but it told me more than I wanted to know."

Children ask probing questions: "If God is good, why are the children starving in Bangladesh?" "But John (in the story) was hungry. Shouldn't he steal?" Children listen, discuss, and perhaps argue when they receive direct, clear, sensible answers. It is vitally important for them to have well-thought out answers. There are good reasons why "we know God is there although, no, He can't be seen." These reasons must be understood, thought about first and along with children. Children like it when we pause and hesitate, saying (truthfully), "What an interesting question! I've not thought about it before," or, "I don't know an answer to that, but I'll find out."

This way of answering is exactly what Charlotte Mason means by saying we are not *over* the child as the source of all knowledge, but *beside* the child, also learning. We usually teach, but children offer a lot for us to consider and learn. The interaction is mutually enjoyable, and both are developing understanding—the "teacher" and "the taught."

Another powerful way Christian life and truth are communicated is by being with people who live by faith. Francis Schaeffer, my father, used to say, "Faith can be caught, not taught." Children sense the genuine and discard the phony. Prayer is powerful. Children who grow up seeing actual answers to prayer in little and big details of life as people pray, genuinely trusting God, will never forget this.

There is no guarantee that a child will choose to believe or want to live a Christian life later on. *And we must not brainwash them in any way.* It will be *their choice.* They need to know why and how the Christian faith is believed to be true—to hear clear answers that demonstrate that Christianity fits into reality like a key into a lock.

They need to be introduced to the living person of Jesus, who is a shepherd seeking them, loving them. He is there; this must be no school lesson. It is terrible to turn this amazing person into a lesson. Children must catch the scent, the scene, the wonder of who He is. If they are used to being interested and moved by other stories, the person or persons in this story will reach them more easily. His Word is the best way to learn about God and His way of working in real history. Love is a great attraction for people, and if children are able to understand this "old, old story of Jesus and His love," their hearts often open to the Savior who is the source of love, goodness, beauty, and abundant life. Children love in return. They appreciate mercy. They respond to kindness. They care passionately about fairness. Jesus is all these things and more.

A few Christian books can be successfully woven into a child's general reading. Children should meet a wholesome range of books and ideas and not always sense they are "being got at" for one particular reason or another.

All children respond to Patricia St. John's books, which can be read to them from the time they are seven or eight to ten years old (one at a time, maybe two a year). Children love Narnia and find it interesting—just to read. They should not be instructed to see this or that in the stories; they will respond in their own way. And don't forget *The Pilgrim's Progress*—an important part of our Christian and cultural heritage. Then the lives of inspiring men and women who trusted in God are important to read. Again, these must be well-told stories, interesting to listen to. Teachers and adults need inspiring too.[14]

It is interesting to consider how children respond to worship. In Charlotte Mason's day, the parish church was Anglican. Children went to a Sunday service where the adults spent much of the time in simple liturgical worship, Bible reading, and prayer. *The Book of Common Prayer* was written in the same century that the King James Version of the Bible was translated (1600s). For lovers of the English language, like Charlotte Mason, both shine out like a gold standard. Their words convey something of the wonder of God's majesty. Too often in churches today children hear only trivial tunes with snappy lyrics that may not stir awe or wonder at all, let alone give them the best of our language.

The words of the Bible and our great hymns can express the majesty and beauty that link us with past generations of believers throughout history. Of course children's attention wandered in the past and wanders today. But they can be helped to follow the readings, and the words of Scripture and the hymns sink in for life.

Beauty strikes into a child's awareness. It is a mistake to reduce all the vocabulary and expressions to a simplified childish level. No, children love the sounds, even the mystery of unfamiliar language (and yet faintly familiar too). They are stilled by the atmosphere of worship and prayer. Slowly as time passes, the words gain meaning, come into focus. A child asks, "What does seraphim mean?" and the answer enlarges their language and their vision of reality.

The beginning of the Te Deum Laudamus ("We praise thee, O Lord") is:

We praise thee, O God; we acknowledge thee to be the Lord.
All the earth doth worship thee, the Father everlasting.
To thee all Angels cry aloud, the heavens and all the powers therein.
To thee Cherubin and Seraphin continually do cry,
"Holy, Holy, Holy, Lord God of Sabaoth;
Heaven and earth are full of the Majesty of thy glory. . . ."

These words have been said or sung in worship for more than 1,500 years. They are part of an early hymn. The child is surrounded by a stream of words and light from long ago. She is part of it now and knows that after her death, Christians will still say and believe the same words—as her grandchildren grow up.

Historical education is not just about dates, treaties, and governments. This sense of a historical stream of believers gives children the perspective that their lives are part of something larger than themselves or their present surroundings. The same benefit is derived from singing hymns that range from the present back into centuries past. We sing with one voice—in the Psalms right back to those who looked forward to Christ before His first coming! A child almost becomes giddy with the distances of time. And yet we all join in the same faith, believe the same truths, sing to and trust in the same God.

This sort of worship and life is not a lesson, although much is learned. Worship tingles with life, hope, and faith. In it we are part of the continuum of believers. It is a precious part of the child's heritage. Ease with the historical usage of language liberates people from feeling at home only in their own narrow century and gives them access to many original texts. They are not even aware of the process, just as a toddler is not aware of learning the complexities of speech. It seems natural.

Worship also includes contemporary expressions of a culture, for it encompasses the *present* as well as the past. It is harmful if we worship only in a way that seems archaic to the person in the street. Not only is our Lord God the God of today, but He is the God of tomorrow as well. Children will enjoy what is current too. The child is aware of the changes in the language but is an educated person and at ease with a variety of historical styles and vocabulary.

Worship inspires creativity. Children enjoy writing, singing, and acting out ideas of their own in response to God's love.

In Marion Berry's PNEU school the children had simple prayer together in the morning, as I've described. They also had about ten to fifteen minutes for memory work at the beginning of the day—a short few minutes to proudly learn until the poem or psalm was known by heart. They enjoyed this time. Memorizing is another way children can possess knowledge and beauty. They respond to the cadences, the words, the thoughts.

Is this sort of educational experience only successful for unusually gifted or privileged children? No, Charlotte Mason is right. All persons respond to this "rich banquet" of a broad curriculum. Of course, like snowflakes, each individual is different from another. But with all the variety in the curriculum, different aspects will strike different children in a variety of ways. This factor demonstrates a relationship. A child has bonded with music or wonderful words. It is as if the child has looked into the eyes of the composer or writer and danced away down a path by the side of that person.

When Marion Berry retired from the school where she was headmistress, she was able to go on educating children. The students in the school had been from families that could pay a fee—a more privileged group. Marion Berry offered to have children from a nearby residential facility come into her home after school for individual help. These at last were the very children she'd most longed to teach! They had a greater need to have the doors into an abundant life opened than the children in the school. (Marion had been wisely told earlier that *all children* needed nourishing—all "are hungry.") Here were your typically less educable children indeed! They had had unhappy experiences previously and were in institutional care. Many were behind in schoolwork. Was the PNEU ideal too high and the material too hard for them? Could it reach them at all? Absolutely. We hear of them responding to her and the hospitality in her home.

She writes in her book:

> I can still see people in my cozy sitting room: Stephen ensconced in a small fireside chair utterly entranced with *Watership Down*. I did most of the reading and he took up the final two paragraphs of each chapter, managing passably well. Sometimes the whole hour was spent like this; sometimes I sensed one chapter was enough. On one occasion, "What next?" brought the answer, "Game of Scrabble with 'Moonlight Sonata' on the record player." Once they had got to know my range I let them choose what to do. I can see Alex on the floor by the fire making up her mind which song to have, "Sur le Pont" or "Au Clair de la Lune," singing softly to herself as she puts on a record. And Jimmy streaking in at the front door, and by the time I've turned on the hall light he's got two chairs drawn up to the fire with a copy of *101 Dalmatians* on each. We read the statutory chapter in the usual way. He snapped the book shut and went to the bookcase saying, "Now poetry. Two each," handing out large anthologies. We rearrange ourselves at the table and get on

with the choosing. He seemed a bit stuck. "What's the matter? Can't you find one?"

"The trouble is I've got THREE."

"We could have an extra, you know." And we're off, sometimes a verse each, sometimes each reading the whole of our chosen poem. Later on he took to *A Puffin Book of Verse*.

"Page 273," he said. "It's really good."

And what did I find on page 273? Psalm 23. By the last few weeks he'd decided we must stop this haphazard choosing and go straight through.[15]

There are several wonderful things about this account, which is a window into a PNEU-type teacher and child relationship. The atmosphere is personal and homey. In this case, it *is* Marion's home, and she gives ample time to these needy children. There is a lot of warmth as she enjoys the different personalities. She's thrilled as they make progress and shares her own enjoyment with them. They have a satisfying time together, rather than just another "lesson" for backward children. They looked forward to coming. Notice her response to the child when he has taken in enough of the story. She does not force-feed him when his appetite is gone.

Her example is a shining one. The very best should not be for an elite. *Those who have been neglected, not nourished with life's richness, need the PNEU approach.* In order to serve their needs, Marion Berry responded to them individually and with experienced sureness. She won them over to a new world—the joy of books, poetry, music, French, and Latin too (appropriately offered for one at least: "No answer needed beyond the radiant face with huge navy blue eyes"). They enjoyed copying beautiful writing patterns. They enjoyed Marion and trusted her. Marion enjoyed them.

Another PNEU distinctive can be identified in Marion's work as headmistress. A unique feature of her school was that it was part of her home. She lived in a few rooms in a large house surrounded by lawn and trees. There was a kitchen where fresh food was cooked every lunchtime, and children ate with teachers joining them around set tables.

In a school like this, the children belonged to a sort of family. They were continually in relationship with each other and the teachers. This is wonderful, simple, and yet precious. The relationships endured—there was real caring and the atmosphere of a community that lives, plays, enjoys, and learns together.

Now we can celebrate the fact that many people are trying to set up schools where this human, personal, and effective approach to education can flourish—a sense of committed folk, parents and teachers, wanting to "pass on the baton" to succeeding generations of educators and children. It is in this spirit of trust and adventure that we invite you to search diligently in the rest of this book for a way forward in teaching the children you know and are responsible for—a thoughtful way forward in the clamor of today's educational world with its competing aims, promises, and techniques.

2

The Child Is
a Person

By Jack Beckman

This first proposition of Charlotte Mason's educational philosophy may seem merely a statement of the obvious. But it is not some minor element of a greater truth. It is a central truth in its own right, and if we ignore it, great sorrow and malpractice can result. Try a simple experiment. Take a small child on your knee. Respect him. Do not see him as something to prune, form or mold. This is an individual who thinks, acts, and feels. He is a separate human being whose strength lies in who he is, not in who he will become. If his choices now and in the future are to be good ones, this person must understand reality and see the framework of truth. . . . We are told by many in our generation that this small child is a cog in a machine, or even that he is a possession, like a pet animal. . . . We must answer: No. You are holding a person on your knee and that is wonderful.[1]

These are the words of Susan Schaeffer Macaulay in her introduction to chapter 2 of *For the Children's Sake*. They are helpful as we come to think actively about Charlotte Mason's first educational principle.

Consider the first two years of the child's life. In the home, the child learns to walk, talk, play, and develop relationships with parents, siblings, and the world at large. He comes to us as a person with an enormous number of healthy affinities (relationships, attractions). Everything around the child is of concern and interest—he gains knowledge from observations and establishes a relationship with the person or thing observed. The child is no mere oyster but fully a person who is learning constantly. If this is true of the infant, what might we see in the school-aged child who has been around a bit? We believe he is moved in much the same way as his adult counterparts, with affinities built in:

> Among these is the Desire for Knowledge, knowledge-hunger being natural to everybody. History, Geography, the thoughts of other people, roughly, the humanities, are proper for us all, and are the objects of the natural desire of knowledge. So too, are Science, for we live in the world; and Art, for we all require beauty, and are eager to know how to discriminate; social science, Ethics, for we are aware of the need to learn about the conduct of life; and Religion, for . . . we all want God.[2]

It is natural, God-given, that the child should thus have a hunger for knowledge like that for food. Only this is "mind food." But what of the child brought up in difficult, disadvantaged circumstances? Surely such a child has lost this appetite. In one community, a pastor and his wife committed to reading aloud to a group of hardened children in a detention center, bringing many books with them to leave for the boys. This couple humbly worked in loving service, and over time relationships developed. They began to see the fruit of their work. *Swiss Family Robinson, Treasure Island, Robin Hood,* and *The Hobbit* opened for the children new worlds of words and pictures. Not only did the boys come to look forward to these reading visits, sitting enrapt as the stories were read aloud, but they soon began to devour all the books offered. Many nonreaders took lessons to gain the tools necessary to begin the joy of reading their own living books. A sense of new life penetrated the desperate world of these children, and from this experience we see that children are built up from the inside.[3]

As the body needs nourishment, so too does the inner person, and this feeding is through ideas found in books. All the child requires is a rich and varied curriculum. He or she has the natural powers of curiosity, attention, retention, and assimilation that comprise the ability for self-education. Our business, writes Miss Mason, is to give the child "mind-stuff." And that mind-stuff is found in the best books by the best minds—first, regularly read aloud to children at home in the early years, and then, as children gain ability, they read on their own. They range among many living books.

In a first grade classroom, six-year-olds are learning the convention of reading. The room is filled with bookcases, and many selections may be

found, to the children's wonder and delight. The teacher make
reads aloud to her students daily from a living book too difficult
of reading (*The Lion, the Witch, and the Wardrobe, Old Mother
Little House on the Prairie*), and thus tunes their ears to the cade   cab-
ulary, and voice of literature. These books they later narrate back with pleasure and detail. The teacher's desire is to so feed her students and whet their
appetites that they will naturally value books and come to feed themselves.
And it is not only from books that children must take their nourishment—
art and music, walks and studies in nature, language and handicraft, movement and physical exercise—all of these are for the feeding of heart, mind,
and body.

We must then come to understand an important principle: "The child's
mind is the *instrument* of his education; his education does not produce his
mind." Life is continual in its progress and learning. Children's speculations,
curiosity, and questions about everything all show this hunger for knowledge.
Robert Coles in his book *The Spiritual Lives of Children* has attested to the
depth and complexity of very young children's philosophically-bent lines of
questioning regarding the nature of God and man. Their "how" and "why"
questions have the ring of a philosopher's quest for wisdom. Like their teachers, children carry about a worldview lens by which they measure and judge
the world.

Miss Mason's definition of an educated child both charms and challenges: "A child who possesses a sound and fairly wide knowledge of a number of subjects, all of which serve to interest him; such a child studies with
delight."[4]

In our imaginings, can we envision such a student? We have witnessed
the dull student, the bored student, the lazy student—but have we observed
the delighted student, the interested student, the capacious student? In an
urban center, one teacher became tired of the sameness of her grade eight
botany textbook, as did her students. After having read about Miss Mason's
ideas for nature walks and notebooks, she decided to use these ideas to make
an urban diary of plants, animals, and flowers. Students' interest in the world
about them increased as they took weekly walks around the school and neighborhood. After completion of the unit, the students' diaries, complete with
notes and watercolor pictures, were displayed in a prominent art museum.

In light of the nature of the learner as a person, the teacher might quake and ask, "What have I to offer?" As the teacher sees the child for who he or she has been created to be, self-acting and self-developing, the teacher's

> . . . dull lessons crumble into the dust they are when he faces children as they are. He cannot go on with his stale commonplaces; he feels that he may not bore them. . . . He knows that children's minds hunger at regular intervals as do their bodies; that they hunger for knowledge, not for information, and that his own poor stock of knowledge is not enough. . . . He is not sufficient for these things.[5]

Teachers and caregivers should be motivated for change in their schools and places of learning in light of these things if they are true. Curriculum and methodology; classroom atmosphere and set-up; policies and procedures; teacher training and oversight; relationship of parent, child, and teacher; home, community, and school all need to be addressed in turn. In view of the Victorian era, Miss Mason asked for no less than an educational revolution. In view of the child as learner, may we do less in our times?

The child's natural relationships begin in the cradle with mother and father and then proceed to the church, school, and community as well. Forces are speaking against this time-honored tradition, but even with many social changes happening, this original pattern is always recognized by professionals and others to be the best for the child. This tradition is one of the ways children come to live in healthy community with others. The scope of each of these natural relationships bears an authority structure that has been deputed from God and is carried out by parents, teachers, and other adults in the child's life. These authority structures serve as models for the child.

THE PRINCIPLES OF AUTHORITY

We, like Charlotte Mason, wish to have children take their places in the world at their best, with every capacity of good in them developed into a power. Children have a vast and rich intellectual and spiritual inheritance to draw upon for their present and future. Living books and ideas; a broad curriculum filled with the realities of truth, goodness, and beauty; and a constellation of natural relationships will put them in touch with this inheritance. What they will become we do not know—but we have hope that they will become all God has planned for them to be, whether parent, artist, factory worker, business owner, doctor, lawyer, or teacher. We hope this because the "who" of children is secure—all we need do is to place them in a large room spread with an abundant feast of learning.

FACTORS THAT AFFIRM THE PERSONHOOD OF THE CHILD

The Learning Space

Physical: The classroom is orderly and neat, reflecting a pleasant atmosphere. Student work, bulletin boards, art prints, and maps are carefully displayed with discernment and a purpose to avoid clutter.

Emotional: The atmosphere is supportive, nurturing, and caring, reflecting a sense of safety balanced with challenge. Good habits of mind and body are deliberately encouraged both in teacher and student. A sense of community is present—praying and feeding on the Word of God, solving problems, and gathering around vital learning together.

Cognitive: Care has been given to the development of a wide curriculum with the selection of literature and other resources reflecting the child's need for "mind food." Narration becomes a daily culture in the classroom. Disciplinary and inspirational subjects are interspersed throughout the day.

The Child

• Responsible for his or her own learning as a scholar, a high calling affirmed by the adult caregiver or teacher.

• Responsible to be under authority as expressed by obedience and teachability.

• Responsible to reflect habits of mind and body (attention, orderliness, reverence, imagination).

• Responsible to cultivate a love for living books and ideas and to make as many connections in learning as possible.

The Teacher or Caregiver

• Responsible to provide an orderly and consecutive broad curriculum steeped in living books and ideas.

• Responsible to affirm her own authority under God and to avoid encroaching upon the personhood of the child by manipulation, suggestion, or influence.

• Responsible to train the students in habits of mind and body as opposed to arbitrary rules.

• Responsible to offer no stray lessons in any subject area that will undermine the learning of the child. Lessons should be well planned and contribute to the whole curriculum.

• Responsible to develop in herself the same things offered to the students—a joy in learning, formation of habits, and an enriched life both inside and outside the learning place.

The initial planning has been done. Desks and chairs have been neatly arranged. Books are set upon the shelf, pencils are sharpened, and hopes arise for a new school year. And then the day arrives, as do the students. The room fills with the sounds of whispered voices ("Is she nice?" "I heard she was strict!" "Sometimes she gives extra recess."), the shuffling of book bags and lunches, and the first furtive eye contacts between teacher and children. Expectancy mixes with a bit of anxiety as this space literally becomes a classroom. What kind of year will it be? What triumphs and trials will occur? Both teacher and students wonder.

This scene is both old and new—it has been happening for a long time, but it also occurs each fresh school season. A teacher sizes up her charges while they also examine her. The teacher has a worldview lens that brings her students and craft into some kind of focus. This worldview is a kind of internalized belief system that speaks to essential questions: Who is the learner? What is the teaching and learning process? What is the role of the teacher? What do I teach? How do I relate to my students?

On a more mundane level, worldview determines methods of discipline and motivation, methods of instruction, and the appearance of the classroom. These beliefs control how the teacher thinks and responds to children, parents, content, learning, and all of life. It is an inescapable fact that the teacher has a view of her students affecting not only how she teaches, but also how she sees them as human beings. This view is a peculiar mix of nature and nurture, personality and training. This is why Miss Green in grade three uses a stoplight to remind her children of the noise level based upon her own tolerance, while Mrs. Brown in the same grade down the hall has trained her students to self-monitor themselves by the development of the habits of attentiveness and respect. Both of these approaches say something about each teacher's view of children and learning.

Most teachers come into education with ideals informed by many sources. Skinner and the behaviorists train in models of child management and efficient methods of instruction. Piaget encourages teachers to understand the stages of developmental cognitive growth and to plan teaching around these stages, which move from concrete thinking to abstract over time. Bruner asks teachers to view the child as journeying toward cognitive insights leading to self-actualization. Freud and Jung desire the teacher to explore the inscape of the child's mind for deeper meaning. Even Christian teachers and counselors create an admixture of Bible truth and secular thinking. The problem lies in the idea that each of these belief systems has a different (and at times, competing) worldview—and a fundamental issue focuses around the view of the learner.

Who is the learner and what is his or her relationship to knowledge and learning? Is he or she basically good or evil (or both)? Passive or active in learning? Capable of choice, or has life already been determined somehow? Motivated internally or externally? An unmarked slate or having unrealized potential? These questions are answered every day in every classroom, day-care center, or basketball court—answered by the way children are viewed and treated by adults.

The teacher's assignment comes complete with guides, workbooks, planners, and a hearty, "Go forth and teach." But what may be missing is something to tie it all together, a "captain idea" (to quote Coleridge), a point of integration that brings the child and learning together in a meaningful relationship. This idea might be termed the missing key to unlock the art cabinet of teaching and learning—a unified philosophy of education that addresses the "who" of the learner and the "why" and "how" of the teaching/learning process. The integrating idea stands against the radical eclecticism in our attempts to blend so many disparate theories of learning in the classroom.

For this unified philosophy we turn to Charlotte Mason. Within the pages of her six volumes of applied educational philosophy, we may feast abundantly—living books and ideas; the primacy of the home in the life and learning of the child; nature studies; art and musical appreciation; the discipline of habits; the knowledge of God, man, and the universe; the centrality of history—all of these and more fill the searching teacher's heart and mind with a perspective, a view of teaching and learning that truly comes together. The fundamental underpinning is the capital idea that *the child is born a person*—not an object to be manipulated as the behaviorist believes. Not a rudderless and morally neutral explorer as the cognitive theorist would think. Nor an animal at the mercy of drives beyond his or her control as believed by the Freudian theorist. But rather *a person* made in the image of God, both active and interactive in his or her own life and learning. Fully a person, not a person "to become."

THE NATURE OF THE LEARNER

As we read *A Philosophy of Education*, Miss Mason provides us with the starting point of her applied philosophy—"that children are born persons." She viewed children as bearing the image of God (Gen. 1: 26), thus capable of reflecting some of His attributes—exercising dominion over the created order, being relational, rational, creative, moral, and expressing mercy and love. The child's person unfolds as he or she relates to God, family, others, nature, books, and knowledge. Note how Miss Mason describes the child for us:

> This is how we find children—with intelligence more acute, logic more keen, observing powers more alert, moral sensibilities more quick, love and faith and hope more abounding; in fact, in all points as we are, only more so; but absolutely ignorant of the world and its belongings, of us and our ways, and, above all, of how to control and direct and manifest the infinite possibilities with which they are born.[6]

Here we see children for who they are in an honest and realistic manner, both with vast potential and yet limits as well. They come to us with natural powers of attention and curiosity, an appetency for knowledge (something like an appetite and a competency), moral and aesthetic capabilities, but also with ignorance and inexperience. Upon a diet of relationships with knowledge found in living books and ideas, God, others, and nature, children must feed to fortify their potential. Children come to us with compelling inborn powers of mind in place, yet also with ignorance, which like an appetite, must be fed on "mind food" from living books and ideas, life and experiences. In this desire for knowledge, they are ravenous.

However, this potentiality is marred by another reality—that of the Fall. Children as persons also bear the effects of the sin nature, being subject to the pull of sin and grace in every aspect of their existence (Rom. 5:12-21). Miss Mason was not unaware of this and wrote:

> . . . every human being comes into the world with infinite possibilities for good; and alas! infinite possibilities for evil; possibly with evil

hereditary tendencies which may be rectified by education, or with good tendencies which his bringing-up may nullify.[7]

And again in A *Philosophy of Education*:

The fact seems to be that children are like ourselves, not because they have become so, but because they are born so; that is, with tendencies, dispositions, towards good and towards evil, and also with curious intuitive knowledge as to which is good and which is evil. Here we have the work of education indicated.[8]

And here we begin to see the reality of the child as both image-bearer and fallen creation—both exist at the same time in the life of the child from beginning to end (Gen. 8:21; Prov. 4:23; Rom. 1:18-32). C. S. Lewis illustrated this duality well in calling man the "glorious ruin."[9] The need of the child is for redemption, a "personal knowledge, that there is a Saviour of the world, who has for him instant forgiveness and waiting love."[10]

Miss Mason, in a practical and realistic manner, describes children as we observe them in the home, the classroom, the playground. We see clearly that they exhibit at times sinful aspects of anger, willfulness, and selfishness, but we also observe mercy, patience, and forgiveness. Our role as parents and teachers is to reflect the model of our Lord Jesus in relationship with these little ones—to come alongside and encourage them in their ignorance and sin toward a better way. In reflecting upon this idea of relationship, Maryellen St. Cyr has written:

When a child chooses to act in accordance with his fallenness, this time is best used to instruct the child in relationship. Let the child see that he bears a holy calling of duty towards self, in governing self and redirecting his behaviors; of duty toward authority (parent and teacher, who are also under authority themselves to God); and of duty in bearing dominion in his world. And let the child experience consequences of poor choosing. And of calling upon God for strength in time of weakness.[11]

It is not unlike the coach of an after-school inner-city basketball team taking the time needed to mentor players in the life skills of communication and conflict resolution as well as skills and strategies on the court. In this, he is helping his players to become more and more persons by both respecting them and providing appropriate discipline and training.

The idea that children are born persons provides a worthy focus for our view of the nature of the learner. The concept is not eclectic or arbitrary in its perspective. It is spiritual and biblical in nature. Our postmodern culture tells us that the child is an individual, set apart from all others, having no limits, with life arrayed about him for his personal fulfillment. His environment and education are designed to "produce" who and what he will become. This fragmented view denies the holistic nature of the learner in all his many aspects, having both vast potential and real limits. In fact, the individual aspect of the child is merely one part of his nature, but it is not all that he is. Issues of community, fellowship, authority, sin, and redemption must be brought into the picture of who the child is—and these principles are understood and developed in Miss Mason's philosophy. Listen again as we quote:

> We have been so long taught to regard children as products of education and environment, that we fail to realize that from the first they are persons; and as Carlyle has well said, "The mystery of a person, indeed, is ever divine, to him that has a sense for the godlike."
>
> We must either reverence or despise children; and while we regard them as incomplete or undeveloped beings who will one day arrive at the completeness of man, rather than as weak and ignorant persons, whose ignorance we must support, but whose potentialities are as great as our own, we cannot do otherwise than despise children, however kindly and even tenderly we commit the offence.[12]

How might we bring principle to practice in this most important of ideas? Are there ways in which children may be respected as persons in our homes and classrooms? If we have read any of Miss Mason's works and are convinced of their efficacy, then we are forced to take another look at our places of learning. Just as she ran against the prevailing mind-set of the Victorian era regarding the child as a passive object in her own learning, so too might we have to run the risk of running counter to the competition and performance-based culture in today's society. At the very least we are confronted with changing or restructuring our attitude toward children.

In the genesis of this restructuring, those in charge of the learning place— school board, principals, governors, classroom teachers, parents, daycare workers, Sunday school teachers—should come together to study and ask some core questions such as:

1. What preexisting ideas about children and learning do these people bring with them to the place of learning?

2. Identify these ideas and compare them to Miss Mason's Eighteen Principles and her Educational Manifesto found in *School Education*, page 214. Read as a group *A Philosophy of Education* for discussion. What philosophical and/or practical roadblocks must be addressed in order to proceed with Miss Mason's applied philosophy?

3. How are the methods and curriculum in the learning place reflective of a philosophy of education, and how might these be redirected to move more into line with Miss Mason's principles? Are those in charge convinced that her approach is a biblical one and worthy of implementation?

4. How might they design a learning community that reflects both the personhood of the child and his need for authority? How might teachers themselves reflect both personhood and authority in the learning place?

5. How are they actively encouraging and providing opportunities to read, study, and discuss not only Miss Mason's works, but other worthy books, including the Scriptures, literature, and other writings in the field of teaching and learning?

AUTHORITY AND DOCILITY

Through relationships with caring and sympathetic adults, children may learn the basic principles of authority, which are natural, necessary, and fundamental. *Natural*, because children are in need of boundaries and standards in order to learn and grow. *Necessary*, due to the sinful nature of humankind and the need for discipline. *Fundamental*, because all earthly authority is under the rule of God and invested by Him. The child's response to authority is docility, which according to Miss Mason may also be termed teachability or obedience. We read this in *A Philosophy of Education*:

> [T]he two principles of authority and docility act in every life precisely as do those two elementary principles which enable the earth to maintain its orbit, the one drawing it towards the sun, the other constantly driving it into space; between the two, the earth maintains a more or less middle course and the days go on.[13]

In observing homes and classrooms, we see these lines of authority and docility being blurred due to a pervasive permissiveness in the culture. Authority has been equated with slavishness, and has given way to models such as the "democratic classroom" where children and teacher stand on equal footing in authority in terms of decision-making and discipline. Within a Christian view an implied equality does exist, however, due to the fact that parent, teacher and child are all under authority in certain spheres of life. Miss Mason writes: "Docility implies equality; there is no great gulf fixed between teacher and taught; both are pursuing the same ends, engaged on the same theme, enriched by mutual interests; and probably the quite delightful pursuit of knowledge affords the only intrinsic liberty for both teacher and taught."[14]

Here we see that the common desire for obedience to authority (the teacher to the principal and board and students to teacher) promotes the exploration of knowledge that ties teacher and child together in a mutual quest. In observing Mr. Green's grade six history class while they research battles of the American Civil War, we note that students and teacher are involved in the process. In fact, Mr. Green is preparing for a presentation to the class on his chosen battle. The class is interested and engaged. On the other hand, Mr. Brown, teaching the same age with the same content, has elected to lecture his students on various battles of the Civil War while they take copious notes. He has taught this content in the same manner for years. The students are distracted and bored.

Authority rightly applied expresses respect for the learner, and takes into account the lines by which he or she is designed. While not abrogating the biblical mandate for obedience, true authority seeks to work *in relationship* with those under its mantle. Thus, the teacher desires to engage students actively as co-learners functioning with respect flowing from a caring and relational authority. In this we are able to observe that Mr. Green takes seriously the nature of his students and adjusts his teaching so as to activate both respect and authority in his methods.

Miss Mason writes about two conditions necessary to secure authority and docility, and if these two conditions are met, the relationship between teacher and taught is unified and peaceful. The first condition is that the teacher must not be arbitrary, but "act so evidently as one under authority" (and ultimately to the Supreme Authority). Notions of convenience or expediency are to be cast aside. The second condition is "that children should have a fine sense of the freedom which comes from knowledge which they are allowed to appropriate as they choose, freely given with little intervention from the teacher."[15]

In one school, we see teachers working together to discuss replacing inconsistent rules and "constitutions" in the classroom with *habits of heart, mind, and body.* Training in the habits of attentiveness, respect, and responsibility is consistently encouraged across the grades. Teachers themselves are inculcating these habits both personally and professionally so that students will witness important modeling. As well, teachers and caregivers should develop in themselves and the child a sense of "ought" and responsibility in life and learning. It is wrong to make children fall under the rule of law while adults are not bound by law as well. How often do teachers lower student grades for late assignments while they themselves are often tardy to school? Or do they require orderly desks while their own is a disaster? Teachers ought to be about the business of doing themselves what is required of the students. As well, all schoolwork should be done in such a manner that children are aware of their own responsibility in learning; "it is their business to know that which has been taught" with no repetition.[16]

This sense of responsibility might be better framed in light of the teacher's and child's high calling in their vocation. If they view themselves as coworkers in the kingdom of God, performing tasks that are worthy in His sight and expressing godly dominion over their work, life, and leisure, then responsibility takes on higher meaning and worth.

Another fallacy found in our homes and schools may be as detrimental in our relationship with children and must be addressed. It is this: The adults may think of themselves as superior and the child inferior, intellectually, morally, and ethically. But if we believe in the personhood of the child and in her vast potential, this becomes a false dichotomy. The reality is that the potency of the child's mind is as great or greater than ours! We see this in a number of ways—parents talking down to their children, the belief that children must be pampered in order for them to be happy and well-adjusted, or the idea that any difficulty in the child's life must be taken care of by the parent.

At times we remove good opportunities for our children's learning by standing in the way. One mother appalled another as they watched their four-year-olds playing at the park. A scuffle ensued between two of the children over a ball. As one of the mothers started to rush over and mediate, the other

calmly spoke: "Oh, let them work it out. Soon they'll be on to other things."
Soon enough play continued uninterrupted by parental interference. The one
mother had an attitude of "masterly inactivity," that of relaxed awareness
and standing aside with wisdom and discernment. And what did the children
learn? That they themselves are fully capable of working out differences without the constant meddling and overconcern of the adults. Certainly if danger
is evident, parents and caregivers *must* intrude, but in most circumstances the
art of standing aside is useful and beneficial to our children's experience.

Parents, teachers, and caregivers must be about the business of affirming
the sacredness of the child's personhood (ignorant and inexperienced though
they might be), respecting them as image-bearers just as we would wish to be
respected. But we will at times use methods of encroachment to circumvent
that personhood in our zeal for "teaching them" or "making them obey" our
commands. We see this tendency in our homes, playing fields, and classrooms.
In *A Philosophy of Education,* Miss Mason states: "People are apt to use children as counters in a game, to be moved hither and thither according to the
whim of the moment. We shall come to perceive that we cannot commit a
greater offence than to maim or crush, or subvert any part of a person."[17]

This need to control children pervades our homes, schools, and playing
fields. In this view the "superior" adult desires for the "lesser" child to be
dependent upon favor, rewards, and approval as motivators for action and
thought. Miss Mason places these forms of control in three categories:

• Manipulation by guilt, fear, or love
• Deliberate control of thinking by strong suggestion or influence
• Undue play upon any one desire

In what ways do we see these things occurring? In our desire to control
children, we have resorted to what Alfie Kohn calls, "If you do this, you'll
get that." This approach is based upon the behaviorist notion that external
rewards will get the desired behavior—it looks very much like bribery.
Parents talk about using tangible rewards to "motivate" children to clean
their rooms or complete homework assignments. Teachers use token
economies, pizza parties, and prize jars to prod students to read, manage
behavior, or keep the noise down. The peculiar thing is that temporarily these
rewards do the trick. Children clean and read, march and finish tasks.
Unfortunately, long-term or heart change does not occur as the power of the
reward diminishes over time and even becomes counterproductive. Miss
Mason realized the destructive nature of suggestion or influence over the child

and its maiming effects on the sacredness of personhood. One private school after having read *A Philosophy of Education* as well as Alfie Kohn's book *Punished by Rewards* was so struck by the rampant behaviorism in their classrooms (stoplights, stickers, stars, extra recess for good behavior, reward systems) that they began to replace bribes, suggestion, and undue influence with the delight of a job well done and an appeal to the child's heart and to the innate longing of the child for learning. Maryellen St. Cyr reflects on this when she writes:

> Seeing that behavior stems from the heart, educators need not take on the role of a behaviorist, modifying and conditioning pupils to act accordingly through elaborate systems of rewards and punishments. There is another way, the way to the heart. Children already possess the capacity for responsible actions and natural curiosity to know and to do good work as a manifestation of who they are; free and responsible agents, in direct relationship to self, God, others and the world around them. When one rewards unthinkingly, the assumption is made that individuals cannot choose to act a certain way on their own. It becomes dehumanizing, treating people like pets or objects. It is the removal of what truly defines us as human.

It is through the process of discipleship and relationship that we must make our plea—calling the heart of the child to duty to self, authority, and dominion-seeking in right ways. It is truly showing the child his own responsibility to choose and to act as a thinking, responding, relational person. And this should greatly impact the way we educate our children if we believe, as Miss Mason wrote, that all children want to know all knowledge and that knowledge is "delectable" to them, that they can be self-motivated to feed themselves with no outside suggestion, influence, or play upon avarice, power, or ambition by the teacher.

This is why we see in Ms. Appling's class of fourth graders an atmosphere of order, cooperation, and care in habit, a broad curriculum with many living books, and students gladly working and playing together without burdensome systems of rewards and punishments. Ms. Appling believes in the innate power of her students to learn—even the "slower" children—and this is reflected in her classroom practice. Students read and narrate with joy and excitement, knowing that they themselves have done the learning.

Mr. Glenn is not so enlightened. He teaches sixth grade biology and has for many years. He has made learning efficient by reducing the content to facts written on the board and then having the students copy them on 3 x 5 index cards. These cards are sent home to be memorized for the weekly quiz. Students are "motivated" by competing over who memorizes the greatest number of cards. These are recorded on a chart, and at the end of the month, the student with the most stars on the chart wins a prize.

Both of these teachers have a worldview that determines how they view children and learning. Ms. Appling believes in the innate powers of the personhood of the child. Mr. Glenn thinks that students must be externally motivated to learn because they themselves are somehow incapable. Our view of the child finds its way into our classrooms by way of methods and practices. It merely takes a short perusal for the observer to make some judgments about the teacher's stance.

FOUR BASIC EDUCATIONAL TRUTHS

Flowing from Miss Mason's view of the child, both in God's image and fallen, and the innate powers of mind, vast potential, and appetency for knowledge, four basic educational truths come forth. These will be sketched out here but fully described in chapter 3.

Education is an *atmosphere*, a *discipline*, a *life*, the *science of relations*—these four truths are foundational to understanding Miss Mason's applied philosophy of education. They are a natural extension of her beliefs about the nature of the learner. In fact, because of who the child is, these four principles must follow. We first define the person; then we move on to describe the "instruments" by which we must engage the child. Teachers and caregivers wonder about the practicality of philosophy, always looking ahead to application and method. Here we begin to see philosophy begin to take on flesh and bone. The idea of the personhood of the child may resonate, but Miss Mason addresses how to take it to implication and application in these four key points.

"Education is an atmosphere, a discipline, a life," read the front of the *Parents' Review*, parading the motto to interested readers. The subscribers of the *Parents' Review* were parents and educators seeking an applied philosophy of education and life. It was here that pithy articles explaining the motto's four concepts (including natural relations) were to be found. Coworkers and collaborators in Miss Mason's grand scheme of education sent forth writings on wide-ranging topics—nature studies, narration, living books, Shakespeare, home education, character, Bible instruction, habit formation, and so on. The reader found tangible expressions of the motto's four truths—all consistent with the view of the child as a person. No wandering off into eclectic realms of thought; Miss Mason's views were focused and consistently thought through in terms of application—nothing left to whim or chance.

Education Is an Atmosphere

By this we take it to mean that the learning place is not a child's environment but rather the formation of proper conditions for learning. These conditions take into account the educational value of the home atmosphere and acknowledge the child's due respect as an image-bearer of God, along with the expectation that the child will think, learn, and act according to that truth.

Education Is a Discipline

The key to supplanting the weakness of will in forming character is the discipline of habits formed definitely and thoughtfully, both of mind and body. To a great degree education is the formation of habits, while trusting divine grace.

Education Is a Life

The mind of the child is not a sack to be stuffed full of information, but an organism that feasts on ideas coming from every area of life; thus the child should have a broad curriculum to satisfy her appetite for knowledge, keeping in mind what subjects, intervals, and recesses are necessary at her age to produce maximum growth.

Education Is the Science of Relations

As a created being, the child has natural relations with a number of things, thoughts, and people; therefore, we must give him opportunity to build these relations to nature, handicrafts, science, art, and many living books.

Implicit in these descriptions is a number of applications. The learner is interactive with his natural relations, engaged in insightful examination of them—nature, books, friends and others, God, and ideas. He then acts according to these explorations in a purposeful manner. The process of learning is dynamic, creative, and imaginative. Learning becomes for the child an act of making connections, combining them into meaningful structures, and then applying those structures to new and novel situations. For optimal learning to occur, the teacher must encourage an atmosphere of challenge and acceptance in the classroom; she must be careful not to over-mediate between the child and his own learning. The child is born a person, and his mind feeds on ideas that he not only assimilates but reproduces in ways touched by his own imagination and thought.

Our starting point is the child and her appetency for knowledge; here is a worthy beginning. As teachers, parents, and caregivers, we become not scientists with microscope and laboratory, but naturalists who observe life and nature within its element—plein air (outdoors)—like the modern day ethnographer observing children in real life to see how and why they learn as they do. In this exploration, we are discovering what moves us forward more and more in line with the learner's nature. Our view of the child becomes a lens to make clear the way we must go.

"I am, I can, I ought, I will"

The reality of who the child is, is well expressed by this Parents' Union School (the early correspondence school) motto. The expression captures in the poet's less-is-more approach the key to the child's nature. Miss Mason writes in *Home Education* these words of explanation:

> "I am"—we have the power of knowing ourselves.
>
> "I ought"—we have within us a moral judge, to whom we feel ourselves subject and who points out and requires of us our duty.
>
> "I can"—we are conscious of power to do that which we perceive we ought to do.
>
> "I will"—we determine to exercise that power with a volition which is in itself a step in the execution of that which we will. Here is a beautiful and perfect chain, and the wonder is that, so exquisitely constituted as he is for right doing, error should be even possible to man.[18]

Or to place the motto in a child-friendly format of more recent years:

I am a child of God,
I ought to do His will.
I can do what He tells me,
And by His grace, I will.

"I am a child of God." How freeing to realize the wonder of the relationship of a child with her heavenly Father—the flow of love and grace in the child's life as she learns to live under His care and authority!

"I ought to do His will." The child has a standard to live by found in the very Word of God. She has a place to go to find out about all the "oughts" in life, but a place of forgiveness and acceptance as well.

"I can do what He tells me." The very real presence of the Holy Spirit in the child's life makes obedience to His precepts possible.

"And by His grace, I will." It is by grace the child has been saved, and it is by grace that the child is preserved and sustained as she walks the walk of faith, life, and learning.

3

Four Pillars of Education

EDUCATION IS AN ATMOSPHERE

By Bobby Scott

It was to Matthew Arnold that Charlotte Mason attributed the saying, "Education is an atmosphere, a discipline, and a life." She called it perhaps "the most complete and adequate definition of education we possess." She considered the statement to be "profound and exquisite" in that it covered what she saw to be the three conceivable points of view regarding education:

1. Subjective (spiritual): Education is a life.
2. Objective (physiological): Education is a discipline.
3. Relative (relational): Education is an atmosphere.[1]

The last of these points, though normally expressed first in her list, indeed finds its emphasis in the realm of relationships of the child—to God, his parents, his teacher, his classmates, his learning, and himself. It is the relationships with all these things, and the ideas that proceed from them, that produce the air the child breathes as his life, either an invigorating draft or a stultifying smog of polluted thinking. Charlotte Mason calls this atmosphere the thought-environment, and claims that the earliest and most important ministry of the educator is to *"excite this (natural) appetency towards things lovely, honest, and of good report."*[2]

This being true, how do we carry out this ministry; how do we produce the atmosphere that does more than just exercise the mind and actually nurtures the heart of the child?

FOUNDATIONAL PRINCIPLES

The Atmosphere of the Child's Environment Inspires an Unconscious Direction for His Life

Charlotte Mason, observing accurately the lifelong effect of a home environment, wrote:

> [T]he atmosphere in which a child gathers his unconscious ideas of right living emanates from his parents. Every look of gentleness and tone of reverence, every word of kindness and act of help, passes into the thought-environment, the very atmosphere which the child breathes; he does not think of these things, may never think of them, but all his life long they excite that vague appetency . . . toward things sordid or things lovely, things earthly or divine.[3]

Plainly we all have a bent toward certain interests in life that were influenced by the atmosphere of our childhood. Authors today such as David Elkind, Michael Medved, James Dobson, and Susan Schaeffer Macaulay stress the importance of a healthy childhood.

The Educational Atmosphere of Schools Either Reinforces or Contradicts the Thought-Environment of the Home

Those of us who have worked with children whose home atmospheres are violent, dysfunctional, or simply chaotic know all too well how true Miss Mason's observations are in this regard. Yet ours is a ministry not of despair but of *hope*. In our best situations we are engaged in schools and in teaching that reinforce a loving and honest thought-environment that already exists in the child's home. In other situations we can become a safe haven for the emotionally abused child, never losing hope that with the power of a loving heavenly Father, it is possible to divert unhealthy thinking and thwart destructive ideas. Children from the most destitute or the most materialistic home environments are not beyond the reach of education in the truth, since they are made as persons in God's image.

The Teacher Has the Central Control Over the Educational Atmosphere

Some teachers caught in very rigid environments with unhealthy structures over which they have no control may refute this principle, but most situations today do leave teachers with the primary responsibility for the learning environment and the ability to create it. Obviously the best situations find the school administration not only allowing the proper conditions to exist, but supporting and encouraging them and preventing outside influences from hindering them.

Of course the teacher's relationship with the children is the first and foremost atmospheric condition. Two *contrasting* examples come to mind.

Rosemary Sutcliff, the accomplished author of children's historical fiction, writes in her biography of her Latin teacher: "He used to stride up and down the aisle between desks, lightly rapping people on the head with the Latin grammar when they got it wrong. I almost invariably got it wrong. I got most things wrong. I did not do nearly as well in any direction." Of her headmistress Sutcliff wrote: "She was a devout, high church woman and tried hard to make us over in her own image, though without much success."[4] It doesn't take some of us long to think back on a schoolroom of our past in which we breathed this type of air.

On the other hand, Ann Puddy, a graduate of the Rickmansworth PNEU school outside London, gave this testimonial about her headmistress Marion Berry: "Oh, I do like Miss Berry, Mummy. Of course, she is soft with us, you know, but we do what she wants just the same. She just tells us not to do so in a very nice voice, and we don't do it anymore."[5]

Does this second example sound too simple, too easy, and certainly not realistic in today's difficult classrooms? Having met Miss Berry personally, I assure you she was no pushover; nor did she possess a magic wand to charm her students into submission. Instead, another principle was operative in her school. It follows.

Atmosphere Is a Living Relationship, Taking Time, Patience, and a Few Bumps Along the Way to Become Authentic

Essex Cholmondeley, the devoted disciple and biographer of Charlotte Mason, in a letter written to Miss Berry in 1964 explained that atmosphere is "that subtle and difficult third part of education. Discipline and life, these can be transplanted carefully, but 'atmosphere' *can only be built up* [emphasis mine] and you have done this to the great happiness of the school."[6]

Miss Berry was respected, obeyed, and enjoyed by her students because of the relationship she had built up with them—that in turn permeated every nook and cranny of the school. Ann Puddy's reflection cannot be credible unless it is placed in the context of her school atmosphere.

*A Proper Educational Atmosphere Can Exist in the Most
Squalid Confines of the Inner City or the Most Regal Classroom
of the Affluent Suburb*

As schools today in American suburbs attempt to capture the refreshing air
of the PNEU atmosphere, one wonders if it is even possible *there*, much less
in the asphalt jungle of an inner-city school. After visiting some of the remaining PNEU schools in England, mostly in small villages, it was easy for me to
come to several conclusions:

• English charm is the primary source of the atmosphere.

• English schoolchildren are brighter and more culturally refined than
those elsewhere.

• Teachers in other cultures will be adverse to adopting any of these
ideas, primarily because change is difficult.

• This atmosphere is impossible to produce in a large school.

• Parents in the West are too committed to their children's achievement
to embrace much of this approach.

In the ensuing six years since these thoughts came to me, all or part of
each conclusion has proved untrue, not because of the great ability of educators to adapt the Charlotte Mason principles, but because of the nature of
the principles themselves. The conditions that produce the atmosphere are:

• cross-cultural

• biblical (and therefore eternal and external)

• spiritually produced and not contrived

• plain common sense (to those who understand children)

In Mason's words:

The ideas that quicken come from above; the mind of the little child is
an open field, surely good ground, where, morning by morning, the
sower goes forth to sow and the seed is the Word. All our teaching of
children should be given reverently, with the humble sense that we are
invited in this matter to cooperate with the Holy Spirit; but it should be
given dutifully and diligently with the awful sense that our cooperation
would appear to be made a condition of the Divine action; that the
Saviour of the World pleads with us to "suffer the little children to come
unto Me" as if we had the power to hinder, as we know that we have.[7]

The culture, the society, the information, and the environments of children do change, but the desire of children to know and to learn does not. Why? Because they are persons created in the image of a God who is unchangeable. And when this is understood and internalized, the teachers who are dutiful and diligent to create the proper conditions can simply *get out of the way*, because that same unchangeable God allows His Spirit to quicken and guide the minds of the children into His truths and beauty in spite of us.

THE CONDITIONS OF A PROPER ATMOSPHERE

In the above quote from Mason, note the statement that "our cooperation would appear to be made a condition of the Divine action." Here the point is made that though it is the Spirit of God who ultimately produces and uses the proper educational atmosphere in the lives of children, we must *cooperate*. And the warning is that if we are uncooperative and hinder the children (i.e., quench the Spirit), we are in serious jeopardy. As stated in the first principle, children may carry the effects of a hurtful atmosphere throughout their lives.

Before we chastise ourselves too much for our past failures, it is good to remember that we have a God who understands our weaknesses, redeems our failures, and can make a garden out of our mess. So many times I lament, "Oh, if I only knew then what I know now! How did those children grow and learn in that atmosphere?" Well, they did grow, and they did learn, because in spite of my poor practices, they were loved. But now with the insights of Charlotte Mason, we can become less of an obstacle to what God will intentionally do in the lives of children. We can provide *conditions* in our classrooms and homes that are consistent with what we know is true about children and about learning. But before we look at those, first we will examine:

The Improper Conditions

ENCROACHMENT ON THE PERSONHOOD OF THE CHILD BY PSYCHOLOGICAL MILLSTONES

In the preface to all her books, Charlotte Mason listed some of these millstones as fear, love, suggestion, influence, and undue play on any one natural desire.[8] Some common examples follow:

The Use of Moralism

Moralism, a seemingly harmless practice, is actually a noxious gas to a child's understanding of God and truth. A favorite example is the misuse of John 6:1-

15, the story of Jesus feeding the 5,000. In a storybook that I read to our teachers in training, the authors focus on the precious little boy who willingly "shares" his lunch of five loaves and two fish with Jesus, who in turn feeds everyone. The book ends with the admonition, "Jesus loves us to share with others."

So is there a problem in this teaching? Isn't sharing taught here? The answers are a resounding yes and an emphatic no! Yes, there is great harm when the truth of a text is manipulated to force a lesson on the minds of children. The practice lacks integrity. No, sharing is not taught in this passage.

But a greater harm than forcing a moral on a text can occur. Children are directed by the author to focus on human actions rather than on the power of Christ. In the long run, a diet of this type of "bread" produces a student who defines himself by what he does rather than who he is. Thus this millstone hinders a true understanding of the gospel. Even those stories that rightfully point out the goodness of a biblical or other literary character should be balanced by acknowledging that character's frailty and need for God.

The Use of Guilt

Though relationships were always of primary importance in the atmosphere of the PNEU schools, care was taken to avoid the misuse of affection and putting students on "guilt trips" for their misbehavior. Wrong responses to students' actions or attitudes can range from a seemingly harmless comment such as "I am so disappointed in you" to "Well, I guess I shouldn't be teaching anymore if that's the best you can do!"

In both cases, the teacher is using his perceived desire of his students to please him as the motivating factor, misusing their affection. Often teachers or parents who practice this method are unaware that their own relationship with their children is also unhealthy, for they define their success at teaching by their ability to win and keep the children's affections. When some students begin to see through these guilt motivation tactics (as they will at about age twelve), these teachers will turn from them to focus primarily on their favorites or "pets."

It should not be concluded that giving a child verbal encouragement should be avoided so that the child is not motivated only by pleasing (or displeasing) his teacher. But as Eve Anderson says, we must avoid praise that is "over the top" and ask for the wisdom to see when a child desires to do right because it is the right thing to do, or desires to do right only to win another's approval or affection.

The Use of Competition

Some years ago some colleagues and I visited a school and observed a situation that illustrates atmosphere. The children were happily celebrating a milestone, cheering at the teacher's prompting the fact that they had completed the math text for their level early in the year and were now to move a grade level ahead. The purpose of the party was to affirm the diligence and academic progress of the children and to make being "a level ahead" the desired outcome of their learning.

Reflecting on what constituted the atmosphere in that classroom, one has to conclude that *competition* was the primary motivator—the desire to be better, to move faster, to be seen as more brilliant than the normal students at that level. Awe and wonder of the truths and challenges of math, even the joy of solving a problem, were replaced with the pride of success. The minds of the children were trained to believe that reaching certain performance levels was the goal of instruction, even to be celebrated as such.

These practices that involve the competition of whole classes as well as those where individual students compete against each other are devastating to a healthy school atmosphere. As a byproduct of rewarding a certain kind of success, they breed pride, self-centered motivation, and great discouragement among the "losers." The atmosphere sought in schools influenced by Charlotte Mason is one where all students thrive in a spirit of cooperation, where the love of learning produces, in the words of Marion Berry, not a pep rally for winners, but "a good time had by *all*."

The Use of Comparison

In a personal interview with Marion Berry in July 1999, I asked her the secret to creating the atmosphere that seemed to exist in her school for fifty years or more, one in which children thrived as persons in proper relationship to so many things. Her reply came quickly, firmly, and with conviction for her ninety-one years. Yet she spoke of what was omitted rather than what was present. The absence of four toxic practices—competition, prizes and marks, stress, and comparison—purified the air for learning.

It is such a temptation in schools, especially where one class may contain a special group of motivated learners (often by design where tracking is implemented), for a teacher to compare the group with a less studious one. Bragging on the better or criticizing the worse is never a motivator for the other, except again as an appeal to competition. As in a family where parents are tempted to say, "Why aren't you responsible like your sister?" or "Your father always made excellent marks!" these comments and attitudes may create an atmosphere where children either strive to improve for the wrong reason or gradually give up in discouragement.

The Overuse of Testing and Evaluation

In Charlotte Mason's lifetime, she faced the challenge of having her House of Education at Scale How approved by state educational authorities in Great Britain for a certified program to prepare teachers for positions in her schools. As described in Essex Cholmondeley's biography,[9] Miss Mason never saw such approval take place in her lifetime. Had she perhaps been willing to compromise some of her philosophy and educational convictions, she might have gained certification. Whether she understood the consequences that such approval may have brought to the PNEU is uncertain. But history has shown that negative consequences would have been inevitable, for school certifications and inspections have increasingly moved from legitimate personal evaluations to impersonal objective assessments based almost solely on the results of student testing and examinations.

The words of the Ministry of Education's 1957 report of the Rickmansworth PNEU school read: "The corporate life of the school is pleasant indeed, in an *atmosphere* of cheery industry and enjoyment of work and play." Today such a report would focus only on how many children passed the required exam or tests and thus on how many were qualified to move to the next level.

The obsession with testing in the United States especially is becoming epidemic, primarily due to the collapse of quality education and the desire to hold schools accountable. Standardized test scores of students are seen as the primary way to judge the quality of a teacher and ultimately of a school.

This trend is leading to calls for a standardized national curriculum so that all assessments can be equalized, a practice already adopted in the U.K. and other Western nations. Surely the tail is wagging the dog when tests and examinations are dictating what the curriculum of schools should contain. In the midst of all this is the unfortunate teacher whose passion for learning and motivation for teaching is brought captive to tests and exams that control the destiny of her students and herself as well! As Alfie Kohn has stated, "Every hour that teachers feel compelled to try to raise test scores is an hour not spent helping kids become critical, creative, curious thinkers."[10]

Marion Berry is right when she says that the greatest deterrent to a healthy atmosphere is the stress produced by striving for marks. So do we mean that schools are not to be evaluated or inspected? No, but they should not be judged on the basis of examinations and tests alone. Nancy Sizer said it well:

> You're asking an awful lot of human beings inside schools if you don't have tests (or exams). You're asking for principals (or headmasters) to be willing to sit down with a teacher and talk to him about things that have gotten out of hand. And you have to reduce the teachers' load so that they can get to know their students better and find out *what will really make each student sing as a scholar.* (emphasis mine)[11]

Charlotte Mason's schools knew this song. The atmosphere of relationship and treating teachers and children as persons is what Sizer is describing. These attitudes lead to "cheerful industry and enjoyment of work and play."

Before we leave this topic, please do not conclude from the analysis of these millstones that we are creating a laid-back atmosphere where children will progress in learning only as *they* see fit. Critics of Charlotte Mason in the United States who make these accusations only show their ignorance of her philosophy. To eliminate the stress of long lessons and long days, to emphasize cooperation over competition, to encourage rather than compare, to motivate by loving affirmation rather than stars and candy—all of these practices create a stronger academic atmosphere because learning becomes a lifelong pursuit congruent with the child's nature and the nature of learning. There is a world of difference in a teacher's admonitions, "Okay, students, let's see how much more we can learn about the amazing habits of spiders!" versus "Let's see, boys and girls, if everyone can make 100 percent on tomorrow's examination." The latter beseeches only the competitive souls and those who perform well on tests; the former excites all the children to know and form a relationship with a part of creation they have all encountered.

After the test, so what? After the lesson, what next?

ANY ATTEMPT TO REDUCE OR ENLARGE A CHILD'S POTENTIAL OR IMPORTANCE

The Limitations of Classical Education

In education, like religion, ideas that seem so novel are more often than not recycled views with a little different packaging. In the Great Britain of Charlotte Mason's day, the proponents of so-called classical education were alive and well, replete with their belief that a child is an empty vessel to be filled with the best of the empire's core knowledge.

Charlotte Mason commented that the children of these classicists are seen to have "little understanding and are only suited for methods that involve memorizing facts, dates, numbers, rules, catechisms of knowledge, and information in small parcels."[12] This reductionism (referred to as the Grammar Stage of the classicist's Trivium) denies the creation of the person of a child in the image of God where all the personality of the Creator is inherent. Though marred by sin, the redemptive and common grace of God allows a child to think, reason, reflect, rule, analyze, and discern truth at all so-called stages of life.

Jesus marveled and commended the faith of little children, not their ability to memorize. Classroom atmospheres that reduce learning to only facts to memorize produce boredom and the need to employ tangible incentives such as candy, stickers, and grades.

The Dangers of a Child-Centered Education

Dr. John Rosemond in his magazine *Affirmative Parenting* states that of all the problems in parenting children over the last thirty years, failure to recognize the importance of children is *not* one of them. In fact, he states that we have overemphasized the self-esteem of children to the degree that they have not learned respect, responsibility, and resourcefulness.[13]

This problem equally occurs in the school classroom. With the contribution of humanism, anti-God environments, and the lack of integrity in leadership, schools have moved toward the children's likes and dislikes as the gauge of programs. Just the comment by a teacher that "my students loved it" cannot be evidence of a good lesson. Sometimes misunderstood, Charlotte Mason's practice of "masterly inactivity" and her restrictions on "teacher talk" did not mean that the students were to control the classroom. Masterly inactivity implies that there is a master—the teacher. It also has other meanings as we see in the following discussion.

The Weakness of a Teacher-Centered Education

Charlotte Mason was very explicit about how the atmosphere of the school classroom is affected by the teacher making herself the "showman of the universe." This type of teaching in effect denies that the child is a person who can act upon the knowledge he receives and retrieves, and that he must be directed as to how, what, and when he should think.

Though the masterly inactivity of Mason does imply a master, it is the role of the teacher to *get out of the way*. The teacher is the master by planning the lesson, having available all the necessary resources, and then deftly guiding the flow. As master, she guards against inappropriate materials or diversions, keeping intact the foundational principles that we discussed earlier. There is never a doubt to her authority, but she never lets herself get in the way of the learning. She is inactive in the sense that she lets the natural curiosity and interest of the students take its course within the confines of the discussion. Often ideas come that lead to connections with truths learned in other subjects, for which she is delighted as students make these transitions.

Overall she lets the living books and other resources speak for themselves and does not consider herself the students' only source of information. Does she share her own stories and information that would benefit her students? Absolutely, but not in a continual lecture format day in and day out that produces an unhealthy attachment of the students. Individual pursuits are encouraged as the teacher realizes that students will not remember or comprehend every detail; nor should they be expected to.

A simple example of masterly inactivity is our school's study of the American Civil War. Interestingly, some students (especially the boys) like the books about the battles and the famous generals, while others (especially the girls) enjoy the relationships, the fashions, the lifestyle, and the plight of the slaves. So the teacher directs students to the living books of their interest. After much research, they report on their findings to the class. The models, diagrams, and live reenactments are superb, aided by the fact that the teacher stays out of the way.

The Proper Conditions

A STRUCTURE AND SCHEDULE DESIGNED FOR THE CHILDREN'S SAKE

The Best Hours for Lessons

In speaking over the years to hundreds of teachers, I have found the unanimous belief that children work best and give the best attention to learning in the morning hours. Charlotte Mason was one of the first to promote such a schedule in schools, doing what was best for children rather than giving in to the pressures of some parents. She wrote, "[T]he morning, after breakfast (the digestion of which lighter meal is not a severe tax), is much the best time for lessons and every sort of mental work; if the whole afternoon cannot be spared for out-of-door recreation [which she preferred], that is the time for mechanical tasks such as needlework, drawing, practicing."[14]

Time for Free Play and Noisy Games Outdoors

Charlotte Mason had a rule of life: "Never be within doors when you can *rightly* be without."[15] This rule was particularly important to her in the children's first years of life when they should be nurtured by their own parents in the home. She believed it was

> a mother's first duty to her children to secure for them a quiet grow-
> ing time, a full six years of passive receptive life, the waking part of it
> spent for the most part out in the fresh air. And this, not for the gain
> in bodily health alone—body and soul, heart and mind, are nourished
> with food convenient for them when the children are let alone, let to
> live without friction and without stimulus amongst happy influences
> which incline them to be good.[16]

When children started school, she said, "the claims of the schoolroom should not be allowed to encroach on the child's right to long hours daily for exercise and investigation. . . . [V]igorous healthful play is, in its turn, fully as important as lessons, as regards both bodily health and brain-power."[17]

The current research confirming the widespread benefits of outside activities makes Miss Mason a prophet of considerable insight and observation. Studies cited in "Running Research News" in the *Journal of the American Medical Association* and by doctors at Columbia University, Tufts University (Boston), and the University of South Carolina have shown the following:

• Outside play has increased benefit over equivalent inside play.

• Simple lifestyle activities like walking the dog, done as little as thirty minutes per day, improve cardiovascular health and blood pressure.

• The amount of sunlight received has a direct effect on moods, depression, and length of stay in hospitals.

• Sunlight also was found to boost the body's immune system.

• The absorption of vitamin D through sunlight facilitates calcium formation and bone health.[18]

But to Miss Mason just having children outside was not enough. While they were there, children should be allowed to be children, again without adult interference. Like Dr. David Elkind in the 1990s, she rejected the pressure for organized games and taught that children should engage in free play. They should be allowed to run and shout and be as loud as they wished.

> The muscular structure of the organs of voice is not enough considered; children love to indulge in cries and shouts and view-halloos, and this "rude" and "noisy" play, with which their elders have not much patience, is no more than nature's way of providing for the due exercise of organs, upon whose working power the health and happiness of the child's future largely depend.[19]

An Atmosphere "Which Nobody Has Been at Pains to Constitute"[20]

In speaking of structuring conditions to help produce an atmosphere, it is very important to note that we are not speaking of creating artificial circumstances to sterilize the environment. Sometimes schools are accused of being hothouses that do not prepare children for real life. As long as schools contain human beings, all the elements are available to produce real life! However, a teacher must have the wisdom necessary to know what real life should be for her class. Real life in a school should look like real life in a home to a great degree.

Miss Mason said that real life should include such natural elements as the student "being taught by his tumbles," learning "how to live with his equals by the chums he gathers round him," enjoying "romps with his father," being "teased by his brothers and petted by his sisters," learning "veneration of the old by the visits of his great-grandmother," and learning "intimacy with animals from his dog and cat."[21] It is easy to apply these same natural elements to the school as the child's classroom becomes his school family for the year, allowing the tumbles, tussles, and triumphs of the school day to become the air of a natural atmosphere.

Field trips, school activities, and daily routines can become the environment for the growth of children if parents and teachers do not magnify their roles unduly. The atmosphere is produced "from persons and things, stirred by events, sweetened by love, ventilated, kept in motion, by *the regulated action of common sense*"[22] (emphasis mine).

AN ACADEMIC PROGRAM PLANNED FOR THE CHILDREN'S SAKE

The Four Tests to Be Applied to Lessons

Charlotte Mason gave these tests to be applied to the subjects in which children are instructed:

- Provide material for their mental growth.
- Exercise the several powers of their minds.
- Furnish them with fruitful ideas (rather than bushels of information).[23]
- Afford them knowledge, really valuable for its own sake, accurate, and interesting, of the *kind that the child may recall as a man with profit and pleasure* (emphasis mine).[24]

If these commonsense principles were applied in schools today, rather than those prescribed by a bureaucracy interested in its own agendas for political and economic purposes, some turnaround might be made in the demise of academics.

Children Given the Right Work for Their Developmental Level

This issue can certainly have a major effect on atmosphere and will be debated as long as schools exist. How much work should a child be given to do? How do you challenge a student without overpressuring her?

Wisely, Miss Mason observed, "The danger exists; but lies, *not in giving the child too much, but in giving him the wrong thing to do*, the sort of work for which the present state of his mental development does not fit him"[25] (emphasis mine). This view provides just the right balance of challenge and pressure. She continues, "But give the child work that nature intended for him, and the quantity he can get through with ease is practically unlimited."[26] In the abundant feast of appropriate ideas, the child's appetite is never quenched.

Children Left Much to Themselves, but Under Proper Authority

It is no surprise to those of us in education that the foundational principle of proper authority carries a great weight in producing the atmosphere of the school. Mason's teaching in this regard reminded parents and teachers that *as children see them responding to their authorities (policemen, employers, government officials, and God), so the children will do the same.* This includes their attitude toward knowledge and the mysteries of God's creation. A humble submission to learning along with the children and giving children permission to work in their own way on the ideas they receive is critical to the atmosphere.

However, this approach does not imply that the children are free without restraint. It is precisely because the children know who is in charge and respect that authority that the atmosphere is healthy. As Mason said, "This element of strength is the backbone of our position. They [the children] are free under authority, which is liberty; to be free without authority is license."[27]

An Eye-Pleasing Classroom Produced for the Children's Sake

The great variety of school classroom situations makes it difficult to be dogmatic in requiring specific decor in a school. Students come to windowless portable trailers in overcrowded United States schools, to classrooms in old converted homes in other areas, and to large, plain-walled multiuse rooms in others. In addition some schools have actual budgeted funds for teachers to decorate classrooms while other teachers are left to their own devices and creativity to dress up a space, all the while knowing that the groups occupying that same space in off-hours may remove things at a whim.

Still there are some things teachers can do to greatly affect the school atmosphere within their own limitations. Some of these might include:

• Playing beautiful music during times of reflection or quiet work.

• Setting aside a place for children to lounge while reading a book or other non-desk activity.

• Exhibiting delightful student work that displays diligence and good execution.

• Finding inexpensive prints of some masterpieces of art to display tastefully.

• Securing living creatures as class pets—and plants and flowers if sunlight is adequate.

• Placing window boxes of flowers in any available space, especially in inner-city schools where asphalt may prevail.

• Helping children develop the habit of keeping their classroom tidy and clean.

• Instilling, where possible, an ownership of the school and classroom that promotes stewardship of all God has given the children.

• Requiring students to show respect for the property of others as well as a reverence for books.

• Having available as many living books as possible in the classroom through library loan, parent donations, student sharing, or whatever means.

• Letting students help create lively educational displays to make the classroom an inspiring place to visit.

• Inviting parents and friends into the classroom for special events (plays, poetry recitals, etc.) with students responsible for hospitality, serving their guests, and creating an atmosphere of warmth.

Permeating It All, a Gentle Breeze of Good Humor

There is nothing perhaps that puts a more splendid aroma in the classroom than the delightful laughter of children and their teacher. All the beautiful displays, the living books, and the proper methodologies can still be stagnant without the joy of the heart that comes from cheerful souls. A good joke is enjoyed by all, especially if the teacher himself enlivens his class with a funny story.

Charlotte Mason said that good humor was a key element in the masterly inactivity of the classroom, where the "wise passiveness" of Wordsworth lends itself to allowing the natural humor and good-natured tendency of children to run its course. It is a teacher to be pitied who cannot laugh at the children's jests and even at his own mistakes and gaffes. This humor should be frank, cordial, and natural.[28] Coarse jesting or silly diversions are not what is meant here, nor are contrived amusements to divert the class from work. The natural environment of the classroom provides many occasions for a good laugh, and the best atmosphere exists when teachers and students are free to laugh at themselves and with each other.

EDUCATION IS A DISCIPLINE

By Maryellen St. Cyr

To bear success in any aspect of one's life, a certain amount of discipline is needed—discipline to order oneself and one's world. Charlotte Mason had attested to this truth through all of her life, but it was not until she had begun to teach that she saw that children lacked consistent discipline and continued to behave as "it was their nature to," with little improvement of faults and weaknesses. She commented: "The faults they had, they kept; the virtues they had were exercised just as fitfully as before. The good, meek little girl still told fibs. The bright, generous child was incurably idle. In lessons it was the same thing; the dawdling child went on dawdling, the dull child became no brighter. It was very disappointing."[29]

The disappointment came in the lack of advancement of the young people in areas of moral and intellectual power. Yes, the children no doubt "got on" a little; they were able to do harder sums and read harder books, but they lacked steady progress in these more vital areas.

From where was this advancement to come?

Miss Mason looked for guidance in the educational literature of the day, but she failed to find an authoritative guide that "embraced the possibilities contained in the human nature of a child, and, at the same time, measured the scope of education."[30] She in turn formulated her thoughts and ideas on this matter of education and devised a philosophy that included the idea that education is a discipline as one of the major tenets. For it was through this strand of the philosophy that she saw successes in children as the discipline of habit was used as a lever to advance them in areas of moral and intellectual power.

In order for us as educators today to have these same successes, it is important that we too "embrace the possibilities" contained in the human nature of a child. It does not take long to recall biblical, historical, and present-day examples of the accomplished feats of children—from the courageous effort of a shepherd boy in defending his nation to the beautiful cursive of an eight-year-old in completing her assignment. Created in likeness of almighty God, the child's possibilities are limitless. The potential of every child exceeds our power of measurement. We need to remember too that children are ignorant and need our knowledge and experience.

Yet it is somewhat astounding to see the limiting beliefs of parents and teachers in identifying children in a school setting. These beliefs are often concealed in educational and psychological jargon whose first intent is to give a description to help in understanding the child, not to excuse or limit the child in responsibility and maturity. For instance, we may say a child is given to inattention, moodiness, laziness, disorder, or unkindness. Does this mean that he or she is enslaved to these behaviors for life and is not able to rise above them? That he or she is only behaving as nature dictates? I have seen these limiting beliefs used by the child, parent, and educator to identify the *person* of the child, rather than being used in an effort of making strong what was once weak. Taken to the extreme, the child, parent, and educator begin to rationalize the behavior and attitudes of children in terms of identity, thereby excusing themselves and others for lack of effort or growth in a particular area: "So and so is such a lazy (untidy, careless, slow, etc.) sort of child."

Charlotte Mason saw the consequences of such an attitude: "When in truth, all persons are subject to weaknesses and faults and these, when left to themselves, become the bane of each of us in our adult years unless divine grace is exerted on the lives with enlightened human effort." She used the following steps ordered by St. Augustine as a motto to rise above the faults and weaknesses to higher things in the formation of habits:

"I am."—We have the power of knowing ourselves.

"I can."—We are conscious of power to do what we perceive we ought to do.

"I ought."—We have within us a moral judge to whom we feel ourselves subject, who points out and requires of us our duty.

"I will."—We determine to exercise that power with a volition that is in itself a step in the execution of what we will.[31]

Miss Mason also considered the literature of the day as failing to reach the full scope of education, in all its varied dimensions and relationships. Some educational literature today reflects the same sentiments as we are urged to identify and measure children to find their niche at a younger age and thereby instruct in a narrow way and to this interest alone. Parents and educators can also display this shortsightedness in looking for areas of natural talent and ability and capitalizing on what is already deemed a strength, neglecting areas in need of real maturation. The idea of education as a discipline encompasses the full realm of education, taking into account its varied relationships—intellectual, moral, physical, religious, and social, as well as the great potential of persons to move in directions of change and growth.

The necessity of forming habits is an integral part of this philosophy as they aid one in functioning in relationships. These habits are not tacked onto one's life as another feat to be mastered in a performance culture, but are used as valuable tools in the intellectual, spiritual, and physical development in relationship to oneself, God, and others. Yet in talking about habits, whether they are intellectual (attention, thinking, or judgment) or physical (neatness or pleasant manners), we can be in danger of saying that some individual children are unable to obtain success in any one of these areas. It is almost believed that these persons are born with inattention, poor judgment, rudeness, disorder, or slovenliness, displaying an utter helplessness in nature with regard to these calamities.

When one sees the learner as an individual created to bear dominion in this world, the necessity of training in habits of "good learning and godly living" becomes a guiding principle. An illustration of this training follows.

The habit of attention comes to the forefront of every intellectual pursuit and ideally is cultivated in the infant through the relationship with mother and father and continues to be worked out in the classroom environment. Children must be held responsible and accountable for learning. They must do the work themselves of listening, of knowing, and of applying. Sometimes attention is the result of a more strenuous effort, and at other times it is a natural response. In either case, the student must see his or her responsibility to the work at hand.

In reading to students of history, fantasy, or poetry, I ask them to "tell back" after a single reading, and the ones who are less attentive will falter in this skill. It is here that I deal with this weakness, alerting the student to his or her responsibility to "tell next" and guiding the child in this way of knowing. As with any debility, consistency of training and accountability will encourage growth and strength. This habit of attention can be attained through reading, listening, and observation. Students are given opportunities to read and listen to literary language, beautiful music, the sounds of nature, as well as to duplicate the works of the Creator and the "masters" through nature studies and picture studies. It is through these means that students are taught "how to see," "how to listen," and, if you will, "how to attend"—not merely to imitate but to "own" the knowledge and contribute their own unique thoughts and skills.

As with the intellectual habits of attending, thinking, and making judgments, so also with physical habits of neatness and order, good presentation of work, and the development of good natural manners. All habit is a result of conflict of sorts, and it is here that the child can learn to live and embrace the realities of life and choose accordingly. These lines of thinking and acting are drawn early, but they can be easily altered through the setting down of new lines of habit with encouragement and tact. This thinking and acting can affect the child both positively and negatively, depending on the habit. Some areas of concern for both home and school would include the habits of reading, paying attention, doing work well, thoroughness, neatness, and accuracy.

How is this education to be developed to be common to all of us, for parents and teachers are in as great a need of life-giving habits as the children in their charge?

THE FORMATION OF HABITS

"The formation of habits is education and education is the formation of habits," Charlotte Mason maintained. "Habit in the hands of the mother, is as his wheel to the potter, his knife to the carver—the instrument by means of which she [the educator as well] turns out the design already conceived in her [or his] brain. The material is there to begin with, his wheel will not enable the potter to produce a porcelain cup out of coarse clay; but the instrument is as necessary as the material or the design." It is the lever to lift a child contrary to his or her nature. Many a child comes into the classroom trained in careful habits of attending faithfully, waiting patiently, writing neatly, working carefully, acting responsibly, and so on. And also many a child comes in trained in discourteous ways or left to his or her nature of disrupting continually, working carelessly, behaving rudely, acting irresponsibly, and so on. It is a rare person who would purposefully train a child in discourteous ways. But children are often "left up to their nature" in hopes that they will grow out of it or in excuse of their youth or individuality. But Charlotte Mason was adamant concerning training in habit. She went as far as to say that almost anything could be accomplished through the correct and consistent training.[32]

When one thinks about training in an educational sense, one can easily think in the realm of the extreme with such examples from the past of Puritan and Victorian schoolmasters who trained children through the use of fear and force—or of present-day behaviorists who train through the use of conditioning and manipulation. Such practices do not line up with Mason's view of education as a discipline. This discipline is instead training that comprises relationships with oneself, one's world, one's God, and others. The parent and/or teacher supplants the child's weakness or affinity through instruction of conscience and the will, along with deliberate effort, that is often painstaking on behalf of both the child and educator to reach the desired outcome. This work expands the scope of a child's education to include the following habits:

1. *Intellectual habits:* attention, concentration, thoroughness, intellectual volition, accuracy, reflection, and meditation,[33] rapid mental effort and application, thinking, imagining, remembering, and perfect execution.[34]

2. *Moral habits:* sweet thoughts,[35] obedience, truthfulness, reverence, and temper.[36]

3. *Physical habits:* self-restraint, self-control, self-discipline, alertness, quick perception, fortitude, service, courage, prudence, and chastity.[37]

4. *Religious habits:* the thought of God, a reverent attitude, regularity in devotions, reading the Bible, praise, and Sunday-keeping.[38]

5. *Miscellaneous habits:* physical exercise, good manners, and ear and voice.[39]

The future character and conduct of children depend on the work of enlightened human effort in forming habits along with the work of divine grace more than anything else. The children will have habits, and we as parents and educators are engaged in forming these habits actively or passively every day, every hour. We cannot escape this fact. But if I say I am responsible, I might have to say I have been irresponsible.

After some personal reflection and study on this matter of habit, I began to work with my teachers in creating a school culture that demonstrated the positive results of schooling in habit. To begin our work, we considered two questions:

- As a school, which habits are we actively engaged in forming?
- As a school, which habits are we passively forming?

It was amazing to each of us that we could so easily identify collectively both the active and passive habits. One of the habits we actively formed was respect for persons in the form of a greeting using the person's name. Each morning children were greeted by a variety of persons, from the older students opening the doors, to myself in morning assembly, to their own teachers and classmates in the classrooms. Some formal instruction was given on how persons reflect the image of God, and our response to all persons at the very least is to demonstrate respect through a formal greeting. In the beginnings of our work, teachers and I took aside children who would not act in accordance with this effort as they were in the habit of ignoring persons or were just plain forgetful. One teacher put a bit of masking tape on the carpet of her classroom to remind such a student that as he approached the tape, he was to go up to the teacher and respond accordingly. Needless to say, the tape disappeared after a time. This habit worked its way into the minds of all of us as quiet and enthusiastic greetings became a part of the life of the school.

Another habit we successfully implemented into our school culture was a display of manners and courtesies during a shared meal. I was challenged by a stay at L'Abri and also by a visit to a PNEU school, Rickmansworth in Moreton-on-Marsh, to see that a noontime meal need not be a hurried time of "fueling," but students and teachers alike could engage in thoughtful, lively conversation with others in a mannerly way, feasting on nutrients for body, soul, and mind. Teachers at our school can be seen toting a blanket out to the lawn to have an outdoor picnic of sorts, or one can step into the classrooms and see desks turned in a table-like way where a shared meal is enhanced by a round of riddles and brain teasers or a topic of interest. Students are trained in basic manners of table and conversation, which have often been lost as they seek to shovel their food down to get to the next thing, which is usually play. To combat this tendency, we do not necessarily have a time of play directly after lunch, and each student is expected to wait until all have finished eating and engage in the conversation at hand. The noon meal has come to be a time of real refreshment as students and teachers break away from their work and gain additional insight into one another's lives.

As a school, we too are passively forming habits along lines that form and compromise our harmony in living. During our planning times, the teachers and I share in times of reflection in which we assess our work and note ways we could instill habits of regularity from car pool to accuracy with regard to the students' work. We look forward to moving beyond ourselves when we become active to what once lay passive in these areas of laying down lines of habit.

To conclude our work in schooling in habit, each teacher assessed herself by answering the following questions:

1. Am I actively engaged in forming:
- Intellectual habits?
- Moral habits?

- Physical habits?
- Religious habits?

2. If so, which habits, and how am I forming these habits?

3. If not, what hinders me from actively forming these habits?

As with any serious endeavor, a sense of humor and a light touch (tact) at the right moment can be helpful in identifying and sharing the burden of a difficult time in a particular child's or school's development.

As a classroom educator of more than two decades, I have seen the application of habit as the line that divides the effective student from the ineffective one. The effective student chooses to do what ought to be done and so, when lacking the power, compels himself or herself to do what is best, and acts out of habit. Proverbs 22:6 speaks to this matter: "Train up a child in the way he should go: and when he is old, he will not depart from it." The Hebrew word for "train" implies a narrowing, a discipline. The Hebrew word for "way" implies a course of life or a mode of action. A paraphrase of this verse using these definitions is as follows: "Discipline a child in a course of life, a mode of action (habit), and when he is old, he will not depart from it." By the very order of God, children are disciples of their father and mother. Discipline is the state of the follower, the learner; thus, it rests with parents and teachers to be consistent in laying down lines of habit as seen in the following example.

Parents and teachers often remarked about the neatness and orderliness of the students' desks in my classroom. The effort was not mine alone, but each student cared for his or her property. I began the first day of school with specific instructions on how to put in order the books and miscellaneous articles inside the desks. And if there were too many miscellaneous articles, these were to be taken back home promptly. I then told the students it was their responsibility to bring their desks "back to order" any time they fell from this arrangement. I would periodically check the desks, and when they did not meet expectations, students would lose their own time of play or be dismissed a bit late to tidy up. One day as we were lined up in the back of the room, it became apparent to me that orderliness had become a real pleasure in the life of my students. One of the boys remarked, "Look how neat the room is! It looks beautiful!" Habit had become a delight in itself!

Yet the labor begun in the classroom or at home is easily lost if one does not bear true to the other. For it is unchangeably true that the child who is not being raised to a higher and higher level will sink to a lower and lower level.[40] There is a certain amount of strenuousness in forming habits as one acts contrary to one's nature. Charlotte Mason admonished the parent and teacher to use tact, watchfulness, and persistence in forming habits with a twofold policy:

• Never let the child slip from his responsibility in the habit.

• Never let the matter be a cause of friction between you and the child (let her suffer the natural consequences).[41]

Therefore, it rests with parents and educators to extend these lines of habit, of power, and of influence to encompass the intellectual and moral life of the child more fully. This disciplining is not all at once, but consists of a steady progress in a careful plan. This careful plan consists of training the will, mind, and conscience.

THE TRAINING OF THE WILL

Some people go through life without many acts of deliberate will. They are amiable, easygoing, hedged in by favorable circumstances.[42] And others go through life falling prey to their senses and slothfulness. Both kinds are unable to live active, vigorous lives because they lack the power of a rectified will. We see this weakness in the school setting in students who display habits of "seeming" rather than "being," who bear motivation out of self-interest or for the sake of appearance. They are the children who desire to please at all costs, namely in expense of their true selves. We also see the weakness in children who approach intellectual and moral endeavors passively, who have an agenda all their own in always looking for ways they can be sensually delighted through amusement and entertainment.

The work before us as parents and educators is to make the child do what he lacks the power to compel himself to do, whether it be in expression of a higher motivation or in possessing a determining will in controlling passions and desires. This steady effort in training the will can be accomplished in the light of the following principle: *Give children opportunities to choose appropriate to their growth and maturity.*

Charlotte Mason quoted from the pulpit of her day that decision-making was the most exhausting effort in life.[43] Children are now being taxed with this effort continually at an increasingly younger age through the clamor of advertising from the media and the peer culture.

In many households, children bear this effort of decision on what to eat, what to wear, and how to spend all of their time. Likewise, in many schools, they must decide how to work, what to read, and how to learn. Choosing requires discrimination, and a child often lacks the knowledge and power necessary to make choices along this line. She resorts to immediate gratification unless she has been trained in habit.

It would be better for the parent to make the ultimate choice of separating out a portion of the child's wardrobe and identifying these as "school clothes," thus allowing the child to choose within perimeters. In the classroom, the teacher draws up the requirements of work well done and allows the child to suffer consequences for his ill choosing. The child should never be given the freedom to not do the work, but instead let her know the choice rests within her as to how strenuous the doing of this may be.

For example, in giving a handwriting assignment, the student is well instructed along the lines of skill in the formation and size of letters with due regard to slant and lines. In preparation of the task, the teacher admonishes the students to follow the instructions within the time period. The teacher also lets them know they are free to redo the assignment as many times as they desire on their own time to accomplish the desired results but states with surety that any one of them could accomplish this in just one try.

Here lies the secret—the child is desirous of meeting the expectations but may be weak in will. Children will look to the teacher to see if he or she is able to make them do what they ought to do. They often beckon the instructor during the assignment with questions like "Is this good?" Such questions should never be answered because it rests with them to make this decision at this time with the knowledge that has been given. For they often know what is "good" or not "so good" but are relying on the instructor's strength or lack of strength to be the determining effort in their choosing. After the student submits the work for approval, the teacher then assesses the work with specific remarks of affirmation or asks the child to redo the work to reach the desired outcome. It is imperative to make the child suffer for his poor choosing, or he will increase in inaccuracy and sloppiness.

Charlotte Mason instructed adults to "[l]ay down lines of thought that shall initiate the thoughts the child should think, the desires he/she will cherish and the feelings he/she shall allow."[44] Ideas are conveyed through a myriad of mediums, from printed pages to visualized pictures. These ideas are clothed in suggestions, which clamor upon us. Thus we begin the daily, ongoing work of education, which is in the realm of these suggestions as we must learn to choose among them. A question we need to answer as parents and educators is, "Who is laying down the lines of thought in our children's lives?" This can easily be assessed by the choices children make with regard to time and money and also in their habits in relationship to others. This work of laying down lines of thought is a deliberate one, which takes much consideration. Here also we see evidences of extremes, from coddling to negligence.

As schools, we have taken on the work of laying down lines of thought quite seriously as we make choices regarding the printed page in the lives of the children. Books are chosen from a variety of genres that emphasize the virtuous deeds of characters, promote the knowledge of histories and sciences, develop the sound and sense of language, and generate the interior education of the learner. With this in mind, the children have set before them "the best thought of the best writers." Our time is limited with the children, and therefore we choose what reflects truth, beauty, and goodness—not necessarily popular culture. The philosophy of Miss Mason consistently impels the educator in this line of action:

> [T]he part of the teacher is to afford to each child a full reservoir of the right thought to draw from. For right thinking is by no means a matter of self-expression. Right thinking flows from a stimulus of an idea, and ideas are stored as we have seen in books and pictures and the lives of men and nations; these instruct the conscience and stimulate the will.[45]

Fortify the Child's Will

Charlotte Mason stated that the fortification of the will was one of the greatest purposes of education and that prior to instructing in this area, the child's eyes should be opened to the possibilities that lay before her as she learns to direct herself.

> They should themselves know of the wonderful capacities to enter upon the world as a great inheritance, which exist in every human being. All its beauty and all its thoughts are open to everyone. Everyone may take service for the world's use; everyone may climb those delectable mountains from whence he gets his vision for the City of God. He must know something of his body with its senses and appetites: of his intellect, imagination and aesthetic sense: of his moral nature, ordered by law and justice. Realizing how much is possible to Mansoul and the perils that assail it, he should know that the duty of

self-direction belongs to him; and that powers for this direction are lodged in him, as are intellect and imagination, hunger and thirst.[46]

In order for the will to take on the characteristic of being fortified, the child needs to be made aware of the temptations before him—the lust of the flesh, the lust of the eyes, and the pride of life. These assaults on the flesh and spirit of persons are attacks on the will, and the greater the effort of decision in any one area, the weaker the will. The child must also be trained to not only will, but to will outside of self in service and duty to God and others. The chivalrous person is one of constant will, for, as we have seen, will cannot be exercised steadily for ends of personal gain.[47] Miss Mason warned that self-culture was not to be accepted as the ideal, for in the service of self in which one responds to each and every appetite and desire, no act of will is required.

Lastly, the child is to know that will is a free agent and is able to do what it likes. The one thing will has to do is to prefer one thing above another. Often when the child is being willful, his attention is focused on the one choice, and he feels as if he is void of choosing. It is important that the child know what he is choosing between when there is a conflict of interest. This conflict causes much strain, and the child may not relax to a yielding point until he seeks recreation or diversion. As Charlotte Mason said, "The will does not want the support of arguments but the recreation of rest, change, diversion. In a surprisingly short time it is able to return to the charge and to choose this day the path of duty, however dull or tiresome, difficult or dangerous."[48]

In the more than twenty years that I have worked in classroom settings, it has been a resolute joy to be a part of educating children in the way of the will. In one instance, the students and I were planning a poetry recital for parents, grandparents, and friends of our class. I gave the responsibilities of distributing programs, holding doors, making introductions, welcoming guests, serving punch, and watching the younger children during the reception time to very eager children. As we conversed about our special day, it was important to me that the children gain some exercise in the strengthening of their will in seeing guests of our classroom as persons we prefer above ourselves. We discussed the conflict that would reside with the tantalizing treats before them and determining the act of the will in preferring others before ourselves. Each act of service from opening a door to declining the refreshments were ways in which we proclaimed to our guests that "you matter more." The guests were privy to the rich ideas and language of poets such as Eliot, Longfellow, and Stevenson as well as to the willing love and service of children that were their own. One need not wait for special occasions to instruct in the will but take advantage of the occasions of everyday living as students exhibit evidence of will with regard to one another, their work, and their play.

I have also seen examples of the waning of the will as numerous parents and teachers explain away a child's irresponsibility toward her work by stating that it was "her decision" to present this work in this manner. I have been dismayed at times with what has been turned into teachers in the name of "work," having the appearance but lacking the form in presentation and content. The natural consequences for the student acting irresponsibly should not be an acceptance of the attempt because of a mere act of volition. For in this way, the child is sowing habits of laxity and slothfulness, which may bring a lifetime of reaping. We easily see this trait in older children who bemoan tasks and depend on others to get their work accomplished. But instead the teacher and parent should make every effort to get the child to do what she ought to do at the earliest possible age.

When Charlotte Mason spoke about education as a discipline, she referred to the discipline of habits formed thoughtfully and definitely in the lives of children. This thoughtful, deliberate training is accomplished in the context of relationships, not mere automation. The training is not fashioned in conduct in the realm of the external, but as the cultivation of internal relationships with self, God, others, and the world, resulting in both character and conduct. In relationship the parent/teacher is able to be the initiator of the thoughts the child should think upon, the desires he cherishes, and the feelings he allows. These thoughts should give the child control over his own nature. This training is in thoughtfulness and responsibility—not in legalism or behaviorism. The contrast is illustrated here:

Training in Habit As:

Building Up of a Person	External Task
Relationship	Task
Responsibility	Achievement
Yieldedness	Control
Effectiveness	Efficiency
Interdependent	Independence
Confidence	Insecurity/comparison
Peace	Hurried

Although the outcomes of training in habits may be similar, they differ at the very core in purpose and motivation. In focusing on performance alone, the child can fall into lines of thought that lead to perfectionism, competitiveness, obsessiveness, guilt, and depression. The educator should be knowledgeable as to how to incite the child to effort through her desire of approbation, of excelling, of advancing, of knowledge, of love, and of duty in such a way that no one set of motives be called unduly into play to the injury of the child's character. Miss Mason firmly believed that the child's natural affinity "to want to know" should not be substituted for any other natural desire for the purposes of education.[49] Habit properly trained in these lines of relationship leads to both character and freedom.

Miss Mason went on to say that perhaps ninety-nine out of a hundred lives are lost because parents "took no pains to deliver their children from sloth, from sensual appetites, from willfulness, no pains to fortify them with the habits of a good life."[50] As the school acts as an extension of the home, not a replacement for it, the parents and educators must work together to avoid giving up on a child who acquiesces to feebleness in these moral and intellectual powers. It would benefit the child's growth and development if the parents' and teacher's first communication would be along the lines of the formation of habits in the life of the child. The parent and the classroom educator must continue an ongoing dialogue to make the unaware informed of the careless habits manifested in the child's life and to work in conjunction with each other's persistent efforts to form habits of right thinking and right action.

We then begin by seeing children as persons of unmeasured intellectual and moral power with a propensity toward growth, and we use the full scope of education to make this possible. Then the child is able to live, to give either of these answers (yes or no) to the solicitations that assail him. And this living means no more than the daily happenings one after another, in the exercise of our minds and wills. These challenges do not come on great occasions, but in the guise of the little matters of everyday life. The duty of this exercise belongs to each of us. Therefore, it is the business of education and the function of the educator to train each child we have been entrusted with in the formation of habits that will allow the child to truly live.

EDUCATION IS A LIFE

By Maryellen St. Cyr

In terms of the development of a curriculum that reflects the idea that education is a life, Miss Mason does not leave us guessing. She has written that just as the body needs nourishment in order to grow and flourish, so does the mind need feeding. "The mind feeds on ideas," she wrote, "and therefore children should have a generous curriculum."[51]

The business of teaching was for the sole purpose of furnishing the child with ideas, and any teaching that did not leave the child with a new mental image missed the mark. A morning in which the child received no new idea, needless to say, was a morning wasted.[52] This wasteful existence goes on and on in many a classroom, on many a day, as the student and the teacher passively interact with information. This need not be, nor should be, as Charlotte Mason has left a rich legacy of thinking and practice that constantly affirms one of her basic tenets that "education is a life." This principle is not a narrow compartmentalizing of facts into one area and life into another, but a rich interweaving of ideas, experiences, and knowledge that leads ultimately to the way in which we all, as individuals, live our lives. She comments:

> This sounds like a stale truism; but, let us consider a few corollaries of the notion that "a child is a person," and that a person is primarily living. Now no external application is capable of nourishing life or promoting growth; baths of wine, wrappings of velvet have no effect upon physical life except as they may hinder it; life is sustained on that which is taken in by the organism, not that which is applied from without.[53]

Charlotte Mason saw the answer not in a contrived system, but in a method of education. This method would allow the educator to have a clearly thought-out end in mind and a step-by-step plan to assist the child's progress both in knowledge and in character and conduct. Again she states: "A person is not built up from without but from within, that is, he is living, and all external educational appliances and activities which are intended to mold his character are decorative and not vital."[54]

She spoke of these external "appliances" as incapable of nourishing life or promoting growth because knowledge is not sensation; nor is it derived in a purely sensory fashion. The capstone of her educational philosophy was the deep conviction that all education rests upon the work of almighty God, whether one acknowledges it or not:

> This idea of all education springing from and resting upon our relation to Almighty God—we do not merely give a religious education because that would seem to imply the possibility of some other education, a secular education, for example. But we hold that all education is divine, that every good gift of knowledge and insight comes from above, that the Lord the Holy Spirit is the supreme educator of mankind, and that the culmination of all education (which may at the same time be reached by a little child) is that personal knowledge of and intimacy with God in which our being finds its fullest perfection.[55]

And again:

> The child is furnished with the desire for knowledge, i.e. curiosity; with the power to apprehend Knowledge, that is, attention; with powers of mind to deal with Knowledge without aid from without—such as imagination, reflection, judgment; with innate interest in all Knowledge that he needs as a human being; with power to retain and communicate such Knowledge; and to assimilate all that is necessary to him.[56]

> Knowledge is not instruction, information, scholarship, a well-stored memory. It is passed, like the light of a torch, from mind to mind, and the flame can be kindled at original minds only.[57]

This vibrant picture of the "lifeward" motivation of children that she draws is most striking and unique. The nature of knowing (learning) begins with *ideas*, the live things of the mind, that strike, impress, seize, and catch hold of one. Ideas are the initiators of habits of thought and habits of action. They originate as the issue from two minds. No one person has the power to produce an idea autonomously, as ideas reproduce after their own kind and in turn generate other ideas. "Ideas are of spiritual origin and God has made us so that we get them chiefly as we convey them to one another."[58] These ideas are conveyed through the natural world, heroic poetry, painted pictures, books of literary tradition, proverbial philosophy, musical symphonies, and the lives of persons and nations. Ideas are the living concepts that undergird, give meaning to, and connect one thought to another.

Children deal with ideas in an easy and familiar manner when given proper support; so Miss Mason lays great emphasis on the responsibility we have to teach ideas carefully: "Therefore, children should be taught, as they become mature enough to understand such teaching, that the chief responsibility which rests on them as persons is the acceptance or rejection of ideas." This is where the proper understanding of education as a life is nurtured. Charlotte Mason spoke of ideas in relationship to education in the sense that they would stir a person to right thinking (instructing the conscience), ultimately leading to right action (stimulating the will).

The mind at work has a threefold activity. It attends; it reflects; it uses what has been apprehended. This threefold activity receives unequal consideration. Much has been said and written upon the power of attention—how to secure it and how to sustain it. Every teacher knows the value of an attentive mind. Much, too, has been written and spoken about the value of expression when the mind has apprehended truth, beauty, or goodness. The value of brush or pen, of decisive action, of criticism, and (in these days) of discussion is pointed out.

Between the initial attention given and final expression, however, lies a whole world of thought, when the mind is active in reflection, seeking knowledge in close contact, resting upon its object, with the same intense activity as a bee on its flower. So little is understood about the way the mind lives. It lives by knowing, by active delight in the ideas, forms, and thoughts with which it comes into contact. The mind must dwell upon its findings, to accept or to reject them. Only then can knowledge come, knowledge of the truth of the thoughts, beauties, and facts it is an individual's concern to know and to show forth and to use in daily life.[59]

The educator's part is to place before the child the daily nourishment of ideas by way of living books that promote "living thought." Scores of thinkers will meet the children mind to mind in books of literary quality. This "mind food" is not served up in dry bits, diluted, or predigested. Instead it is offered in abundance with all its savory delights. Each child eats what he wills and leaves nourished and contented.

Thus, as an avenue in the learning process, facts are clothed in *ideas*. Facts are taught in relation to a vast number of thoughts and integrated into a body of knowledge (part to whole). The learner assimilates this knowledge when it is reproduced or carries a meaningful connection. Learners can *act* upon information seen or heard through verbal and written narration, individual or cooperative relationships, or visual demonstrations of art and movement. These applications are not trite rehearsals. The learner is challenged and responds with creativity. Throughout the process the learner experiences responsibility, accountability, and a bit of tension as he or she grasps understanding of new ideas and knowledge. This information then comes forth as something known, something personal, something private. This is the act of knowing.

Throughout Charlotte Mason's work with the PNEU, "thousands of children were educated and developed capacity, character, countenance, initiative and a sense of responsibility."[60] It was an education fit for the children of both miners and professors. They were fed sumptuously from a varied curriculum consisting of multiple subjects sustained by the best thought of the best writers, allowing them to continue in self-education long after the happy days of schooling at the PNEU.

Here is hope for education in a new millennium, one in which, could we but understand and truly believe, children *will* attend, reflect, and apprehend knowledge out of a natural desire to do so. Some of the current educational research not only shares this same hope but suggests some of the same means of attaining it. Caine and Caine in their book *Making Connections* characterize lessons according to how the brain works. The brain works optimally when:

• Retelling or talking about learning.
• Using the vocabulary of the subject.
• Listening, reading, viewing, and acting.
• Drawing relationships through the use of metaphor and simile.
• Experiencing rigorous content and intellectual challenge joyfully.
• Eliminating rewards and punishments.
• Focusing heavily on teacher not technology as the main facilitator in learning.
• Processing part and whole learning simultaneously.
• Delaying gratification to achieve success.
• Searching for meaning is innate.
• Involving focused attention.[61]

One can see the congruency of thought a hundred years later as Mason and Caine and Caine come to the same conclusions on how the mind works and on what activities the learner should be involved in. Mason often referred to her method of education as a *discovery*, not an invention, for we each know that truth transcends time, tradition, and taste.

The Way to Reform Educational Practice

When one thinks of the educational panacea before us, one is reminded of learning styles, "whole language," standardized testing, "hands-on" learning, phonics, ability grouping, core curriculum, accelerated programs, great books—almost amounting to each and every way in getting at what it means for a child to "know." And when he still does not know, maybe there is yet another untapped resource to explore. For we are looking for a system into which the child can lock and that guarantees that a child will be "educated."

It is important to think of Charlotte Mason's practice of education not in an eclectic sense, as a selection of good practices from all systems of philosophy, but rather, as the outgrowth of a particular philosophy. The practice is significant because of its philosophical underpinnings, not because of trend, tradition, or tastefulness. Practices are manifestations of beliefs— beliefs the educator has concerning the nature of the learner, the role of the teacher, and the nature of knowledge. This work of reformation is not a single act in investigative thought, but an ongoing inquiry into the beliefs expressed in the classroom through various choices regarding books, activities, methodology, and resources. To begin this inquiry the educator might take a hard look at the quality and quantity of knowledge set before the learner each day.

The Quality and Quantity of Knowledge

Children should be put in touch with original minds, not a text that has been watered down or predigested or served in small morsels. Books of the highest literary quality are appropriately chosen to introduce mind to mind. Materials used to help in understanding can be, for example, carefully selected maps, atlases, timelines, art prints, CDs, and so on. These materials will allow the children to have a direct path to the knowledge afforded them.

Looking at the timetables of the PNEU, one can readily see the diverse number of inspirational and disciplinary subjects used with each child. Children were engaged in study of the Bible, literature, Shakespeare and poetry, science and nature study, music composers, picture study, citizenship, history and geography, and the practice of English grammar and English composition, mathematics, music theory and singing, dictation and repetition, handwriting, drawing and handcrafts, reading, foreign language and Latin, physical education, and real work.

When one looks at the quality and quantity of work in the PNEU, one's mind immediately moves to present-day examples of preparatory schools, accelerated programs, and gifted education. Yet the schools that practiced Charlotte Mason's philosophy did not fall into these categories. All students participated in the feast set before them—some generously, others less so. Grades were used on examinations alone; assessments and ranks were not calculated, comparing one student to another, making prominence over others the main goal. Instead, students reached full potential in many areas, motivated by natural curiosity rather than by self-glorifying desires.

THE PREPARED LESSONS

The important implications of how the mind is nourished and works need to be brought continually to the forefront of the instructor's lesson plans. Seeing that the mind requires daily nourishment and exercise just as the body does, the educator must carefully plan and prepare lessons that provide varied and abundant sustenance. Charlotte Mason urged the educator to apply four tests to the students' lessons:

Does the lesson
- Provide material for mental growth?
- Exercise several powers of the mind?
- Furnish fruitful ideas?
- Afford valuable, accurate, and interesting knowledge?[62]

The educator concerns himself with putting the students in the way of information clothed with ideas that they in turn will know. This new knowledge will add to their storehouse of knowledge, which in turn will generate further ideas that lead to fruitful action. In developing these lessons sustained by ideas, one must search for the ideas that come forth naturally in the teaching of content and in the introduction and reinforcement of skills. Let the words themselves sink in. Don't chew up the ideas yourself and then hand them over half-digested to the child. Let him have direct access to the source. One must also be careful not to superimpose ideas in a contrived way. Some examples of how ideas come to light through the instruction of content and skills are listed below. These examples are somewhat lengthy, as they have been copied in their entirety. A thorough study of these lessons will allow one to see the thoughtful preparation of the material studied. The examples have been taken from *School Education* and from my own teaching experience.

ALEXANDER THE GREAT
History Class
Time: 30 minutes
Age: Eight and Nine

Objectives:

To establish relations with the past.

To introduce a fresh hero.

To stir them to admiration of the wisdom, valor, and self-reliance of Alexander the Great.

To increase the power of narration.

Lesson: (A step-by-step progress)

(Neutral gender has been established for clarification as some of these lessons were taken from single-gender classes.)

Step 1—Begin by connecting Alexander the Great with the time of Demosthenes, of whom the class has been reading recently.

Step 2—Draw from them some account of the times in which Alexander lived and of Philip of Macedon.

Step 3—Arouse interest in Alexander by the story of the taming of Bucephalus, which must be read, discussed, and then narrated.

Step 4—Ask the students what is meant by a hero. The old meaning was "demigod"; the Anglo-Saxon meaning, "a man." Both really meant a man who was brave and true in every circumstance.

Ask: "What qualities make a hero?" Draw from them how far we can trace these qualities in Alexander. We notice:

• Wisdom—"What a horse they are losing for want of skill to manage him!"

• Perseverance—He kept repeating the same expression.

• Self-reliance—"And I certainly could." This was justified by the fact that he could.

• Observation—He noticed that the horse was afraid of its shadow.

• Courage—Seeing his opportunity, he leaped upon its back.

• Prudence—He went very gently till he could feel that he had perfect control of the animal.

These are not all the qualities one looks for in a hero, but as they will be learning all about Alexander next term, they will be able to find out for themselves what others he had (or did not have). They will see, for instance, how he never imagined a defeat, but went on, conquering as he went (hope).

The name of Alexander has never been forgotten because he was so great a hero. Owing to him, the language and civilization of Greece were carried over a great part of Asia.

Show map illustrating his campaigns. He tried to improve the land wherever he went. Owing to his travels, people began to know more of geography and natural history than ever before.

Himself a hero, Alexander reverenced heroes, keeping "the casket copy" of *The Iliad*.

Step 5—Recapitulate Step 4 by means of questions.[63]

NORMAN ROCKWELL
Picture Talk
Time: 20-30 minutes
Age: Eight and Nine

Objectives:

To acquaint students with the boyhood of Norman Rockwell.

To familiarize students with Rockwell's relationship with The Saturday Evening Post.

To develop an appreciation for Rockwell as an artist and an illustrator.

Lesson

Step 1—Begin connecting Norman Rockwell with the students by having them tell what they already know about him and his time and place in history.

Step 2—Read the description of Rockwell's purpose of illustrating American life as he did.

> I guess I have a bad case of American nostalgia for the clean, simple country life as opposed to the complicated world of a city. . . . I would not have dwelt so long upon these summers I spent in the country as a child, except that I think they had a lot to do with what I painted later on. . . . The view of life I communicate in my pictures excludes the sordid and ugly. I paint life as I would like it to be.[64]

Step 3—Read and narrate pages 12-17 on Norman Rockwell concerning his boyhood and early influences (Dickens, Pyle, Remington, Rackham).

Step 4—Show several covers from *The Saturday Evening Post* and allow students to tell the story first with a quick glance and then with a more thoughtful look. Use *Boy Pushing Baby Carriage, Happy Birthday, Miss Jones,* and *Triple Self-Portrait.*

Step 5—End lesson with final quote: "If you do something well, stick to it. Don't go off on a tangent just because people tell you you're old-fashioned or narrow. . . . I know [modern art's] not your kind of art." George Horace Lorimer, editor of *The Saturday Evening Post* from 1912-1936.[65]

PHONICS AND SPELLING
Time: 15 minutes
Age: Nine and Ten

Objectives:

To use syllable and phonics rules as tools to aid in pronunciation and spelling.

To allow students to bear the responsibility of their own spelling.

To learn the spelling of two to four new words.

Lesson:

Each student will have a copy of *Black Beauty* for use in this exercise. The text used has *already* been read and comprehended.

Step 1—Ask students these questions:

• What is the purpose of the five-syllable rules in our work of spelling and pronunciation?

• Is any other tool necessary?

• If so, what other tools are available to aid us in accuracy in pronunciation and spelling?

Step 2—Review syllable rules orally.

Step 3—Read paragraph three on page 172, seeking a word or words that you could not spell or pronounce if called upon to do so.

Step 4—Draw on your resources to learn the spelling of the word or words from your reading.

Step 5—Call on each student to share his knowledge.

Step 6—Repeat this exercise for the remainder of the time, using paragraphs that are tightly packed with challenging vocabulary.

The forms of these lessons are indicative of the philosophy that the learner is *active*, not passive, and bears the responsibility for his learning. He is called upon to attend to the readings and the observation of maps and pictures, as well as to reflect upon the questioning and the knowledge already gained from previous and current lessons. Finally, the learner is asked to apprehend information and ideas from the text, self, others, pictures, and so on, and make it *his* knowledge.

THE EDUCATOR'S ROLE

In reading Charlotte Mason's philosophy of education, one might conclude that all this education "stuff" is easy enough, that just about anyone can teach children. This is sure enough in one sense, the sense that just about anyone can cook, parent, befriend, care, love, encourage. But then one's mind moves to the particulars when the need is for food, direction, friendship, comfort, security, and strength, and not just anyone will do. A certain person comes to mind. So in teaching too.

Charlotte Mason stated that a person, a teacher, must not depreciate the office of teaching or have a narrow view of the child. Teachers depreciate their office when they do the work of learning for the child by preparing lessons that have been diluted, predigested, and are void of thought. This truly is a depreciation of teacher and child—to conscientiously apply the "habit" and "discipline" idea of education and then to sit students down routinely to meals of sawdust. The work of the teacher is secured in preparing lessons with "prophetic power of appeal and inspiration." The communion develops from mind to mind, and the teacher acts as guide, philosopher, and companion. An obstacle persists when children are viewed as products of education and environment, not as persons. And we lose the way into the mind when "we have embraced the belief that 'knowledge is sensation,' that a child knows what he sees and handles rather than what he conceives in his mind and figures in his thoughts."[66]

A teacher, like any person, must be willing to examine her beliefs at any time and begin the hard work of change in regard to unproductive thinking.

Let children feed on the good, the excellent, the great. There is no need to get in their way with little lectures, facts and guided tours! It is salutary to be reminded that Abraham Lincoln spent only one year in school. The rest of his youth, he read books, he worked, and on the Mississippi River he met all sorts of people. He knew them. In fact, his life educated him.[67]

The office of the educator was highly esteemed by Charlotte Mason and the PNEU. Charlotte Mason herself examined educational theories of the day through personal reading and travel, and she was not willing to put thoughts into print until she had arrived at a comprehensive plan. Teachers who had been educated by the House of Education were sought after with an ardent zeal. The training at the college was respected and seen as too strenuous to lightly pass on to others in relationship without enrolling in the college formally. Charlotte Mason looked at education as serious business!

Most educators would immediately agree that their aim is for students to know. As we have already stated, this is the work of the mind, not the educator. The work of the educator is to put the child in the way of knowing by providing a living way through worthy thought and worthy work. Yet we have all at one time or another bought into the idea of systematizing knowledge through a curriculum package or program, relying heavily on *it* to do the work rather than on the mind. We spend large amounts of time and money implementing these resources and evaluating learning from the prescription laid forth in teacher guides and manuals. Using these guides, we look at lessons in view of what the learner should do instead of what the learner should know. And then we engage the learner in large amounts of paperwork consisting of rote answers, busy work, reporting, copying, testing, and quizzing, which is easily evaluated in terms of "success" because a number or letter grade is given.

Once we engage the learner in a system of achieving results instead of obtaining knowledge to understand and make sense of life, the method and means of education easily take on competitive values focusing on finishing first and obtaining the highest marks. The emphasis moves from the process to the product. Students become anxious to finish tasks and do the next thing rather than participate in the work of attending and reflecting. The teacher then bears the weight of adjusting lessons so that they can be assessed objectively. The learner sees himself as one whose work is to adapt from one scheme to another in order to gain the promised result. Knowledge is no longer seen as a human response to the great inheritance before us, but as a commodity to be gained in order to procure whatever it is one desires.

In saying this, it is not enough to offer living books and narration to the student and then characterize the lesson as one that will provide mental growth, exercise several powers of the mind, furnish fruitful ideas, and afford the child with interesting and accurate knowledge. These lessons described here can only be the result of *careful, thoughtful planning.* Eve Anderson, former head-mistress of Eton End (PNEU), firmly attests to the importance of prepared lessons needing to be brought before the students. Unprepared lessons wander aimlessly and are directed by the clock, tangents, and unrelated questions. They begin and end abruptly, and the next thing is attempted but rarely achieved. Prepared lessons have objectives in mind (content and/or performance), questions to be asked, ideas to be discussed, skills to be introduced or reinforced, and sympathies to be gained. Yet in all this preparation the educator is careful not to do the mind work for the students, but thoughtfully moves toward an aim so as not to get in between the living books and things and the child.

In spending time and effort in preparing lessons, the educator moves into the realm of instructing by way of ideas. At times ideas are imparted directly through the words or questions of the teacher. At other times they are communicated through other means—more literary language and the thought environment that surrounds the child by way of "every look of gentleness and tone of reverence, every word of kindness and act of help."[68]

Mason also speaks of ideas in *general* terms, as even in the atmosphere,

> [t]he idea may exist in a clear, distinct, definite form, as that of a circle in the mind of a geometrician; or it may be a mere instinct, a vague appetency towards something, like the impulse which fills the young poet's eyes with tears, he knows not why. To excite this appetency towards something—towards things lovely, honest, and of good report—is the earliest and most important ministry of the educator.[69]

She speaks of ideas in more *specific* terms as Coleridge's "captain" ideas and initial ideas, which may strike as a weapon or a sudden impulse. These first ideas are ideas on various subjects that move the person to pursue knowledge along these lines with intention and delight. Captain (leading, main, or chief) ideas are sustained by other fitting ideas, resulting in constructive habits and conduct of living.

Once we recognize that all thoughts that breathe and words that burn are of their nature spiritual, and appeal to the spiritual within us—that, in fact, all intercourse of thought and feeling belongs to the realm of ideas, spiritually conveyed, the great mysteries of our religion cease to be hedged off from our common experiences.[70]

Education is the assimilation of these ideas, and it is the educator's work to ensure that the children with whom he has been entrusted are fed well and not undernourished by the provision of "mind food" through living books and living things. As education is an applied philosophy, it is important that the work of the classroom truly reflects the values and beliefs of knowledge in the principle that "education is a life." A panacea for education is nonexistent. But consider a plan rising out of principles, and each such principle being a part of an educational philosophy. This is education as Charlotte Mason ascribed it to be.

Our Lord spoke of "abundant life." He said, "Man does not live by bread alone." Nor does he live by being reared on a computer printout, or scientifically planned workbooks that build skills by reading comprehension exercises based on isolated paragraphs, or any of the horrors that sometimes go under the name of the "education process."[71]

What we are about is not some misty future preparation for our children. Education is not a life later; it is life now.

Sample of Student Work: Drawing of Homer

EDUCATION IS THE SCIENCE
OF RELATIONS

By Jack Beckman

WE ARE EDUCATED BY OUR INTIMACIES

In 1903 Miss Mason penned a letter to her students commending the work of the Parents' Union School. In it she wrote:

> The first effort of the Parents' National Educational Union, continued through ten years of its existence, was to impress upon its members the definition of education contained in our motto, "Education is an atmosphere, a discipline, a life." By this we mean that parents and teachers should make sensible and prudent use of a child's circumstances (atmosphere), should train him with tact in habits of good living (discipline), and should nourish his mind with ideas, the food of the intellectual life. These three we believe to be the only instruments of which we may make lawful use in bringing up children.[72]

Here we see clearly the means by which children are to be educated. Atmosphere, discipline, and life all take their places as instruments to be used gently and carefully for the training of the child. Taken together definitely and deliberately, as others have described in this book, we can see a logical end in sight. What will these three working in unified fashion bring to the child? For this we turn again to Miss Mason's letter:

> The union, having devoted, as I have said, ten years of its existence to learning how to use the three instruments of education (circumstances, habits and ideas), took a new departure some five years ago, and asked what should be the end in view as the result of a wise use of due means.
>
> What is education after all? The answer came in the phrase, "Education is the science of relations." We do not use this phrase in the sense that things are related to each other, and we must be careful to pack the right things in together so that, having got into the brain of a boy, each thing may fasten on its cousins and together they make a strong clique or "apperception mass." What we are concerned with is that the fact that we personally have relations with all that there is in the present, all that there has been in the past and all that there will

be in the future—with all above us and all about us—and that fullness of living, expansion, expression and serviceableness for each of us depend upon how far we apprehend these relationships and how many of them we lay hold of. *Every child is heir to an enormous patrimony, heir to all the ages, inheritor of all the present.*

An infant comes into the world with a thousand such embryonic feelers, which he sets to work to fix with amazing energy: he attaches his being to mother, father, sister, brother, nanna (granny), the man in the street, cat and dog, spider and fly; earth, air, fire and water attract him perilously; his eyes covet light and color, his ears sound; his limbs movement; everything concerns him and out of everything he gets:

That calm delight
Which, if I err not, surely must belong
To those first-born affinities that fit our new existence to existing things,
And, in our dawn of being, constitute
The bond of union between life and joy.[73]

Later, we step in to educate him. In proportion to the range of living relationships we put in his way, will he have wide and vital interests, fullness of joy in living? In proportion as he is made aware of the laws which rule every relationship, will his life be dutiful and serviceable: as he learns that no relation with persons or with things, animate or inanimate, can be maintained without strenuous effort, will he learn the laws of work and joys of work? Our part is to remove obstructions and to give stimulus and guidance to the child who is trying to get into touch with the universe of things and thoughts which belong to him. Our deadly error is to suppose that we are his showman to the universe, and, not only so, but that there is no community at all between child and universe unless such as we choose to set up.[74]

Children are born with natural affinities and intimacies with numbers of things: the out-of-doors (trees, grass, field and stream, parks and ponds), parents and others (authority, community, and society), God (author of life, heavenly Father, dispenser of grace and justice), and many living books and ideas (a broad curriculum, putting the mind of the child in the way of great minds, informing thoughts and concepts that serve to feed the mind). The three instruments of education working together provide the proper environment in which to breathe and learn (atmosphere), the habits necessary for self-control and regulation (discipline), and the delightful mind-stuff of a broad curriculum (life). From here it is natural to see that these make for a learning place in which many living relationships are formed between the child and his intimacies.

Consider the second grade teacher who has thoughtfully applied these instruments to her classroom. The atmosphere of her class is warm, supportive, and caring. There is a sense of ownership between teacher and student regarding learning and responsibility. The teacher understands the nature of the young learner and alternates inspirational (literature, art and music, history) and disciplinary (mathematics, spelling, grammar) subjects, as she is aware that the minds of her students will tire. Teacher and child work together to solve problems, explore content, and ask questions. Habits such as attentiveness, respect, and responsibility are foundational to the workings of the class, with both child and teacher developing these traits together. The structure of authority is clear, but manipulation or control does not abrogate the personhood of the child. Life in the classroom is real and vibrant: Student work is neatly displayed, literature selections and resources are carefully selected and used, and students have time to read on their own day by day. The teacher also reads aloud to her children. This is indeed a gentle and growing time for the children.

Atmosphere, discipline, and life can open the door to a wide room of many relations; these become the conditions that must be satisfied before a child can fully apprehend all the relations and intimacies available to him. One can imagine the opposite is also true. If the circumstances are such that the child is viewed as an empty vessel or that he is only bad, if rules and control are the methods for obtaining good behavior, and if the vitality of education is strangled by rote learning, workbooks, and drill, then the result may be (not discounting the indomitable spirit of the child to learn in spite of everything) that learning will be meaningless, incoherent, disconnected. Education will then become the science of fragmentation.

THE HOUSE OF EDUCATION
An Example of Relationships in Life and Learning

With the publication of *Home Education* in 1896, Charlotte Mason increasingly gained status and success as an educator of some influence in educational and religious communities. From this beginning came the formation of the PNEU (Parents' National Educational Union) and the creation of a monthly magazine called *The Parents' Review* in 1890. In 1891 Miss Mason made a move to Ambleside in the Lake District of England, a place that was to become a metaphor illustrating the ideas of the life and intimate relationships of education. It was here in Miss Mason's home that the constitution of a learning community for teachers called the House of Education was born in 1892. Young women came here to work and study, to share meals and sleeping quarters, and to live out daily themselves and later with others an applied philosophy of education, all the while remaining under the watchful care and discipleship of a wise and discerning (and demanding) mentor, one Miss Charlotte Mason.

It was in Ambleside that students would be exposed to the wonder and joys of intimate relationships and healthy rhythms of life. In her own words, this was a setting "of natural beauty. A country rich in flowers, mosses and ferns. They [her students] will learn to know and love the great individuality of great natural features; mountain pass, valley, lake and waterfall." The surroundings of her training college would encourage in the students a common love of nature and inspire them with awe and wonder toward the created order.

A sense of mutual trust, care, concern, honesty, and service would soon emerge among these young women as they lived and worked together. The life and training of these students would also make them aware of the intimacies and relationships in learning that come from "being persons," relationships beginning with God—the author of knowledge—and extending to nature, books, and living ideas; handicrafts; maps and local geography; the sweep of history with its people, places, and events; the beauty of art, music, and poetry; the very real day-to-day existence of people in community. These are the very intimacies they would later bring to their own students. The preservice teachers at Ambleside did not stand outside the curriculum, in a vicarious manner, but lived out the relationship of life and learning in daily practice. And all the while, Miss Mason was there to provide counsel, advice, direction, encouragement, and exhortation—the role of a mentor.

It was the living and learning together daily in this home (for that is what the House of Education was) over the course of two years that developed teachers who came to understand Miss Mason's philosophy of education and then practice it in their own teaching and lives. They came to realize that the child is born a person, that she has a great capacity for learning, that the curriculum must be steeped in living books and ideas, that education is an atmosphere, a discipline, a life, and the science of relations. They knew because this is the manner in which they themselves had been taught at Ambleside by Charlotte Mason. The significance is unmistakable: As these young women were trained up in the intimacies of learning based upon an applied educational philosophy—in relationships with God, knowledge, nature, and others, and within a harmonious community—so too would they take the intimacies and relationships of learning with them into homes and classrooms scattered across Great Britain. In fact, the ideas of relationship and community worked in concert to make concrete the metaphor found in Ambleside: The House of Education, in bringing together the intimacies of learning, was indeed a life, one in which these students were immersed and by which they found themselves changed.

A "CAPTAIN" IDEA

In the science of relations there must be a worthy starting point, an arch that brings unity to the whole. This starting point is the nature of learning, and that is theological at heart. In *School Education*, we read:

> This idea of all education springing from and resting upon our relation to Almighty God is one which we have ever labored to enforce. We take a very distinct stand upon this point. We do not merely give a religious education, because that would be to imply the possibility of some other education, a secular education, for example.
>
> But we hold that all education is divine, that every good gift of knowledge and insight comes from above, that the culmination of all education is that personal knowledge of and intimacy with God in which our being finds its fullest perfection.[75]

Essex Cholmondeley comments on Miss Mason's passion for spiritual things and their rightful place in our lives:

> The love and knowledge of God, of Jesus Christ the Saviour of the world, of the Holy Spirit as supreme educator of mankind, these themes are never absent from [Miss Mason's] thoughts. To reach such knowledge each person must feel the need to know. A keen desire, a full attention given to the words of life, the will to receive them, to ponder, to keep them—this attitude of mind gives entry into the world of truth which is the life of the world to come, the Kingdom of Heaven,

for the mind fully given is a humble mind, free from self-concern, ready to enter, to receive and share with others the bread of life.[76]

Therefore Miss Mason places the knowledge of God on the leading edge of her curriculum, with the knowledge of man and the universe following in order. God has revealed Himself, His being and purposes, through the pages of living Scripture, which has its focus and meaning in the life and work of Jesus Christ. Because of this starting point, we must infer that all of life has a theological or religious base. A purpose of education begins to emerge, that of developing an understanding of God and His created reality and to use that understanding in exercising a creative-redemptive dominion over the creation in which we live.[77] The child is not passive in his education; he experiences, understands, and acts upon that understanding in ways that show the image of God in him—creating, exploring, making choices, building relationships.

In Charlotte Mason's book entitled *A Philosophy of Education*, the German philosopher Johann Herbart (1776-1841) is examined in great detail. His theory of learning revolves around the thought that the child has no personality in the sense that Miss Mason described or believed, that ideas contend to find entrance into the threshold of the child's mind, and that once in, these ideas form themselves in related groups called apperception masses. It becomes the role of the teacher to arrange appropriate ideas within the curriculum, to make the best relations between ideas so that cognitive connections may be facilitated. It is like the arranging of mental furniture in the mind's household, with the teacher playing the part of interior decorator. In this model the teacher is the active player, choosing the ideas, arranging the correlations, planning out every contingency. The child becomes a new creation as he comes forth from the hands of the teacher.[78] These well-planned units of instruction were called concentration schemes.

One such plan was designed around Robinson Crusoe. It was here that the plans of a teacher-centered effort came forth: The whole unit was systematized, arranged, and packaged for the child's consumption, for consumer he is, in Herbart's way of thinking. As these elementary-aged students read a child's adaptation of the original classic work, they were provided with integrating experiences that connect art, handicrafts, writing, recitation, and arithmetic. Students drew Crusoe's island, wrote about his experiences, counted wine casks, and built models. In these tasks Miss Mason noted seeds of inanity, as she believed the content to be trivial indeed. The same might be said of units centered on themes such as apples or teddy bears, topics that find their way into many classrooms. Her word for this would be twaddle, and an answer to the concentration scheme approach is as follows:

> As I have said elsewhere, the ideas required for sustenance of children are to be found mainly in books of literary quality; given these the mind does for itself the sorting, arranging, selecting, rejecting, classifying, which Herbart leaves to the struggle of the promiscuous [indiscriminate] ideas which manage to cross the threshold.[79]

It is to the potency and personhood of the child that she beckons us to look, not to the power and ability of the teacher and her bag of tricks and methods. If current brain research is correct, then the mind of the child is made to search out connections in life and learning, to appropriate ideas and relate them in novel ways to new avenues of learning, and to gain insight in an environment of trust and mutual respect. True education should not stand in the way of the science of relations by having the teacher become the child's showman of the universe. Rather the process has the child and teacher working side by side, delving into the world of books and ideas together for connections that surface in the search for knowledge and meaning.

One such natural connection is the real link between literature and history. One does not need to stretch and make artificial ties to hold these two together. Miss Mason often placed a classic literature selection alongside the study of history. She believes this arrangement made history come to life as the child looked through the eyes of historical figures in their own places and times. We must beware the Herbartian error—that of so arranging the curriculum for the students that the connections are merely handed to them.

THE PRIMARY STARTING POINT OF EDUCATION

The child is rooted in the reality of the fall of man and the created order and in the redemptive work of Christ in space and time. He has both a natural intimacy with an inbred sin nature and a potential for intimacy and relationship with his Savior. This then becomes the primary starting point of education. The science of relations works to our detriment (the fallen nature and relationship with Adam and sinful mankind) and as a boon (the image of God in the child and his affinities for spiritual things, nature, life, people, and ideas). It is as Al Wolters has written in *Creation Regained*, a set of relationships affected by the directional pull of sin and grace.

As the child enters this world of truth, whether it be at the knee of the parent, at Sunday school or Bible club, or even at a Christian school, a perspective of the world comes into view—a lens the child uses to evaluate and judge, peruse and wonder upon what she sees, hears, and reads. The worldview is developed as the child comes more and more into relationship with her primary Source found in the Savior and Scripture. And this worldview becomes the foundation for understanding and enjoying many other aspects of knowledge. Built upon this foundation are the knowledge of humankind as expressed through history, literature, citizenship, morals and ethics, composition, languages, art and music, as well as the knowledge of the universe through science, geography, mathematics, physical development, and handcrafts. Through these three aspects of knowledge, we begin to see the richness and variety found in a broad curriculum. In fact, the curriculum of the school must be structured around these three relationships as they encompass in an orderly way the intimacies and affinities inherent to the child. In Part Two of this book, we shall see how the knowledge of God, humankind, and the universe works itself out in terms of curriculum, scope, and sequence.

However, the leading or captain idea is this—education is the science of relations. The broadness, diversity, and fruitfulness of this motto is evident when Miss Mason writes:

> A child should be brought up to have relations of force with earth and water, should run and ride, and swim and skate, lift and carry; should know texture, and work in material; should know by name, and where and how they live at any rate, the things of the earth about him, its birds and beasts and creeping things, its herbs and trees; should be in touch with literature, art and thought of the past and the present. He must have a living relationship with the present, its historic movement, its science, literature, art, social needs and aspirations. In fact, he must have a wide outlook, intimate relations all around, for it depends, not upon how much is learned, but upon how things are learned.[80]

At the beginning of a new millennium, we might look at this ideal state wondering if it is possible to create a space where running, climbing, exploring, and living the good life are feasible, realistic, or affordable—not to mention the resources needed for such an enriched curriculum. The truth is that

Miss Mason lived in a day in which city factories blotted out the sky with smoke and soot. The sameness of the architecture, the long hours of work for adult and child alike, and the dreariness of an impoverished existence made for a mind-numbing life. But it was to these places, as well as to the more well-to-do homes, that Miss Mason made her plea for an educational revolution. She did not simply issue a call to others. She personally developed schools in the industrial cities of Victorian England for the children of the workers—with amazing results. She believed in the infinite possibilities of the child's mind, including the minds of children of the slums:

> [A] limited vocabulary, sordid surroundings, the absence of a literary background to thought are not hindrances; indeed they may turn out to be incentives to learning, just as the more hungry the child, the readier he is for dinner. This statement is no mere pious opinion; it has been amply proved in thousands of instances. Children of a poor school in the slums are eager to tell the whole story of Waverley, falling continually into the beautiful language and style of the author. They talk about the Rosetta Stone and about treasures in their local museum; they discuss Coriolanus. . . . they know by heart every detail of a picture by de Hooch, Rembrandt, Botticelli.[81]

Let us be encouraged, for in this field (the science of relations), small efforts are honored with great rewards. Consider the inner-city Bible club in St. Louis where middle school girls come to eagerly hear stories from God's Word and then give eloquent and detailed narrations to the committed and caring adult leaders. Or the elementary school in the Amazon delta region where ten-, eleven-, and twelve-year-olds are listening to the music of Bach or Vivaldi while they work. Or the suburban Ontario grade six teacher who leads a literature club for parents, students, and coworkers in her home on a monthly basis. Or, finally, the small school in the bayou of Louisiana that has decided to perform an adaptation of *A Midsummer Night's Dream* involving students from grades one to five. In any or all of these cases, teachers and children took the risk of daring to make education the science of relations through broadening the curriculum by placing people in the way of their natural affinities. The atmosphere, discipline, and life of these situations opened the door to a wider room of learning called the science of relations.

The information age in which our children live has its own slough of despair with the advent of the Internet, super-fast computers, satellite links to the world, violent games and simulations, and virtual reality. Our children are hit with a constant barrage of images from terminals, television, and movies—all in the staccato fashion of the age. Attention spans continue to decrease as we can no longer keep up with the speed at which information passes us. Movies such as *The Matrix* attempt to make sense of the world of the near future, but they merely serve to confuse and promote hopelessness. It is into this world that we must make our foray for the children's sake. Caring and committed adults in the many and varied learning places—urban, rural, suburban; upscale or under-resourced; multicultural United States or the Third World—may begin in a modest fashion by reading aloud a whole living book, placing on the walls of the classroom works of art, playing music during the time of work or quiet, bringing parents in to share about their lives and experiences, taking a walk outside, or visiting a local museum. It is important that we begin somewhere, however modest, for indeed small efforts are honored with great rewards.

THE BROAD CURRICULUM

More specific to a school setting, the broad curriculum is where the child finds her sustenance. Miss Mason carefully laid this out for her students at the House of Education as they themselves participated in a broad curriculum during their two years of training. And what better way to place within the hearts of those young teachers the love of the intimacies of learning than to have them experience firsthand the mind-stuff and "life-stuff" of a curriculum steeped in the science of relations? It was not toward methods that Miss Mason pointed her students; it was to the depth and breadth of a broad and rich curriculum founded on many living books and ideas. Hers was always an *applied* philosophy of education—the "knowing and doing" to be lived out with real integrity. Provide the student with an abundant feast of learning, and she will educate herself—the powers of curiosity, attention, retention, and expression naturally turned on to the meat of this curriculum.

A broad curriculum will place the child in the way of vital relationships and will be orderly and consecutive in scope. Although it is broad in nature, it is not haphazard or incoherent. During a term's work (ten to twelve weeks) in most of the former PNEU schools, the students would range among many books carefully selected to expose them to many minds and ideas. Students gave an oral or written narration at the end of each lesson, a requirement for the development of the habit of attention, as well as an opportunity to reproduce the assimilated knowledge from each area of content or from each book read aloud to or read by the students themselves. Note the content-rich atmosphere: *The Bible for the Young, Parables from Nature, The Pilgrim's Progress, Andersen's Fairy Tales, Our Island Story, The Ambleside Geography Book* (by Charlotte Mason), six pictures by Durer, the keeping of a nature notebook (six wild fruits, ten birds, five other animals), musical compositions by Brahms, two Christmas hymns, Psalm 150, verses from Joshua and the Gospel of Mark, and *The Fairy Queen* for recitations, along with mathematics, physical education, practical work (gardening, knitting, paper-folding, and modeling), French, and music lessons. Each lesson was set forth with book, idea, and page numbers for the parent or teacher to follow. The child was free for the afternoon to continue developing the many other essential nonbook relations and intimacies with tree and rock, stream and pond, cloud and sky, friend and playground, backyard or playroom.

THE TEACHER'S PLACE IN THE SCIENCE OF RELATIONS

As with Miss Mason's view of the nature of the learner as a fully made person and not a person-to-be, we come to the question of the teacher's place in the life and education of the child. Miss Mason's approach, rather than falling prey to a humanistic child-centered philosophy, places the teacher and child into a proper relationship of authority and accountability. The teacher provides direction and guidance, feedback and exhortation (discipleship, if you will), and then stands back in an attitude of masterly inactivity. The child responds by dominion-seeking according to his nature, learning habits of heart and mind, and cultivating his love of learning through books.

Over and over Miss Mason reminds us to beware the tendency to overwhelm the child with an adult's personal influence and manipulations; she reminds us that education is the science of relations—those relations natural and proper to the child in his great capacity for knowledge and for making connections. As a challenge to the educator in any learning place, Mason wrote:

> We consider that education is the science of relations, or, more fully, that education considers what relations are proper to a human being, and in what ways these several relations can be best established; that a human being comes into the world with a capacity for many relations; and that we, for our part, have two chief concerns, first, to put him in the right way of forming these relations by presenting the right idea at the right time, and by forming the right habit upon the right

idea; and, secondly, by not getting in the way and so preventing the establishment of the very relations we seek to form.[82]

The fulfillment of this credo must be found in a proper relationship between child and knowledge and teacher. This connection becomes vital in the process of life and learning. The child finds himself in an interesting position, that of one under authority and at the same time made to express dominion and choices. The teacher has another dynamic—that of a balance between being the purveyor of wisdom and knowledge and remaining a learner herself, who is willing to at times stand aside or to be a part of the process of learning. Either way, there is risk—and fulfillment.

The teacher may then take the natural role as discipler, as co-learner, as both authority, habit-builder, and fellow pilgrim in this journey of faith and learning. The idea to keep in mind (and heart) is a theological one that has immense implications for educators: Both we and our students are fallen creatures who will continue in the lifelong battle of flesh against Spirit. For the children and students, the teacher's role as godly mentor and keeper of accountability (a bit like Miss Mason and her young teachers) becomes for his charges a spiritual and necessary relationship.

Consider William Golding's *Lord of the Flies*, a cautionary tale about stranded schoolchildren who descend the scale of civilized human behavior very rapidly when trying to survive on their own without guidance from a teacher or moral authority. A structure must be in place in the classroom that takes into account both the image of God within and the fallenness of the child and his need for dominion with direction and guidance from an earthly authority—the parent, and, by extension, the teacher.

Charlotte Mason believed that every child should grow in wisdom and in the knowledge of the many relations about him. Essex Cholmondeley summed this up well when she penned in 1960:

> [Miss Mason's] books remind readers of their children's needs and powers, of the laws of authority and obedience, of the helpful stability of good habits, of the joyous living that comes with minds well supplied and occupied. All this, established half a century ago, stands firm in truth applicable to the swiftly changing circumstances of new generations.[83]

4

Distinctives of a Charlotte Mason Education

LIVING BOOKS

By Maryellen St. Cyr

Charlotte Mason introduces the reader to living books and living things as the only form of "mind food" that provides the daily nourishment for the mind to do its work. "For the truth of the matter is that babies and young children explore new experiences with tireless enthusiasm. A girl or boy has a mind which is hungry for ideas. They have an appetite for knowing and experiencing."[1] If a book is not living, Mason refers to it as twaddle, something dry, diluted, predigested, void of vital thought. It seems as if there is nothing in between; books and things either do the work of nourishment, or they do not. Yet I've spoken with many a teacher who might argue otherwise, who might give justification for a book not necessarily living but not nearly dead either. Looking at each book in view of these principles may aid the reader in characterizing books as either living or dead.

• Books are to be well written, not dependent upon illustrations for the story to unfold (*Ourselves*, Part II, p. 11).

• Books must contain literary language to make a direct appeal to the mind, to stir the imagination, and hold the child's interest (*A Philosophy of Education*, p. 248).

• Books must be enjoyed. The ideas they hold must make the sudden delightful impact on the mind, cause the intellectual stir that marks the inception of an idea (*School Education*, p. 178).

• Books are not to be too easy or too direct. If they tell the reader straightway what to think, he will read but not appropriate the information (*A Philosophy of Education*, p. 303).

• Good books are able to be narrated. The child is able to recall the ordered sequence with graphic details (*School Education*, pp. 179-180).

I have seen children of all ages well fed on thought from direct relationships with living books. Third graders went back to read the "dry parts" of Scriptures as they became familiar with geography and genealogies. Students begged for more history during the lunch hour after an already lengthy lesson. Books of geology and gemology were packed away to be read at home and brought back with students zealously retelling what they knew from the evening's reading. And the daily time of reading a book to students of all ages usually ended in a sigh as the clock reached the final hour of school.

As a school, we carefully choose each book presented to the students in order that these meet the criteria of such living books, whether they are textbooks, read-aloud books, literature books, or resource books. For we desire to give children a full diet of living thought in order to approach life actively, to be in touch with vibrant interest with whatever they see and hear wherever they go. In turn, we want them to reflect upon their thoughts and conduct of life, to be able to value what is good, true, and beautiful. We, as educators, have at times put aside our personal preferences in the way of books and have also been challenged by some limiting beliefs that we have held to, for both our students and ourselves, regarding the level of difficulty or interest of a particular book. There have been times when a book has been contested because of its difficulty or lack of emotional appeal. In response, we have asked the instructor to comply with the demands of the curriculum. And more often than not, the educators have been surprised and delighted with the manner in which the students responded to this living book when presented more carefully.

And then there are other times when a teacher or parent desires a book for the child because he delights in it, but we deem it unfit. Delight alone does not determine whether books are appropriate for the child or for the adult.

We need not ask what the girl or boy likes. She very often likes the twaddle of goody-goody story books, he likes condiments, highly-spiced tales of adventure. We are all capable of liking mental food of a poor quality and a titillating nature; and possibly such food is good for us when our minds are in need of an elbow-chair; but our spiritual life is sustained on other stuff, whether we be boys or girls, men or women.[2]

I know that we are living during a time when it is not a usual practice to say no to requests that do not bear an evil intent. Yet the question is not what the book does *not* do, but instead what silly stories and twaddle *does* cultivate in children. What enthusiasms are generated by this kind of thought? What tastes are cultivated?

Children must grow up on the best. There must never be a period in their lives when they are allowed to read or listen to twaddle or reading-made-easy. There is never a time when they are unequal to worthy thoughts well put and inspiring tales well told.[3]

Miss Mason often reminded the educator that he was educating the child to be a man or a woman. We look at the child's requests today and see no harm in letting him read carelessly for an hour or two a day. Yet what would become of the child as a man? And yet further, what would become of the child as a man if the child read first-rate books, the best books of the best authors?

Children brought up largely on books do better than those educated on a few books and many lectures. Wide reading produces children with generous enthusiasms, keen sympathies, a wide outlook, and sound judgment because they are treated from the first as beings of "large discourse looking before and after." They are persons of leisure too, with time for hobbies, because their work is easily done in the hours of morning school.[4]

Daniel Defoe, Louisa May Alcott, Robert Louis Stevenson, Mary Mapes Dodge, William Shakespeare, and the list goes on and on,[5] are friends to my students and myself because we spent many a day in meeting mind to mind.

We do not wish to claim more for the vital importance of good literature in the life of a child than it can bear, but we are nevertheless aware that, if neglected, a child's life can suffer inestimably. Literature, books, education, and life all go hand in hand. The best literature is the human heart of education.

NARRATION

By Maryellen St. Cyr

NARRATION DEFINED

Narration is considered the sum total of Charlotte Mason's philosophy and practice of education. She had discovered narration as the foundation stone of learning. Practiced with the right books, narration would provide the food upon which the mind can grow and thrive.[6] Charlotte Mason defined narration, this fundamental human activity, in the following ways:

> Narration is an art, like poetry-making or painting, because it is there, in every child's mind, waiting to be discovered and is not the result of any process of disciplinary education. A creative fiat calls it forth. "Let him narrate"; and the child narrates, fluently, copiously, in ordered sequence, with fit and graphic details, with a just choice of words, without verbosity or tautology, as soon as he can speak with ease.

And again:

> Narration is the children telling back what they read, hear, see, and let this action of the mind be habitual. The small ones go over in their minds their pictures, their tales, their geography and other readings. As they do so they use their own words, they "tell back" aloud, giving each incident, each point in their own way. If there are several children, they take turns, until the whole is told back.[7]

Narration is retelling. It is not memorization or parroting. It includes feelings and reactions. It is not word for word, but point to point. It is a type of essay response to a broad open-ended questioning, a recall of information.

In the strictest sense, narration is an immediate recall of information seen, read, or heard. In a more liberal sense, it is often used as a quest for information that has been seen, read, or heard after a period of time in the form of exams or evaluation of a child's knowledge on a particular subject. But even in the latter sense, the work of oral narration must have gone on before in order that the child retain the knowledge in question.

The goal of anyone who teaches is for the learner to possess this comprehension and knowledge from a body of information. That is the beginning stage for further development in the use and discussion of this information. In light of this, the learner must first acquire a degree of knowledge to act upon her experience in a valuable way. Once this knowledge is granted, the mind can be stirred to fuller and clearer knowledge through discussion and further inquiry. The value of these activities depends upon what has gone on before, upon the amount of attention and the quality of assimilation and reflection. As Miss Mason said, "When the mind has not attended or had the leisure to do the work of the mind, only superficial activities of impressions and less thought can be the result of dealing with this information."[8]

Therefore, the goal of any learner must be *attention*. Attentiveness is a vital part of understanding and remembering, for one does not know what one has not attended to. The practice of oral and written narration is a way for the learner to acquire knowledge as well as to be held accountable in an active way for what is seen, read, and heard. The practice of narration is explicitly described below:

• Prepare the passage carefully beforehand, thus making sure that all the explanations and use of background material (vocabulary, dates, and geography) precede the reading and narration.

• Write all difficult proper nouns on the blackboard prior to the lesson. One should never stop in the middle of the reading to explain the meaning of a word or particular map work.

• Read the literature *once*. The child listens carefully with a view to narrate. It is impossible to fix attention on that which we have heard before and know we shall hear again.

• Regulate the length of the passage to be read to the age of the children and the nature of the book. Narrate less before you narrate more. If you read a fairy story, you will find that the children will be able to narrate a page or two if a single incident is described. With a closely packed book, one or two paragraphs between narrations are sufficient. Older children will be able to tackle longer passages, but the same principle should be applied; the length varies with the nature of the book.

• Never interrupt or prompt a person narrating even if a person mispronounces a word. Persons soon forget what they were going to say next when interrupted.

• Correct any mistakes after the narration through your instruction or the prompting of other students. After a child is finished narrating, you may say, "Does anyone else have something to add to the narration?"

- Begin a lesson with a short narration of the previous lesson.
- Use written narration after a child is fluent with oral narration. Keep a record of the written narrations as a way of noting the child's progress. Written narration is not evaluated for spelling and grammar, but for content alone. Special care should be taken that certain spelling and grammar is covered as the need becomes apparent.
- Follow up written narration with the child reading his work aloud to the teacher or to other students.
- Use narration to assess comprehension of the listener, how the child constructs meaning with new knowledge derived from the text put together with background knowledge in ways that make sense.
- Follow the narration with guided questions posed by both teacher and students.

As a multidisciplinary tool, this method of narration is used with individual students, groups of students, and whole classrooms in different contexts, from picture studies to nature studies.

An example of narration across the disciplines follows: Students narrate the antics of *Pinocchio* in the first grade, a biographical sketch of E. B. White in the second grade, problem-solving strategies in word problems in the third grade, the region of the Mesopotamian Valley in the fourth grade, the leadership of Justinian in the fifth grade, the description of van Gogh's *Irises* in the sixth grade, molecular structure in the seventh grade, and the tale of Boaz and Ruth in the eighth grade.

THE BENEFITS OF NARRATION

Narration is the practical outworking of Charlotte Mason's philosophy of education as implied by the statement, "Education is a life, an atmosphere, and a discipline." Narration is underpinned by the view of the learner as a person capable of attention, accountability, insight, and expectation. For it is here that the manifold benefits of narration are seen as characterized in the following:

- Narration instructs the conscience. The interior life of the child is developed through listening to stories and myths that are repeated over again. "Every time a child rattles one off, he taps deep into those emotional roots, for the stories get told from their 'inner senses' out."[9]
- Narration allows the learner to take on an active role. Studies have shown that when the learner is held accountable through retellings, compre-

hension and enjoyment are increased. This role puts the student in an interactive role as an active listener to her own voice, the writer's voice, and/or the reader's voice.[10]

• Narration gives food for the mind. The work of cognition can only take place when the mind is nourished upon real food. This food for the mind can be found in a variety of subjects, not just literature. A history text can teach history in a literary form, as a narrative. The same can be said for studies of science, music, nature, and other subjects. Texts such as these are not as readily available as ones that are diluted or dry but can be sought in a variety of disciplines.

• Narration increases brain activity. The culmination of current research suggests that brain activity is enhanced when learning involves challenging tasks and information, a tolerance for ambiguity, literary language, and intrinsic motivation. When narration is used with literature that encompasses "the best thought of the best writers," we have this optimal state of the mind.

• Narration provides far more information about students' comprehension than answers to questions. Narration incorporates individual constructs, organization, meaning, and vocabulary without the support clues provided by the questioning.[11]

• Narration moves the learner from rote or taxon memory to locale memory. Narration is a strategy in which the learner rehearses, relives, modifies, and integrates interpretations of the author's messages into her own reality, thus bringing about a greater degree of transfer and meaning.[12]

• Narration brings about social interaction. "Knowing is how we make community with the unavailable other, with realities that would elude us without the connective tissue of knowledge. Knowing is a human way to seek relationship, and in the process, to have encounters and exchanges that will inevitably alter us. At its deepest reaches, knowing is always communal."[13]

• Narration maximizes the process of comprehension and meaning. Studies show that children who narrate comprehend far better than those who do not, regardless of the age factor. Younger children who narrated gained more insight and comprehension than older children who did not narrate.

THE QUINTESSENTIAL ASPECTS OF NARRATION

Narration can be seen as a novel idea in which it is approached with younger children more than older children, is infrequent in use, and lacks deliberateness as a methodology to sustain comprehension and retain information. The education secretary for the western county of Gloucestershire in the 1920s, Mr. H. W. Household, addressed this issue of the infrequent and halfhearted use of narration. A teacher hastily replied, "My children read to themselves, and reading is followed by narration. There is nothing new in this."

Household responded, "Perhaps not. But let us be quite clear. Does the child always learn from the book? Does narration always follow? Is there never more than one reading?"[14]

In point, the student who readily narrates after a single reading will have command of the knowledge read. There will be no getting on with the work of learning with continual aid from the text, prompting from the teacher, or a second and third reading.

There is a danger of supplementing the method of narration with general talking and questioning, losing the clarity of a point-by-point argument posited by a writer. Thus, the burden of our schools is before us, bringing forth passive, inactive minds in students. If the mind is to be active, it must do the work of attending, reflective thinking, and expression through the work of narration. One cannot omit that part of the lesson where the *child* puts *his* mind to the task of retelling through reflective thinking, where he performs the "act of knowing" through verbal or written expression.

The lesson can offer fruitful ideas; thought-provoking questions; enumerations from the reading; analysis of characters, ideas, observations, and much more; a tracing of cause and effect, as well as a multitude of other activities to further knowing and understanding. "[W]e must never forget that without narration the mind will starve; whatever disciplinary exercises we use, they should be *in addition to* and never instead of narration." Physical exercises for the mind are appropriate at times, and the children will benefit from them, but exercise will not take the place of nourishment. In actuality, one cannot exercise what one does not possess, knowledge.

Miss Mason believed that children possessed unmeasured powers intellectually, morally, and spiritually. She defined children as persons—persons who are described as fully human with the power to create (Gen. 1:26), to relate (1 Cor. 12:12), to choose (Rom. 3, 5, and 6), to love (John 13:34-35), to know (Ps. 46:10), to reflect (Gen. 2:19), and to access the supreme Creator, the King and Priest of men and women (Matt. 19:14). She attributed the aspect of mystery to persons as God's image-bearers and said that our attempts to define persons did nothing more than bind them, for people often exceed forms of measurement. Persons have potential for both good and bad exercise of the natural and fundamental principles of authority and obedience.[15] Miss Mason did not therefore limit children because of class or state. She saw each child as a person who could do the work of learning through the constant effort of attention and observation because of how the created mind works, as well as the innate desire to know.

Here are two educators' statements verifying the beneficial use of narration after a time of disbelief. The first, a country teacher, said:

> The most pleasing fact of all has been the eagerness among the older scholars to narrate, a thing I could never get them to do previously, and, greatly to my astonishment, scholars I thought to be almost helpless are in many cases the most exact and fluent narrators. Because of the oral work the scholars have enlarged their vocabularies, can express their ideas more exactly, and exercise a greater amount of intelligence in answering problems and questions based upon the work studied.[16]

A headmaster of a boys' school stated:

> What has surprised us most is the ready way boys absorb information, and become interested in literature which we have hitherto considered outside the scope of primary school teaching. A year ago I could not have believed boys would read Lytton's *Harold*, Kingsley's *Hereward*, and Scott's *Talisman* with real pleasure and zest, or would study with understanding and delight Shakespeare's *Macbeth*, *King John*, and *Richard II*; but experience has shown that we had underrated the abilities and tastes of the lads; we should have known better.[17]

It seems as though all teachers at times profess limiting beliefs regarding their students and their work. Some of the studies manifested this as well in students eliciting cues from the teachers and teachers providing "instructional support" until the students figure out what the teachers want. Charlotte Mason stated that we as educators must recognize that children are not ruminants (contemplative) intellectually any more than they are physically. "They cannot go over the same ground repeatedly without deadening, even paralyzing results, for progress, continual progress is the law of intellectual life."[18]

The role of the teacher is that of one who gives direction and elucidation in lessons, one who shares sympathies in studies, speaks a vivifying word here and there, provides a full reservoir of right thought, lays down lines of habit, exercises several powers of the mind, and sows opportunities for learning.

The teacher relies not upon approbation, avarice, emulation, or vanity to bear undue influence upon the learner, but upon the child's innate ability to know. The educator does not manipulate, taking on the responsibility for the child's knowing, but provides a fitting environment wherein the mind is sustained upon ideas, thus continuing the act of education, self-education. And this education is produced from living thought found in living books. The life of thought needs a nourishing, plentiful diet, a diet of ideas. Miss Mason said, "An idea is more than an image or a picture; it is, so to speak, a spiritual germ endowed with vital force—with power, that is, to grow, and to produce after its own kind."[19]

These ideas are the progeny of minds, the work of God among men and women (James 1:17). While these living ideas come from living books, "it is accepted as the nature of a school-book that it be drained of living thought. It may bear the name of a thinker, but then it is the abridgment of an abridgment, and all that is left for the scholar is dry bones of his subject denuded of soft flesh and living color, of the stir of life and power of moving—void of life. It cannot be too often said that information is not education."[20]

Books are to be well written, not dependent on illustrations for the story to unfold. They are to be classic works containing literary language that sparks the child's interest and opens the door to the child's mind. Miss Mason held out the vision: "We shall train a race of readers who will demand literature—that is, the fit and beautiful expression of inspiring ideas and pictures of life."[21]

PERSONAL REFLECTIONS CONCERNING NARRATION

Teachers' Experiences in a Classroom Application

In view of its far-reaching benefits in transforming mere information into vital knowledge, a plan was devised at Parkview School to institute narration as a commonplace practice with children. Each student in the school would be held accountable to narrate both orally and in written form consistently. Students would be called upon daily to narrate orally throughout the disciplines. Students would participate weekly in a written narration, either written by the students themselves or in the younger grades dictated to an adult recorder. It was our goal that each child would narrate skillfully and naturally.

Some of the educators that have been implementing this plan share the following thoughts:

> Narration is an excellent tool to assess a child's understanding. Many times it is difficult to determine how much a child is absorbing strictly through observation, for often the child who is quiet and seems to be listening has not understood as much as a fidgety child has. Narration makes a child an active, responsible party in the learning process. At the kindergarten level, some students have not had to be accountable for listening for a prolonged period of time. The short, colorful picture books and fast-paced TV programs that children are accustomed to do not allow them to internalize what they have seen or heard. However, narration does this and should be used as soon as possible in developing the habit of attentiveness in children. (Carol James, kindergarten)

> In the years I have worked with narration, I am convinced about its benefits. First, using books with living ideas written above the grade level produce food for thought. I have enjoyed teaching vocabulary in conjunction with narration. It brings connectedness in the learning of words. It is also a wonderful tool to strengthen the habit of attention, thinking, and imagination. I have also taught the elements of literature through narration because the story is so much a part of students. They recognize the various elements with ease. And, lastly, writing assignments have also been a success with narration. The students have been "romanced" with living thoughts, judgments, and predicaments. They are chomping at the bit to write! Narration meets each child at his or her own level and allows each to grow—each one is successful. (Rebecca LaPointe, grade one)

> Narration holds students accountable for the story as a whole. They are not just required to recall the plot, the characters, or the setting. They are accountable to create the same mental pictures the author did through retelling. Narration is an active process as the listener interacts with another's thought in history, science, or math—creating mental masterpieces! (Nicole Dolan, grade three)

> I have seen the benefits of using narration in history. I would present the history lesson to the students as a story with many details and references on maps. Throughout my telling of the story, I would have the students narrate back to me. It was remarkable how they remembered

the tiny details and even pointed to the map as they were retelling events. Then at the end of the lesson they would narrate the whole story in their "Book of Centuries." Because they had narrated the story in smaller sections, they were able then to write a complete and thorough summary of the story. They did so with great accuracy and attention to details. I believe if they had not narrated throughout the whole process of the lesson, they would not have been able to write such detailed, accurate summaries. This comprehension was not short-termed. On tests weeks later they were able to answer essay questions covering all the king's successes, reasons for war, and other broad questions. Again they would write with great attention to details and summarize points not typical for a fifth grader. Narration greatly improved their comprehension of history. (Mischa Gunn, grade five)

The nature of narration does not lend itself to second-rate, poorly written literature. As I've incorporated narration more and more into my teaching, the quality of literature and written text has risen proportionately. Using narration was somewhat discouraging to me at first because I did not get the results I wanted right away. It also didn't seem "to fit" the usual fast-paced, high-entertainment, gimmick-dependent methodologies I was used to using. After consistent practice, however, the children were remembering better, comprehending more, and as a result enjoying their lessons. (Rebekah Brown, middle school)

The Students' Experiences

The students also experienced a degree of success in attending, in listening, in assimilating, in thinking, in remembering, in reflecting, in sorting, in comparing, in deciphering, and in expressing their mind-stuff through narration. Read what follows:

One morning you could see the clouds coming to each island one by one. And then they come to you on your island. You hear the boat pulling, the rudder going "brum, brumm, brummmm." The ripples in the water reach the sand. You smile because the water didn't touch your toes. You could hear seals in the distance, and you know you're not alone. The trees look like ghosts, and you can hear something, but you know it's not your heart. You hear the green plants growing and breaking through the weeds. Then the clouds broke away and the sun shone. All the children went out to the beach to play and jump in the water. "Wheee! Kersplash!" Then they lied down in the sand and made the form of their body. After everyone is gone, you row out and put the flashlight on the water and see the crab that is left when the sea rode up. The stars look like a hundred pair of eyes. But one pair of eyes was looking everywhere! (A kindergartner on *A Time of Wonder*)

In the cool of the evening, Templeton was hungry and thirsty. So Templeton went out to find some food. Charlotte yelled to him, "Bring me back a word!" Templeton did not like being treated like a messenger boy. "I didn't come here to get newspapers like a newspaper boy," he replied. "I came to enjoy myself." Templeton found an old newspaper behind the cattle barn. In it he found a ham sandwich, a wormy apple and some Swiss cheese. He ate it. Then he tore a word out and went back to the pigpen. "Here," said Templeton. "What does it say?" asked Charlotte. "I need you to read it for me." "It says humble," said Templeton. "Humble has two meanings. It means not proud and close to the ground. That's Wilbur all right," said Templeton. "He's close to the ground and not proud. Now, I'm going to enjoy myself." (A second grader on *Charlotte's Web*—excerpt from the narration)

Butterflies are interesting creatures that have entertained you many times with their bright colored wings. Now, let's take a closer look at these interesting creatures and you'll find out that there is much more to them than just their interesting wings. After mating the butterfly has to find a certain kind of plant to lay its eggs. Once the egg hatches, the caterpillar, also known as pupa, has to eat its host plant. Actually, the caterpillar spends most of its time eating, crawling and resting. Thus, the miracle called metamorphosis begins. The caterpillar grows rapidly as it eats. After a while the caterpillar sheds or slips out of an old skin into a new. Even a new head capsule comes. During a caterpillar's life it sheds four times. Then the pupa forms into a larva, also known as a chrysalis. It takes about two weeks for an adult butterfly to come out of the chrysalis. The adult butterfly wings are lepidopteron meaning scaly wings. If you've ever handled a butterfly, you know how easily these scales come off on your fingers. A butterfly lives off of nectar and its tongue is like a straw, it helps it reach those hard to reach places where the nectar is. There is a hole on the bottom of the butterfly's tongue so it can sip nectar. There are about nine thousand different types of butterflies. (Third grader, nine years of age, on *The Butterfly*)

In evaluating our work with narration during the school year, I have been pleased with the teachers' responses to this methodology and all the implications of philosophy and practice that have also been a part of this implementation process. We have all exercised the attitude of co-learners with the children in a spirit of teachableness and enthusiasm. The students are avidly narrating from living books and are growing in knowledge and in relationship with persons of the past, the world, their fellow classmates, teachers, parents, and God. As a school, we are in the beginning stages of incorporating narration. We are in the process of change from a view of the learner and of teaching and learning that focused on tradition, text, and technique to a view that embraces relationships, living thought, and principles. Through this transition time, I am indebted to the pioneer work of Charlotte Mason who left a sound and relevant treatise to help us in the work of change.

Summary

Children brought up narrating living books "see" what they have conceived in their minds, producing manifold benefits to them as narrators. Narration:

- Provides much more exercise for the mind than is possible under other circumstances.
- Crystallizes a number of impressions, psychologically, completing a chain of experiences.
- Adds to a storehouse of information that can be referred to, built upon, and assimilated to equal the sum of a child's knowing on a topic.
- Gives an opportunity to secure attention, interest, and concentration on a great many subjects.
- Creates the habit of getting mental nourishment from books.
- Presents the child with a wide vocabulary, and her vocabulary increases as she narrates.
- Develops discrimination and love of books.
- Forms a capacity, character, countenance, initiative, and a sense of responsibility in students as good, thoughtful people.
- Grants generous enthusiasms, keen sympathies, wide outlooks, and sound judgment because students are treated as beings of discourse, responsible for knowing.
- Kindles the imagination.
- Develops the style and rhythm for writing in quantity and quality.

IDEAS FOR NARRATION IN THE EARLY YEARS OF THE ELEMENTARY SCHOOL

Third Grade

BIBLE

Tell about the creation of the world in six days.

Give the context in each case, and describe the occasion on which these words were used: "Say, I pray thee, thou art my sister."

Tell about the Israelites' work. How was it made more oppressive?

ARITHMETIC

Tell about the rules of borrowing in subtraction. Use this problem: 25-8.

Tell about using zero as a place holder.

LITERATURE

Tell about "The Boy Who Cried Wolf."

Tell about Robert Louis Stevenson's childhood.

Tell about Hilda's attitude of feeling cross and sulky in chapter 11.

Narrate chapter 7, "Little Quekle Friends."

Tell the story of Medusa.

HISTORY

Tell about the buffalo hunt from *My Indian Boyhood.*

Tell about the Pilgrims' dreadful winter.

Explain the name Continents of Nature.

Tell about the onset of Patroklos.

Tell about Odysseus as the Stranger.

NATURE STUDY

Gather three kinds of leaves and tell all you can about them.

Tell about two kinds of wildflowers.

Tell about a bird and its chirping.

How many kinds of bees are in a hive? What kind of work do they do? Tell about it.

PICTURE STUDY

Tell about Rembrandt's being commissioned to paint portraits.

Tell about Benjamin West's first portraits.

Describe Renoir's *Girl with a Watering Can.*

POETRY

Tell about Henry Wadsworth Longfellow's "The Children's Hour."

Tell about your experience in the recital.

Describe the village blacksmith.

IDEAS FOR NARRATION IN THE LATER YEARS OF THE ELEMENTARY SCHOOL
Fourth, Fifth, and Sixth Grades

BIBLE

"And Jonathan loved him as his own soul." Of whom was this said? Tell a story of Jonathan's love.

"For they saw that the wisdom of God was in him." Give an account of an incident that displays David's wisdom.

ARITHMETIC

Define perimeter. Tell how to find the perimeter of a rectangle. A square. A triangle.

Explain to another student the principal steps in adding, subtracting, multiplying, and dividing fractions.

LITERATURE

Describe your favorite scene in *Heidi*.

Describe a journey to Narnia.

Contrast Jeannette and Jo in Mary Mapes Dodge's poem.

Describe the mood in John Greenleaf Whittier's "In School Days"—relate incidents, thoughts, and setting.

Tell about one tale from Chaucer's *Canterbury Tales*.

HISTORY

Describe a walk across the eastern seaboard of the United States.

Tell fully how Abraham Lincoln acquired the title of "Honest Abe."

Tell about riding an immigrant train in the late 1800s out west.

Tell about the towns, rivers, and other sites you would see while traveling around Atlanta.

SCIENCE

Tell how the following seeds are dispersed: birch, pine, and dandelion. Give descriptions.

Make a diagram of the eye. Explain how we view the world around us.

PICTURE STUDY

Tell about Claude Monet's *Women Seated Under the Willows*.

Tell about the use of arrangement and color in Vincent van Gogh's *Sunflowers*.

Mary Cassatt is known for painting peaceful, loving moments shared by mothers and their young children. Tell all you can about one of these paintings.

INFORMATION FOR PARENTS

How You Can Assist Your Child's Education

Dear Parents,

Throughout the elementary school, students will be receiving assignments in narration each week that are to be assisted by a parent. It is our desire to increase the student's manifest power of attention and clarity of thought, as well as to strengthen their abilities to deal with many subjects. These skills will prepare them to compose not only orally but also in writing. The answer to some questions you may have regarding this process follow.

What is narration?

Narration is retelling. It is not memorization or parroting. And it may include feelings and reactions at times. It is not word for word, but point to point. It is a type of essay response—broad, open-ended, questioning with a recall of certain information.

What does the student narrate?

A specific assignment will be given by the teacher each week. Narration can be the result of the student's, teacher's, or parent's reading aloud; or it may be the result of an oral lesson or something observed.

What part do I, the parent, play in narration?

The parent is the recorder. The child narrates to the parent, who writes down each sentence. (The child is recalling the sequence of events, arguments, main points, items of interest, graphic details—mentally asking what next?)

Some Guidelines to Follow:

• The child is told *prior* to the reading that he or she will narrate, to encourage careful listening/reading.

• The literature is read once.

• The child's response is to be respected. No promptings. No interruptions.

• After the child is finished, read back to him or her what was written. Ask the child if he or she would like to say anything else.

READING AND LITERATURE

By Jack Beckman

Miss Mason believed that children must be educated on good books. "No education," she wrote, "seems to be worth the name which has not made children at home in the world of books, and so related them, mind to mind, with thinkers who have dealt with knowledge."[22]

It is in the lap of the parent that the child first explores the universe of the printed page, and it is in the school atmosphere that this relationship with living books is extended into new frontiers. In recent days, whole-language theorists have encouraged what Miss Mason knew all along: Children of all ages must be immersed in the world of literature. For younger children working through the mechanics and convention of print, the teacher read-aloud becomes the vehicle for them to enter the world of living books. They listen to the cadence of the language, become friends with the characters, and see the events with the mind's eye. And this experience should not only happen in the first few years of school; children of all ages should be listening to literature being read aloud. Each grade should have its own book list of read-alouds for the purpose of enjoyment and delight.

LEARNING TO READ

Let us take a closer look at the younger child's learning to read. On this topic Miss Mason had definite ideas. First of all, in the nursery at home prior to grade one (age six), the child had been given a daily diet of reading already—in the lap of the parent. Then comes the day when the child is taught to read, most likely at age six or so. Little Bobbie has had this first lesson in reading, described in *Home Education*. We listen in on one mother recounting to another her experience with Bobbie in the nursery ("Two Mothers Confer," pages 207-214). A quick reading provides us with some assumptions about Bobbie:

- He knows his letters and sounds (in fact, it appears that Bobbie has "caught" these from playing with older siblings at a sand table and by using letter squares).
- He has a large receptive vocabulary already.
- He finds some words more interesting than others.
- He has an amazing capacity for apprehending words visually.

If we have done any reading at all of Miss Mason's thoughts on children, we must note that Bobbie is a normal child in her eyes. Using a chalkboard, several copies of a nursery rhyme (some cut up word by word), and Bobbie's natural mental powers, he is able within thirty minutes not only to read the twelve different words that make up the nursery rhyme, but is able to generalize those words to other print. The method goes something like this:

• Mother writes "Cock Robin" on the blackboard (for this is the nursery rhyme) and then tells Bobbie that the words are "Cock Robin."

• Bobbie is told to look at each word until he is sure he knows it.

• He then makes the words "Cock Robin" from memory, using loose letters.

• Bobbie finds the words "Cock Robin" in a bag containing the words of the rhyme.

• He is then shown the rhyme written on a sheet of paper and asked to find the words "Cock Robin."

• The other words of the rhyme are taught in the same manner. As the words are found, they are set aside where they can be seen and reviewed.

• Once all the words have been learned, mother dictates the rhyme line by line as Bobbie finds the words in his "word bank."

• Bobbie then reads off the rhyme line by line to mother from his words.

• Bobbie reads the selection from the sheet containing the full rhyme.

• On the next day, mother does word-building from the selection— "sparrow," "arrow," "narrow," "marrow."

From then on, the mother offers a day of reading alternating with word studies. In this session we see that phonetic work is combined with a "look-say" method. This ability to visualize and focus the powers of the mind is reinforced further in school through the use of narration (retelling after a single reading), picture talks, musical appreciation, nature notebooks, and dictation.

Teachers of young children should take time to learn from this mother's methods.

Miss Mason sets forth this question for us to consider:

[W]hat is it we propose in teaching a child to read?

(a) that he should know at sight, say, some thousand words;

(b) that he shall be able to build up new words with the elements of these.

Let him learn ten new words a day, and in twenty weeks he will be to some extent able to read, without any question as to the number of letters in a word. For the second, and less important, part of our task, the child must know the sounds of the letters and acquire power to throw given sounds into new combinations.

What we want is a bridge between the child's natural interests and those arbitrary symbols with which we must become acquainted, and which, as we have seen, are words, and not letters.[23]

How Miss Mason would have detested the teaching of meaningless "sound bite" parts like *sta, ste, sti, sto, stu* or nonsense words such as *crub, stame, flig*. She believed that the child "should be taught from the first to regard the printed word as he already regards the spoken word, as the symbol of fact or idea full of interest." The length of the word is of no consequence; it is the interest of the word that matters and sets up associations in the child's mind that "couple the objects with their spoken names."[24] Although Miss Mason uses interesting words such as *buttercup* and *robin redbreast*, we may find others to our students' liking and interest. Nursery rhymes and children's poetry provide good starting points for reading, and certainly a number of publishers on the literature-based track for reading offer alternatives to the purely phonetic-based approaches so prevalent in today's educational climate.

In schools where Miss Mason's principles of reading are being followed, I have seen young students eagerly making connections in receptive to expressive vocabulary (both in sight and phonetic sound), using chapter books, children's literature, nursery rhymes, and "big books" to foster a lifetime love for books and the needed strategies for growth in reading (fluency, understanding, expression). Very importantly, there are the literature-based read-alouds on a daily basis so that while our children are developing the tools of reading, they are not missing the beauty and depth of a well-told story.

READING FOR THE OLDER CHILD

The child over nine is moving into fluency and independence in reading; we see the student reading to know for himself rather than being read to by another. Inflection, phrasing, depth, and complexity mark this transition. These students also have a greater capacity for narrating in sequence and detail, pulling the author's vocabulary, style, and voice into the retelling. Whereas with the child under nine we might read several paragraphs and up to a page before asking him to narrate, we begin requiring the older child to read a chapter for himself before narrating. But it is always a single reading with an immediate retelling; at this age oral and written narrations are both used.

As we read *A Philosophy of Education*, it becomes obvious that Miss Mason's students had exposure to great literature even in the young years. Reading lessons were taken from such books as Andrew Lang's *Tales of Troy and Greece, The Heroes of Asgard, Aesop's Fables,* and *The Pilgrim's Progress* for students ranging in age from seven and a half to nine (pp. 180-181). Once the student had the tools of reading and was developing fluency, expression, intelligence, and regard for punctuation (about age nine to eleven), literature and history converged. Names such as Homer, Shakespeare, Stevenson, Scott, and Bulfinch began to emerge, and a much higher purpose for reading than simple enjoyment came forth. The reading of great literature led to two avenues of knowledge—that of God and that of man. Both were mirrored in the great works by the great minds. "Literature" wrote Miss Mason in *A Philosophy of Education*, "not only reveals to us the deepest things of the human spirit, but is profitable also for example of life and instruction in manners" (p. 338). One school in which I was the head-master reoriented its curriculum for the purpose of concertedly integrating history and literature for grades 4 to 8. Literature was used to make history come alive for the students, for them to experience the life and times of the people of the past, and to think through the ideas of the ages. Therefore, students in grade four would read *The Golden Goblet* in conjunction with a study of Egypt, while children in grade five would read (among others) *Adam of the Road* to support a study of the Middle Ages. As the students were dealing with the general content for history by project and copybook, they were also encountering the cultures of the past through literature.

When children have grown up with a steady diet of living books from the beginning, they will not clamor in later years for what Miss Mason calls twaddle. "As for literature—to introduce children to literature is to install them in a very rich and glorious kingdom, to bring a continual holiday to their doors, to lay before them a feast exquisitely served. But they must learn to know literature by being familiar with it from the very first."[25] From the lap to the school desk, students must be at home in the world of books.

It would appear that the teacher offers little in the way of literature instruction; instead the responsibility lies in the relationship between the reader and what is read. "Given a book of literary quality suitable to their age," Miss Mason writes, "children will know how to deal with it without elucidation" after a single reading.[26] But as teachers, we feel there must be some appropriate manner in which to find out what our students are taking in by all this reading! But Miss Mason goes on to write (to our utter consternation):

> Treat children in this reasonable way, mind to mind; not so much the mind of the teacher to that of the child,—that would be to exercise undue influence—but with the minds of a score of thinkers who meet the children, mind to mind, in their several books, the teacher performing the graceful office of presenting the one enthusiastic mind to the other.[27]

The teacher's role becomes that of providing the time and the "score of thinkers" to the child for her edification. And from this the reader has a responsibility—that of a single reading and a retelling of what has been read, either orally or in written form. It is by this retelling that the student expresses what she knows, for what one cannot tell, one does not know.

What bears scrutiny is our choice of books. Certainly today the pendulum has swung back to what we call the classics,[28] as we see by the popularity and success of the homeschool curriculum purveyors who have plumbed the heights and depths in pursuit of the best literature available. We are even seeing the resurgence of old friends from our own childhood—Rosemary Sutcliff and G. A. Henty, to name two. Resources such as *Let the Authors Speak* by Carolyn Hatcher provide exhaustive lists of living books for all ages based on history. Books out of print may be searched for on the Internet (an expensive proposition if you need ten copies!). The responsibility of the school is to decide its course of study with definite literature selections for each grade level, read-alouds and independent books. Miss Mason has much to say about what makes a worthy and living book; it is to her you may go for book selection criteria.

SOME FINAL THOUGHTS

At some time on the school calendar, principals and teachers should sit down to work through a number of vital questions. What might a review of our school reading and literature curriculum reveal to us? Does our philosophy of education match up with the methods and books we have selected for our children? How is it that we teach our younger students to read? Are our students choosing to read outside of school as a leisure activity? What do our literature lessons in upper grades look like? What criteria do we use to select worthy living books for our students? How do we deal with vocabulary, comprehension, and fluency? What is the place of narration in the scope of things? Each school might develop a presenting list of questions grade level by grade level, or a bibliographic list of the books both read by students and read aloud by teachers could be compiled for analysis. This is important and worthy of our consideration as a school staff.

We cannot overemphasize the importance of the home with regard to books and reading. The very culture of the homeplace must be challenged not only to acknowledge the necessity of reading, but to discover the changes necessary to place books back into their rightful place there. "It is our part," penned Miss Mason, "to see that books take root in the homes of our scholars and we must make parents understand that it is impossible to give a liberal education to children who have not a due provision of various books."[29] The application of this principle is problematic and often falls upon the school's shoulders, but there are creative first-step solutions to get books into the home: school-sponsored parent literature clubs, book fairs, class-wide home literature read-alouds, and parent workshops.

SPELLING AND COMPOSITION

By Jack Beckman

"Writing, of course, comes from reading," wrote Miss Mason in *School Education*, "and nobody can write well who does not read much" (p. 233). Within books we find the whole storehouse of knowledge in literary form— the grist of the young scholar's mind mill. At the first he collects, gathering ideas and knowledge while the hand is learning the mechanical convention of the written word. But he is not without a natural capacity for bringing forth a wordy "composition" from his books, as we shall see. As the child grows in wisdom and stature, he will come to naturally place pen to paper in an attempt to respond to those many and varied ideas he has found in the treasure trove of books. In reality, for him, "composition comes by nature."[30]

THE YOUNGER CHILD (NINE AND UNDER)

In a small class of second graders, the teacher is asking the students for a "composition" to be done on a portion read from *Charlotte's Web*. But here now . . . we see no pencils brought out, and where is the paper for writing? However, the students are eager to share their "composition" with the teacher and each other, and so we must begin. Lovely words and sentences flow forth from the students. A sequence from beginning to middle to end emerges as the students compose for the teacher from what was read only once and to which they have listened attentively. What we might believe to be a written composition in fact turns out to be oral—a narration.

"For children under nine," says Miss Mason, "the question of composition resolves itself into that of narration, varied by some such simple exercise as to write a part and narrate a part, or write the whole account of a walk they have taken, a lesson they have studied, or of some simple matter that they know."[31] Miss Mason believed that the conventions of composition had no place in the child's learning until much later in her school career. Until then it was enough for her to draw from her books mostly in oral narration form. What the child was asked to write was of concrete things from her books and her immediate experiences; the rules of punctuation and capitalization were taught as the child came to notice them herself in books. For children who have listened to the syntax, language, and expression of stories well told and well written, there is a natural reaping of what has been taken in through the child's abilities to retell—first in oral form, then in written. "If we could believe it, composition is as natural as jumping and running to children who have been allowed due use of books. They should narrate in the first place, and then they will compose, later, readily enough; but they should not be taught 'composition.'"[32]

This thought of writing being the handmaiden of reading is a "captain idea" and must motivate us to encourage the home and school not to neglect our duties of making our children at home with books.

Little need be said here regarding formal grammar. Miss Mason saw the study of grammar as abstract and difficult for young children to understand.

Still students in the first years of school may be given the idea of the sentence versus its component parts and pieces: "[E]very sentence speaks of someone or of something, and tells something about that of which it speaks.

> *So a sentence has two parts:*
> *The thing we speak of;*
> *What we say about it.*"[33]

As a young teacher, Miss Mason was convinced that she could teach seven- and eight-year-olds the nominative case. And so summoning up her powers of persuasion with which she might influence these little ones to a point of understanding . . . she failed miserably. She wisely writes, "Their minds rejected the abstract conception just as children reject the notion of writing an 'Essay on Happiness.' But I was beginning to make discoveries; the second being, that the mind of a child takes or rejects according to its needs."[34] Let us keep this in mind as we make our attempts at instruction.

The act of teaching our little friend Bobbie to read opened a door to an area that does bear comment—that of spelling. You will remember that mother had Bobbie look at the words "Cock Robin" until he could "see" them in his mind's eye and then reproduce them using letters. She was accustoming him to see the letters in the word for the purpose of retaining and using them in some manner, in this case reading. The use of the power of the eye is central to spelling:

> The eye "take[s]" (in a photographic sense) a detailed picture of the word; and this is the power and habit which must be cultivated in children from the first. When they have read "cat," they must be encouraged to see the word with their eyes shut, and the same habit will enable them to image "Thermopylae." This picturing of words on the retina appears to me to be the only royal road to spelling.[35]

We find the same concept in picture and nature study, that of training and focusing the powers of the eye to "take in" and then reproduce by narration or brush. But what of poor spellers? A partial explanation by Miss Mason is that "illiterate spelling is usually a sign of sparse reading,"[36] but may also be caused by the confusion of the misspelled word with its correct form. She writes:

Once the eye sees a misspelt word, that image remains; and if there is also the image of the word rightly spelt, we are perplexed as to which is which. . . . Every misspelt word is an image in the child's brain not to be obliterated by the right spelling. It becomes, therefore, the teacher's business to prevent false spelling, and, if an error has been made, to hide it away, as it were, so that the impression may not become fixed.[37]

Therefore as our students miscopy words from the board or from each other or see the teacher's red marks under misspelled words, an association is being set up in the mind's eye of the incorrect form. Even in the face of the tried and true method of multi-copying the correct spelling, a lingering uncertainty may still remain. Miss Mason has resolved this conflict for us by offering a method that capitalizes on the mind's ability to picture, namely dictation. She sets out for us in clear form the steps:

A child of eight or nine prepares a paragraph, older children a page, or two or three pages. The child prepares by himself, by looking at the word he is not sure of, and then seeing it with his eyes shut. Before he begins, the teacher asks what he thinks will need his attention. He generally knows, but the teacher may point out any word likely to be a cause of stumbling. He lets his teacher know when he is ready. The teacher asks if there are any words he is not sure of. These she puts, one by one, on the blackboard, letting the child look till he has a picture, and then rubbing the word out. . . . Then the teacher gives out the dictation, clause by clause, each clause repeated once. She dictates with a view to the pointing [punctuation], which the children are expected to put in as they write; but they must not be told "comma," "semicolon," etc. After the sort of preparation I have described, there is rarely an error.[38]

If for some unforeseen reason there is an error found by the watchful teacher on the child's copy, she must be quick with a Post-it slip to cover the errant word so that its impression may not set into the mind's eye. The student would then study the correct spelling and write it on the Post-it.

Two questions may arise from this approach to spelling: What of the student under the age of eight? From what source might I find the topic(s) for dictation? For younger students, it would be advisable to use the resources close at hand—the reading curriculum word lists, nursery rhymes, and short poems. For students ages eight and older, a ready-made source would be the essays, poems, psalms, and Scripture verses used as recitations. These may be memorized at home for class retelling but are also useful for dictation. For example, if students in grade five were to learn "The Canticle of Brother Sun" by Saint Francis as a recitation, the actual work of memorizing could be done at home while the teacher used one stanza or two per week as a source of dictation. Dictation may be used once a week in the classroom.

This method of picturing words in the mind's eye may be used in other areas of the curriculum with equal results—proper names of people and places, scientific terms, and so on. These may be written on the chalkboard and then erased when the students can "see" them.

THE OLDER CHILD (OVER NINE YEARS)

Here again Miss Mason stuns us. She believed that composition (writing) should not be taught as a formal subject for a student until she was at least age fourteen! Instead the student should continue her course of worthy reading in a wide manner, responding to what she has taken in by narration (in a movement from oral to written as the child advances—for us, grade four is a grand transition from heavy emphasis upon oral to more written forms). The writing the student does takes its sentence-building, style, voice, and vocabulary from the literature and poetry that form the core of the curriculum. Miss Mason believed that as students read Shakespeare, Dumas, Scott, Stevenson, Herbert, and others, they would reproduce something of these writers but touched with their own imaginations. Or to paraphrase the computer maxim: "Beautiful words and ideas in; beautiful words and ideas out." Miss Mason tells it with more power:

> Children (ages 9-12) have a wider range of reading, a more fertile field of thought, and more delightful subjects for composition. They write their little essays themselves, and as for the accuracy of their knowledge and justice of their expression, why, "still the wonder grows." They will describe their favorite scene from *The Tempest* or *Woodstock*. They write or "tell" stories from work set in Plutarch or Shakespeare or tell of the events of the day. They narrate from English, French, and General History, from the Old and New Testament, from *Stories from the History of Rome*, from Bulfinch's *Age of Fable*. . . . In fact, Composition is not an adjunct but an integral part of their education in every subject. . . . The exercise affords

very great pleasure to children. . . . But let me say again there must be no attempts to teach composition.[39]

The same may be said for students to age fourteen! What Miss Mason is telling us is that student writing should be primarily taken from their reading in narrated form, but that students may also write their own "creative" pieces based on interest and upon subjects that have "warmed their imaginations." She also emphasizes writing across the curriculum. So it is not the writing itself to which she objects, but the formal teaching of writing as its own subject.

The sad thing we find is that students today do not bring with them the rich and varied background of reading necessary for them to tap into these avenues of expression. What they do bring is a culture of television, pulp trade books, and a lifestyle too busy for quiet times to read. My experience has shown that children raised from the beginning in the world of books (both at home and school) are well able to "compose" for themselves with words and sentences showing knowledge well expressed.

But the opposite is also true: Children who have an impoverished "book world" are less likely to develop a lifestyle of reading, and they have a distaste for writing. We see these students all the time in our classrooms. It is with patience and love that we must deal with these children, remembering Miss Mason's words, "We spread an abundant and delicate feast in the programs and each small guest assimilates what he can."[40] When the vagaries of convention get in the way of student composition, one helpful method (that comes to us from journalism and was popularized by the whole-language folk) is the writer's cycle or process. The student is provided a vehicle for expression, but with a form that addresses various "issues" such as content, form, spelling, structure, and so on. In short form, it goes like this:

1. The student writes a rough draft.

2. The draft is edited by teacher and student.

3. A final copy is written based upon the edits. The relationship between teacher and student is strengthened as well as the relationship between the student and the written word. This turns composition into a process that gives the student more opportunities for success.

Grammar becomes a formal study for the student beginning at age nine and, along with mathematics, is a disciplinary subject. These subjects, Mason writes, depend largely on the power of the teacher, though the students' power of attention is of use in these too. Whether this teacher power is due to her holding the mysteries of the arcane, or whether it is wielded like a club is unknown. Possibly the clue lies in the need of the student to exercise great habit of attention while dealing with these subjects. Grammar tends to the abstract, and for this Miss Mason makes some recommendations for the older child:

> English [grammar] is rather a logical study dealing with sentences and the position that words occupy in them than with words and what they are in their own right. Therefore it is better that a child should begin with a sentence and not with the parts of speech, that is, he should learn a little of what is called analysis before he learns to parse. It requires some effort of abstraction for a child to perceive that when we speak, we speak about something and say something about it; and he has learned nearly all the grammar that is necessary when he knows that when we speak we use sentences and that a sentence makes sense.[41]

For this formal study, a suitable book on the subject was used. For beginning grammarians (aged nine and ten), Miss Mason created her own lesson book, First Grammar Lessons, Parts I and II, which put students into contact with subject and predicate, noun and verb, prepositions, and so on. This particular lesson book has been reprinted in the United States by Karen Andreola under the name *Simply Grammar*. Following up this introduction, any number of publishing companies produce books that extend and deepen the child's experience with grammar. Of appropriate use also are the various writer's guides that wed the function of writing with the form of grammar.

Though Miss Mason knew that few students take pleasure in grammar, she believed that it could not be neglected either. "The time will come," she wrote in *A Philosophy of Education*, "when they will delight in words, the beauty and propriety of words; when they will see that words are consecrated as the vehicle of truth and are not to be carelessly tampered with in statement and mutilated in form" (p. 151). How is this possible? Again we must return to the steady diet of many worthy books that fill the student's mind with words and sentences—the stuff of grammar.

For spelling and the older child, we must be reminded of that "royal road"—dictation. The methodology remains the same, but the length of the selection increases to between one and three pages. Dictation may be paralleled with recitation. The piece is sent home for memorization, but is used during the month as the means for dictation. The use of dictation once or twice per week is usually sufficient.

POETRY

By Maryellen St. Cyr

Some years ago my third grade students and I were in relationship with an elderly woman in her eighties. We all happened one December morning to be in her home bringing gifts of food and hands for helping. During the interval between helping and giving, the students shared some carols and poems that they had been learning in school. It was then that our dear friend also wanted to participate in this demonstration of knowledge. Tucked away in the recesses of her mind, she eloquently came forth with a very lengthy poem she had memorized in the third grade. What an indescribable joy to share in this mutual love for the poetic!

"We could hardly do better than lead children to reflect on some high poetic teaching,"[42] for it is here that the young and aged mind continue to feast, providing food for moral understanding, reverence, imagination, and true loveliness. Charlotte Mason maintained that this reflection on poetic teaching takes place each and every day. This teaching need not encompass whole class periods, but just times of repetition in which memorized poetry is recited, or stanzas read (here a little, there a little), or a formal lesson given using poetry classified as the lyric, epic, or ballad.

Upon reading Miss Mason's advice to read poetry each day, I began to make time to share some of the poets such as Longfellow and Stevenson. Beginning the day, after recess, or prior to dismissal, I began to acquaint the students at different times on different days with "the poets and their songs." It can truly be said that the students and I began to inwardly digest the poetry, and as Miss Mason said, "[R]everence comes to us unawares, gentleness, a wistful tenderness towards the past, a sense of continuance, and a part to play that shall not be loud and discordant, but a piece of a whole."[43]

The students and I developed this reverence for Longfellow's beloved wife in "The Cross of Snow":

There is a mountain in the distant West
That, sun-defying, in its deep ravines
Displays a cross of snow upon its side.
Such is the cross I wear upon my breast
These eighteen years, through all the changing scenes
And seasons, changeless since the day she died. *

We also loved the delicacy in color of the barren woods and sounds of freshly fallen snow in "Snow-Flakes":

Over the harvest-fields forsaken,
Silent, and soft, and slow
Descends the snow. * *

We appreciated the gentleness at the end of a day in "The Day Is Done":

The day is done, and the darkness
Falls from the wings of Night,
As a feather is wafted downward
From an eagle in his flight.
I see the lights of the village
Gleam through the rain and the mist,
And a feeling of sadness comes o'er me
That my soul cannot resist. * * *

* "Cross of Snow" (www.web-books.com)
* * "Snow-Flakes" (www.moonfairye.com)
* * * "The Day Is Done" (www.bartleby.com)

Note the wistful tenderness toward the past in "My Lost Youth":

> *Often I think of the beautiful town*
> *That is seated by the sea;*
> *Often in thought go up and down*
> *The pleasant streets of the dear old town,*
> *And my youth comes back to me.*
> *And a verse of a Lapland song*
> *Is haunting my memory still.*
> *"A boy's will is the wind's will,*
> *And the thoughts of youth are long, long, thoughts."* *

There is a sense of continuance in *A Psalm of Life*:

> *Lives of great men all remind us*
> *We can make our lives sublime,*
> *And, departing, leave behind us*
> *Footprints on the sands of time:*
> *Footprints, that perhaps another,*
> *Sailing o'er life's solemn main,*
> *A forlorn and shipwrecked brother,*
> *Seeing, shall take heart again.*
> *Let us, then, be up and doing,*
> *With a heart for any fate.*
> *Still achieving, still pursuing,*
> *Learn to labor and to wait.* *

As we read the poetry, we assimilated these poetic thoughts and a myriad of others, making intimate relationships between poets and students, students and teachers, developing the inner person.

This intimate and searching teacher, poetry, may only have its way if we bring it before the students void of preconceived notions that may interfere with the students' enjoyment and learning. Therefore, here are some practical requests to the instructor when teaching a particular poet's works:

• Awaken the students' interest and enthusiasm from the beginning with short lessons introducing the poet. For example, the students are introduced to the poet Henry Wadsworth Longfellow in a short biographical sketch

---

* "My Lost Youth" and "A Psalm of Life" (www.bartleby.com)

including his boyhood, schooling, and adult life. They begin to see the poet as a person—the days on the shores of Maine watching ships come into the harbor, the letters from his parents when he was abroad, and the hours spent in translating and composing his life's work.

- Accompany these biographical sketches with poems from the particular periods of his life.

- Prepare the students with any background information that may be needed to heighten their understanding of the poems. *Note:* This is not a lesson in criticism but a brief (five minutes or less) introduction.

- Acquaint the students with these poems through a careful reading. Attend to what is really there. Pause at punctuation. Read silently. Read aloud. Read individually. Read chorally.

- Learn to *enjoy* the poem, and share this enjoyment through reflecting upon:

Feelings the poem suggests.

Ideas brought to the reader's attention.

Literary forms used.

Words evoking rhythm or the sound and beauty of the language.

Connections and inferences to one's own life experience.

- Store a child's memory with a good deal of poetry without a good deal of labor. Hearing and reading the poems frequently allow the child to take in the words and meaning naturally without the great effort of memorizing.

- Train the students in the art of recitation, the fine art of beautiful and perfect speaking. "The child should speak beautiful thoughts so beautifully, with such delicate renderings of each nuance of meaning, that he becomes to the listener the interpreter of the author's thought."[44]

- Share the works of poets that afford the best thought of the best writers with your students. There is so much noble poetry; the child should not be allowed to learn twaddle.

- Introduce the older students to the epic poems of Longfellow such as *Hiawatha, Evangeline,* and *The Courtship of Miles Standish.*

As the students became well acquainted with poetry, they gained experience with verse—its forms, meter, rhythm, and language. Hence, they not only had an acquaintance with the subject of poetry but a working knowledge of poetry. However, the students of the PNEU were not only proficient in the knowledge of poets and their works, but they also developed the ability to compose in verse for examination questions regarding descriptions of nature and persons, in addition to writing narratives.

Poetry can easily take on a less prominent role in our classrooms than in the days of the PNEU and even be relegated to an elective for a myriad of reasons. Yet it is poetry, "the line that strikes us as we read, that recurs, that we murmur over at odd moments—this is the line that influences our living."[45] And it is poetry that makes "us aware of this thought of the ages, including our own. Every age, every epoch, has its poetic aspect, its quintessence, as it were, and happy the people who have a Shakespeare, a Dante, a Milton, a Burns, to gather up and preserve its meaning as a world possession."[46]

"Poetry is the noble and profound application of ideas to life," wrote Matthew Arnold. "Poetry is one of the means by which we hand on the torch of the human spirit," said Monk Gibbon. One cannot neglect so great a gift!

THE TEACHING OF SHAKESPEARE

By Maryellen St. Cyr

Charlotte Mason spoke of children participating in "the banquet which is Shakespeare," according to their needs and desires; "there is enough to satisfy the keenest intelligence, while the dullest child is sustained through his own willing effort."[47]

Miss Mason familiarized the children with the bard in each form (grade level) and during each term. The third and final term concluded with the performance of a Shakespearean play. A review of current research and my own experience in teaching children from kindergarten to the eighth grade has strengthened my belief that children should be introduced to this "banquet which is Shakespeare" as a vital part of the classroom experience. My interest in teaching Shakespeare was kindled by Mrs. Olive Norton, the headmistress and teacher of a PNEU school in England some years ago. Children from ages five to twelve held an unabridged text in hand and reviewed and memorized lines varying from fifty to over five hundred. The spirit and pride of the children in their work was exemplified through their practice and eagerness to recite on and off stage. In truth, Mrs. Norton remarked that in her fifty plus years in education, the learning of Shakespeare was the sole subject former students spoke of when she became reacquainted with them. It was a memory that lived beyond the classroom.

The students, Miss Mason, Mrs. Norton, and a number of enterprising teachers have only reflected William Shakespeare's intent in performing his plays as stated in the introduction of the First Folio published in 1623: "To the great Variety of Readers, from the most able, to him that can but spell. . . ."[48]

"Shakespeare is for all students: of all ability levels and reading levels, of every ethnic origin," states Peggy O'Brien, the head of education at the Folger Shakespeare Library, which is the chief repository for Shakespeare scholarship and education in the United States and England. Yet the teaching of Shakespeare has been somewhat limited to children in gifted and talented programs as well as high school and college level programs, effectively excluding a wide range of young people. In the foreword of a text designed to instruct elementary teachers in Shakespeare, Fred C. Adams responds to the question of age appropriateness this way: "I believe that the moment a child takes pleasure in a humorous incident, is frightened by a suspenseful occurrence, or is warmed by a human experience—that child is ready for Shakespeare."[49]

Living during an era in which the market for children's products exists as never before, one is tempted to play into the idea that children are in need of an undemanding, diluted text to furnish food for the mind in the way of great literature, including Shakespeare. Today's research on the brain and Charlotte Mason's insight regarding the mind at work both concur with the idea of challenging the student through the use of worthy thoughts in the form of literary language. There are manifold benefits in putting children in the way of beautiful language and vivid ideas. The younger child develops listening skills and appreciation for the beauty of language as he or she tells back what was heard. "Children take pleasure in the 'dry' parts, descriptions and the like, rendering these quite beautiful in their narrations."[50] Children also become confident readers and writers through the hearing and reading of well-written texts. Also through questions and discussion of the use of figurative language, characterization, elements of plot, setting, and themes, the student and teacher alike exercise the full power of the mind in analyzing, comprehending, reflecting, and synthesizing. These questionings and discussions generate an interior life as through contemplation and thought students come into relationship with the past, the present, and the transcendent.

PREPARING THE BANQUET

"If to do were as easy as to know what were good to do, chapels had been churches, and poor men's cottages princes' palaces."[51]

In preparing the banquet which is Shakespeare, I have been involved in working independently in the individual classroom and also working alongside twelve teachers and parents in a school-wide performance, both bearing positive influences in the students' relationships with Shakespeare. The individual classroom experiences consisted of six-week studies in which middle school students became acquainted with Elizabethan culture and history, William Shakespeare, and a play read in its entirety, culminating in a one-hour performance with each student taking a role in the play. The school-wide experiences consisted of a four- to five-week study in which eleven individual classroom teachers acquainted the students with Elizabethan culture, music, dance, art, and history, William Shakespeare, and three Shakespearean plays to be performed by students in grades three through eight. These formal times of instruction resulted in a fair of sorts, lasting three to four hours, with each student actively participating both in music and drama. My purpose here is to share with you as a classroom educator some "tried and true" methods of acquainting children with Shakespeare, whether you choose to set your table in an elaborate or simple fashion.

PRESENTING THE FEAST

"If ever fearful to do a thing, where I the issued doubted, whereof the execution did cry out against the non-performance, 'twas a fear which oft infects the wisest."[52]

As an educator, the most important component you bring to the classroom is your *enthusiasm* for this endeavor. Therefore, any fears or barriers you bring should be discussed and dispelled and never, ever communicated to your students. I have worked with various teachers, some who have had training in literature, drama, and Shakespeare, and others with little or no experience with these. Each one has been capable and effective in instructing in this area because of a spirit that was open, teachable, and committed. The following list depicts some of the content covered and methods practiced successfully with students from five to fourteen years of age:

• Acquaint students with the culture of Elizabethan England. Look at pictures and art; listen to histories, stories, and music; read poetry, rhymes, and prayers; play games of that day; practice dances; sing Elizabethan songs; play recorders; make a book illustrating drawings and narratives.

• Present students with the geography and history of England.

• Acquaint students with the life of Queen Elizabeth from childhood to the throne and discuss her contributions to the theater.

• Familiarize students with William Shakespeare, his life, his plays, and his contribution to drama.

• Inform students about the theater in Shakespeare's day (players, audience, merchants, hired men, and the Globe).

• Prepare students to receive the story as presented in the play through Lamb's *Tales from Shakespeare* or Nesbitt's *Beautiful Stories of Shakespeare for Children.*

PARTICIPATING IN THE FEAST

"Hope to joy is little less in joy than hope enjoyed."[53]

The teachers and students alike are active participants in the feast. For the educator, the primary work has been in the preliminary tasting of these delights both individually and collectively with other teachers prior to presenting them to the students. It is here that the teacher inquires, dialogues, and rehearses with colleagues. As for the student, he or she becomes an active participant daily in all that is Shakespeare. The following is a list of some of the ways the student partakes of a Shakespearean play, using a variety of mediums:

• Read the language of Shakespeare from a variety of plays (quotes and brief dialogues).

• Form a written record of the study in a copybook.

• Hear the language of Shakespeare from a professional audio recording.

- Read the text together as a class.
- Narrate scenes and acts in both a written and oral manner.
- Memorize excerpts in the language of Shakespeare.
- Experience the words of Shakespeare through dramatic improvisations of "play acting" diverse characters and scenes.
- Identify oneself with a character from a play for the presentation of a formal performance.

The student has thus become fully immersed as a reader, listener, narrator, artist, and actor in experiencing and expressing the words of Shakespeare through the study of a particular play. Upon finishing the reading of the text, the students prepare to present the play to an audience. The text now acts as the script. Parts of some speeches and scenes are deleted because of difficulty, appropriateness, or time constraints. The performances last from a minimum of forty minutes to a maximum of ninety minutes, in which each student participates as a speaking character. Thus each student feasts at the banquet of Shakespeare, which so often is reserved for the gifted and talented.

Although the culminating event to this study is the performance of the play itself, the many joys of grasping meaning and understanding from the printed page should not be overlooked. Some examples that come to mind from the experiences of my students are:

- Students sympathizing with Queen Elizabeth as they began to see the effects of the murder of her mother by her father and the discomfort and insecurity manifested in her life.
- Four eleven-year-old girls eagerly and enthusiastically writing the music and melody of the fairies' lullaby in *A Midsummer Night's Dream*.
- Students discussing the kinds of conflict in *Hamlet* from man versus self to man versus man and the resolutions and outcomes of the conflict.
- Boys, who were at times considered timid and reserved, approaching the reading of the text with varied inflection and then volunteering for main parts in the play.
- An eight-year-old girl who rushed to the library to check out audiotapes on none other than Shakespeare's plays for holiday travel in the car.

As anyone who teaches knows, there are countless other examples of learners interacting with the knowledge offered in the day-to-day intercourse of teaching and learning. As educators, might we concur with the research and experience of Charlotte Mason and a host of educators in the possibility of teaching Shakespeare in the elementary classroom.

HISTORY

By Jack Beckman

History falls into the category of the knowledge of the human race. Students should develop a sense of time and place; a relationship with people, places, and events of the past; an understanding of the captain ideas of great men and women; an awareness of past and present historical, geographical, and cultural relationships. And whether the student reads *Plutarch's Lives,* Tacitus' *The Histories,* or Thucydides' *Wars of the Peloponnesus,* he will come to find that history is not neutral in its ethics and morality, but offers numerous life lessons from those who have gone before us. History's viewpoint should be broad, sweeping, and panoramic, and yet it must come alive in its detail. Here is what Miss Mason wrote regarding what she deemed the pivot on which her curriculum turned:

> It is a great thing to possess a pageant of history in the background of one's thoughts. We may not be able to recall this or that circumstance, but "the imagination is warmed"; we know that there is a great deal to be said on both sides of every question and are saved from crudities of opinion and rashness in action. The present becomes enriched with the wealth of all that has gone before.[54]

History makes a worthy focus for our curriculum, for under its broad umbrella fall all the aspects of life: literature, science, geography, art, music, religion, government, family. The final outcome of the study of history is the child's grasp of its flow and his place in that flow. The wise choosing of books lays a groundwork of relations with people, places, and events that have life and reality for the student. Human history is a living story to be heard, enjoyed, and pondered.

SOME SUGGESTIONS TOWARD A CURRICULUM OF HISTORY

Miss Mason offers advice and counsel from her writings in *Home Education* and *A Philosophy of Education* that bear looking into. Generally speaking, young children first learn the history of their own country in the earliest years of their formal schooling. Good books that tell the story of history and offer interesting stories of people, places, and events are to be employed. Solid biographies offer the students intimate and delightful scenes from which they may narrate. Of young children and history, Susan Schaeffer Macaulay comments:

> Charlotte Mason urges us to give the young child leisure to explore an age in detail. Choose a history of a period that actually introduces one to people who lived then, the great and the small. As much as possible, use source material. I feel I have met someone when I am able to read his own account, not merely what someone else tells me about him. Let the tale live, flow. The child will breathe life into the past. His imagination will be touched, and he will bring judgment on it with his own mind.[55]

This use of source material includes biographies, diaries, or other living books that depict the age studied in a holistic manner. The child is to come away having seen the sights; tasted the foods; experienced the struggles; appreciated the culture, life, and times of the real people of history. Living history presentations, where the students dress as characters from the past, offer a true hands-on background for historical studies.

As students progress in years, European and ancient history is gradually added. By way of example, looking at the flow of the history curriculum of a former school may be of help. It was our contention that history should form the core of the curriculum, particularly for grades four to eight. We, of course, realized that many other schools used different (and successful) methodologies in history. However, history became for us the unifying "discipline of choice" due to our belief that all aspects of life fit under its broad sweep. Along with this belief was the conviction that a proper education must place children into relationship with God and others, nature, art, history, and all that life in Christ has to offer. This is what we take the phrase, "Education is the science of relations," to mean. And so, as the student ponders the Renaissance, she will be challenged by the works of Donatello and Titian (art), the thoughts of da Vinci (science, medicine, technology), and the words of Petrarch (poetry). Thus, we employed a learning methodology that was history-driven and thematic in nature. Using Miss Mason's idea that history and literature are connected, there was a concerted effort by teachers to collect many books (literature, biography, and so on) that would undergird and support the curriculum for the various grade levels. This, then, is how the plan looked in basic form:

Grade One

History of student's own nation

Grade Two

History of student's own nation continued

Grade Three

History of the world overview (including China and India), local and world geography

Grade Four

Antiquities (Old Testament times, Sumer, Mesopotamia, Egypt, Greece, Rome, life of Christ)

Grade Five

Middle Ages and Renaissance (500-1600)

Grade Six

Reformation and Age of Discovery (1400-1600)

Grade Seven

Age of Expansion and Revolution (1600-1800)

Grade Eight

Modern times (1800-present)

A few comments may be in order. Grade three becomes a transitional year in which students are exposed to the world at large, beginning with their own local geography (school, home, and state), moving to the home country, and then to the continents of the world. Emphasis is on the cultures of the people, the habitats of the earth, the oceans, landforms, weather, and use of maps and globes. Grade four opens the door for students to delve into the broad stroke of history's pageant—beginning with antiquities and ending in grade eight with modern times. Within each time period the great ideas and people, works of art, music, literature, invention and discovery, culture and geography are researched and sought out. Many living books are relied upon—these include biographies, literature selections, Jackdaw portfolios (source documents), and other books for pleasure and knowledge.

Two other related areas need mentioning—timelines and copybooks. In each classroom, teachers have placed a simple chart divided into 100-year segments beginning with prehistory and ending with A.D. 2000. This timeline is mounted near the ceiling of the classroom and usually takes up two and one-half walls in its layout. The purpose of the timeline is to give the child some conception of the panorama of history, its key events and people. The central point of the timeline is the birth of Christ. The timeline has some basic information posted: the age of Greece and Rome, Middle Ages, Renaissance, Reformation, Age of Discovery, and so on. As the students study various time periods, new information is added—pictures of famous people, wars and battles, discoveries and developments. The timeline reinforces a biblical and linear view of history from beginning to end.

Students also keep copybooks of the time periods under consideration. Miss Mason was of the opinion that children must reproduce knowledge to show that they had indeed assimilated it. This is the purpose of narration and the purpose of copybooks as well. The copybook is used for the student to record her findings in an orderly and neat fashion, using beautiful handwriting and illustrations. It is a book that she herself has produced—not a collection of consumable worksheets—and will keep for her own. Copybooks begin as a bookmaking activity—using either wallpaper or fabric (many how-to books are on the market telling how to do this). The student illustrates the outside of her book relative to the time period—Egypt, Greece, Rome, and so on. The pages of the book are left out until the end of the study. Once they are fully edited, they are placed into the book for binding. A title page and table of contents are also included.

And what are the contents of a copybook? The teacher and students identify the areas to be researched for copybook entries. For Egypt, the list of entries might include such things as religion, daily life, art and crafts, mummy making, the pharaohs, architecture, agriculture, science, family life, occupations, geography, and commerce and trade. These become the focus for study, reflection, and research. As information is found, it is recorded in rough draft form, edited, and then put into a final draft for placement into the copybook. As well, the student's narrations, timeline for Egypt, and any special projects are placed in the copybook. Once completed, the student has produced his own book of the particular time period under study. The book is of his own creation, reflective of his own imagination and personality, in combination with the knowledge gained from his readings. The capabilities of the student are illimitable:

> Let a child have the meat he requires in his history readings, and in the literature which naturally gathers around this history, and imagination will bestir itself without any help of ours; the child will live out in detail a thousand scenes of which he only gets the merest hint.[56]

MATHEMATICS

By Jack Beckman

Mathematics comes under the category of the knowledge of the universe. Though she is dealing with an area of the curriculum that has absolute standards based on scientific and irrefutable truths, Miss Mason again dares to invoke the science of philosophy to make her point:

> We make strong ground when we appeal to the beauty and truth of Mathematics; that, as Ruskin points out, two and two make four and cannot conceivably make five, is an inevitable law. It is a great thing to be brought into the presence of a law, of a whole system of laws, that exist without our concurrence,—that two straight lines cannot enclose a space is a fact we can perceive, state, and act upon but cannot in any wise alter, should give to children the *sense of limitation* which is wholesome for all of us, and inspire that *sursum corda* which we should hear in all natural law.[57]

However, in the midst of truth and beauty, a practical value must emerge:

The chief value of arithmetic, like that of the higher mathematics, lies in the training it affords to the reasoning powers, and in the habits of insight, readiness, accuracy, intellectual truthfulness it engenders. There is no one subject in which good teaching effects more, as there is none in which slovenly teaching has more mischievous results.[58]

Within this short statement are two insights—that mathematics has a higher set of purposes than we may realize, and that the teacher in this subject area exercises a good deal of influence for good or ill. Miss Mason goes on to tell us that even mathematics must have its appropriate proportion in the daily curriculum—no more and no less than other subjects.

In the past five to ten years, the publishers of mathematics curriculum in the United States have made sweeping changes, many based upon the recommendations of the National Council of the Teachers of Mathematics (NCTM). Whole companies have reoriented their materials based upon the standards drawn up by the NCTM. Use of manipulatives to make concrete the many abstractions (although these have been in place for much longer), emphasis on metacognition and thinking strategies, the application of mathematics to real life, the concerted use of calculators, open-ended math problems (!), along with the basic forms and functions—place value, estimation, multi-digit algorithms, word problems, measurement, and so on—constitute the modern-day math curriculum. Many publishers' materials are indistinguishable, but some are surely better than others.

What Miss Mason offers us is not the name of a particular mathematics curriculum that we may select and implement. Even in her day, the various curricula used in classrooms across England mostly met with Miss Mason's acceptance. What she offers is a filter of sorts by which we might make some assumptions about curriculum, and so move toward choice. It is very much the same today. Many math curricula have similar components, scope and sequence, strands and spirals of skills and strategies. It becomes a matter of what is taught when, how often things are reviewed and tested, and what kinds of resources come with the teacher's materials. Some publishers emphasize the processes of math, while others push facts and products. And all are concerned mainly about standardized testing. Let me leave you with a final view through Charlotte Mason's looking glass.

What follows is a gleaning from *Home Education* and *A Philosophy of Education* that the reader may find practical.

"Nearly right is a verdict inadmissible in arithmetic" (*Home Education*, 255).

"Children should be given problems which they can work, but which are difficult enough to cause some mental effort" (*Home Education*, 255).

"Students should be trained, before starting a problem, to consider what kind of function will produce the correct answer" *(Home Education,* 254).

"Everything that can be demonstrated should be demonstrated" *(Home Education,* 255).

"Use of weights and measures, rulers and tape-measures encourages accuracy and judgment, neatness and quickness" (*Home Education*, 256-260).

"Students who have been taught to concentrate by the method of a single reading followed by a narration will find it easier to concentrate on the disciplinary subjects such as mathematics" (*A Philosophy of Education*, 230-233).

"Students must realize that there is a law in mathematics, that in giving an impossible answer to a sum, they are laying themselves open to Euclid's 'which is absurd,' as absurd as it would be if a man were to say that his apples always fell upwards from the tree" (*A Philosophy of Education*, 152).

"The training in exactness and ingenuity which mathematics affords does not always necessarily carry over to other subjects" (*A Philosophy of Education*, 231).

With respect to a curriculum, Miss Mason wanted teachers to implement one that was carefully graduated with "only one difficulty at a time being presented to the mind" *(Home Education,* 262).

"Let his arithmetic lesson be to the child a daily exercise in clear thinking and rapid, careful execution, and his mental growth will be as obvious as the sprouting of seedlings in the spring" *(Home Education,* 261).

With so many competing agendas, how do we come to a place of agreement? We find ourselves back at the beginning—gazing through the lens of our philosophy of education. Agreement may be found as the interested parties of the school—parents, teachers, board, principal, students—use the lens to view the nature of the learner, the nature of knowledge, and the purposes we attach to teaching and learning. This is the starting point, the arch of our decision-making, whether it be the mathematics curriculum or discipline policies. Our classroom practices are indeed born out of our philosophy of education. Miss Mason reminds her readers over and over again that the *doing* of education relies upon the *knowing* and *believing* in certain things about children, about books, about life and learning. Let me leave you with a final view through her looking glass:

> Now we must deal with a child of man, who has a natural desire to know the history of his race and of his nation, what men thought in the past and are thinking now; the best thought of the best minds taking form as literature, and at its highest as poetry, or as poetry rendered in the plastic forms of art, as a child of God, whose supreme desire and glory it is to know about and to know his almighty Father: as a person of many parts and passions who must know how to use, care for, and discipline himself, body, mind and soul: as a person of many relationships—to family, city, church, state, neighboring states, the world at large: as the inhabitant of a world full of beauty and interest, the features of which he must recognize and know how to name, and a world, too and a universe, whose every function of every part is ordered by laws which he must begin to know.[59]

NATURE STUDY AND NOTEBOOKS

By Bobby Scott

"But, Mr. Scott, we can't find anything!" Such was the lament of a small group of thirteen-year-old girls on our first nature walk on the back eighteen acres of our school property. The other students were off down the stream or wandering through the underbrush, each desiring a "find."

Feeling a bit frustrated at their lack of diligence, I walked calmly toward them, reached down to the ground, and picked up a live box turtle that they had almost been standing on! "Well, perhaps you weren't looking closely enough," I replied, actually as surprised as they were, while remaining the confident nature guide.

This was one of my students' many experiences on nature walks. Charlotte Mason devotees such as A. C. Drury and Karen Andreola have written at length about nature study, nature notebooks, and the like. My purpose here is to tell how our school has practiced this area of study in a way that has proved to be a delight even for hard-to-please early adolescents.

Beautiful nature books are increasingly popular in the United States today, from the drawings of Marjean Baskin to Maryjo Koch. Part of the reason may be the increased effort of environmentalists to deify nature and preserve its beauty. As I see it, though our presuppositions and ultimate purpose for doing nature study may be different, contemporary nature books have been sources of inspiration and joy to my students in their research. It's a shame that their delight in design is usually not transferred to the Designer, since most see the intricate features, beautiful colors, and interesting structures as only chance mutations or adaptations. Nevertheless, the increased interest in nature motivates us all the more to "consider the lilies" as a worship of God the Creator.

At our school, nature study consists primarily of these components:

- A series of nature walks
- A collection of specimens for onsite and laboratory observation
- Dry-brush watercolor paintings of selected specimens
- Research notes from living books and handbooks on the same

In grades one and two (six- to eight-year-olds), these activities take place, led by both classroom teachers and parent volunteers, on our weekly enrichment days. In grades three to six (nine- to eleven-year-olds) the classroom teachers take the lead, and currently, because of my personal love for the practice, I as headmaster assist with the seventh and eighth graders (twelve- to fourteen-year-olds). Some of the details vary by grade, but here is how our classes operate.

Beginning in first grade, the students receive a spiral-bound notebook for nature study to last two years. Being very careful as to what is collected and where it is collected, children at this age love to walk, explore, and collect interesting specimens. Occasionally these objects are observed closely, discussed, and even painted outside, but we've found the best place for the least distractions is to return to the classroom. In third grade, each student purchases a hardbound nature notebook to last the rest of his five years at our school. At these ages a class period of thirty to forty-five minutes is spent walking somewhere on the large acreage of our school. But lest some of you despair, some of our best studies came from a basket of sea shells provided by my art teacher. Even in the asphalt jungle, nature study is possible. In our case, the walk, observations, and watercolor painting can take three to four class periods, which we schedule apart from regular science classes. The final class period, after paintings are completed, is spent in library research, finding the formal and common names of the specimen, its common locale, its use, as many interesting facts as possible, and personal notes of the circumstances surrounding its discovery. The grabbing of a snake by one brave student produced good fodder for notes from one of our walks! He was placed in an aquarium for further observation (the snake, not the student!).

Our method is not too different from the principles presented by Charlotte Mason for nature study as the prelude to science. Her procedure and principles follow:

1. One afternoon a week, the children go for a nature walk with their teachers.

2. The children notice things for themselves, and the teacher gives a name or other information as needed.

3. The teachers are careful not to give scientific instruction on these walks, as the emphasis is on observation with very little direction.

4. The children are given the opportunity to delight in natural and living things, as in the familiar faces of friends, which in turn becomes the motivation for scientific study.

5. The epitome of a living education would be for all schoolchildren, of whatever grade, to have one-half day in the week, throughout the year, in the fields.

6. Children should watch and note in their notebooks the procession of the seasons from week to week.

7. Schools should take advantage of local naturalists who would be willing to give their help in these nature walks.

8. After the walks, children are put in the right attitude of mind for scientific observations and deductions, and their keen interest is awakened.

9. The challenge is then to put the students in touch with the right books to make discoveries for themselves.[60]

With most beginning students, I have had to constantly emphasize neatness in recording notes and observations in their notebooks. Some beautiful paintings have received sloppy notation. But as students have progressed year to year, more care is now being given, though a far cry from the *Diary of an*

Edwardian Lady! Yet at the same time, the nature notebook should be very "catholic," "a traveling companion wherein the 'finds' of every season, bird or flower, fungus or moss, is sketched and described."[61] As such they may become a little worn but hopefully not messy. My great hope is that many of my students will desire on their own to continue to observe and illustrate their nature notebooks, that these may become a treasure for life. Eve Anderson, the former Eton End PNEU school headmistress, inspired me to pursue nature painting and study in my forties. It is never too late to begin to appreciate beauty in this way. And as with so many of Charlotte Mason's methods, the teacher need not be an expert; in fact, we learn right along with the students.

Our goal the first year was modest—for each of our third to eighth graders to take many walks, but to complete only one nature painting and study per month. Others may do more, but this was an appropriate goal for our school. Encouragingly, I have found my older students to be motivated to these studies without the threat or enticement of a grade or exam, which some say is necessary to motivate this age. However, I'm sure having the head-master as their teacher has helped motivate some! At the end of the term I ask what aspect of nature study they most enjoy. Consistently two-thirds enjoy the walks best, and the other one-third put the painting first. And when asked how to improve the course, they say without exception, "We need more time" to walk, to paint, and to research. Perhaps other schools can provide such time; for now, we are delighted about the enthusiasm of our students and hope they will take more time in their lives outside of school to gather the rosebuds while they may.

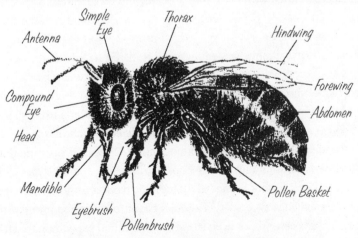

Sample of Student Work: Honeybee

SCIENCE

By Bobby Scott

To enter the land of Narnia, the daughters of Eve and sons of Adam had first to go through a magical wardrobe. It seemed a sort of natural entrance into a supernatural world of wonder. Likewise, the student in a PNEU school was taken first through the practice of nature study into the wonderful world of science.

When we look at how science was approached in her schools, we see how Charlotte Mason avoided having bored students swamped in a bog of dry scientific fact. As Miss Mason said, "The way into the secrets of nature is not through the barbed wire entanglements of science, but through field work and living books."[62] The importance of ideas rather than information is perhaps more critical in science than any other subject. And the path is made straight and prepared by the study of nature.

The specifics of nature study were discussed earlier, but the key element is that first students learn to observe, examine, and delight in living and real things without letting scientific "tidbits" destroy their enthusiasm. All this observation is "incidental, easy, and things are noticed as they occur."[63]

Once introduced in this manner to living things, primarily on nature walks and field trips, the student is taken to the living books on the subject. The ideas that naturally arise in the child are fed by the teacher through these resources. "Our business is to give children the great ideas of life . . . of science . . . ideas clothed with facts as they occur, and leave the child to deal with them as he chooses."[64] So we see that the facts are not ignored, but they are given their proper place.

On a nature walk, one student happens to detect a camouflaged insect on a twig. This discovery leads to a natural curiosity of how and why the camouflage is used. Given a living book on the subject, the interest deepens and broadens until the whole class is eventually enthralled by the knowledge shared by the observant one. In the reading and sharing, scientific facts become a natural part of the ideas, like unobtrusive clothing that receives its proper interest. We need to work hard at finding science books written in a literary style—difficult but possible. Look for books that tell of individual scientists in pursuit of some particular knowledge or discovery; books beautifully written and illustrated about the life of bees, fish, or deer; stories of travels and expeditions to strange, new lands with diverse land forms, climates, plants, and people.

The enthusiasm for science pursued in this way is protected by avoiding a strictly utilitarian approach to its subject matter. Nothing can kill the sense of awe and wonder in science more quickly than to teach the subject simply as practical preparation for another level of schooling or, as is most prominent, solely as preparation for a standardized examination. Miss Mason quotes Sir Richard Gregory, a leader in British education in her day: "School science, therefore, was not intended to prepare for vocations, but to equip pupils for life. Reading or teaching for interest or to learn how physical science was daily extending the power of man receive(s) little attention because no credit for knowledge thus gained (is) given in examinations."[65] This is sadly more true and more common in schools today.

Thus separating science teaching from the initial awe and wonder of nature, from the necessary field or laboratory work, and from the living literature on the subject (not dry textbooks) destroys a love for science. Why is this true? Because our fact-intensive, classical approaches to science have forgotten who the child is and how he learns. Miss Mason reminds us:

> I am considering a child as he is, and am not tracing him, either with Wordsworth, to the heights above, or, with the evolutionist, to the depths below; because a person is a mystery, that is, we cannot explain him or account for him, but must accept him as he is. This wonder of personality does not cease, does not disappear, when a child goes to school.[66]

Why is it that we can observe how wonder, truth, and beauty attract the interest of the younger child and yet let this interest be swept away by boring details in oversized textbooks when he or she enters a school? We must have the courage to teach for the sake of the children rather than for the system. When taught properly, science can be our students' favorite subject.

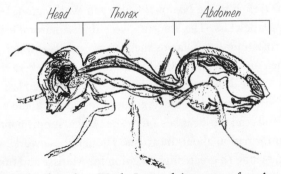

Sample of Student Work: Internal Anatomy of an Ant

PICTURE STUDY

By Bobby Scott

"Why did that boy have to wear a dress for the picture?" asks an inquisitive second-grade boy on observing the painting *Master John Heathcote* by Joseph M. Turner. Seeing a background that includes dogs and trees, he continues, "I'll bet he's not smiling on purpose; he wants to go play!" First graders looking at Degas's *Rehearsal on the Stage* dance describe two slouching men on the side of the stage as dads who were tired and wanted their daughters' practice to end so they could go home!

These are typical comments from our students engaged in what the PNEU schools described as Picture Study. As principal, I had asked the teachers to let me substitute for them a time or two, not only because I love to teach the children, but also because it takes no expert to lead this area of art appreciation; in fact, it is good to enter in with little background save some knowledge of the life of the artist. Masterly inactivity here requires carefully directing the students to practice reading the pictures, learning by practice to see detail and draw the beauty of the work into their souls.

Indeed, appreciation of art involves acquiring not technical knowledge, but what Mason calls "reverent knowledge of what has been produced. Children should learn pictures, line by line, group by group, by reading, not books, but pictures themselves."[67] Just as in reading a book, we all may be diverse in our favorite parts, so it is in reading pictures. The teacher's favorite aspect might be, and often is, different from the students'. So a spiritual harmony takes place where teacher and pupils enjoy the details together, learning from one another how to see the artist's work.

I recall traveling to the National Gallery in Washington, D.C., with my son's eighth grade class. The students were drawn naturally to the rooms where the artists more familiar to them were found—Monet, Rembrandt, Seurat, Turner, and others. I elected to go to the wing where the twentieth-century artists were displayed, primarily because I have had less appreciation for their work. As I joined a guided group, I found the guide gifted in helping us to see and read the ideas behind the paintings, supplementing her comments with information about the artists. Though these works were still not my favorites, I gained a greater appreciation for Matisse and others by being encouraged not just "to see a picture, but to look at it, taking in every detail."[68] Without telling us what we should appreciate or being adamant about what the painter was trying to say, the tour guide helped to inform our seeing. Teachers in schools with a little reading of the author's life can do the same thing. In fact, they should do no more.

My training in Picture Study came from Eve Anderson, the author of the foreword to this book. Eve believes, and has taught me to believe, what the poet Robert Browning said—that we really learn to see things when we see them painted, "things we have passed perhaps a hundred times nor cared to see." Students can develop a relationship, indeed a spiritual one, with artists and their works that grows out of their reading of pictures. Eve outlined for me a typical Picture Study lesson to use at our school, which is presented here. As she reminds us, this procedure is not the *only* way, but practiced regularly, it will give the children a lasting memory of pictures and reinforce their habit of observation.

PICTURE STUDY LESSON

1. Prior to studying a specific picture, children should have been read a story or information on the life of the artist, when he lived, where he should be placed on the timeline of history, and perhaps the general subject or type of his pictures.

2. Introduce the title of the picture and distribute prints facedown on cleared desks. Note: Eve taught us that it was crucial that each child have her own print of the work to be studied; so we made color copies at the 11" x 17" size. It's expensive but worth it.

3. Have students turn over the pictures and study them silently for several minutes. Then ask for first impressions and major parts first. Direct them to look closely at foreground, background, details, color, feeling of movement, and so on.

4. Children then silently look at the picture again for one minute, eyes down. Suggest that they shut their eyes. Can they see a complete colored picture in their minds? If not, they should have another look.

5. Everyone (the teacher too!) turns the picture over facedown. Now have children describe in as much detail as possible, listening carefully to each other, and not repeating what has already been said. With practice they will be able to give vivid, detailed descriptions.

6. Turn over pictures and look again to see if any parts have been left out or if any details are not clear in the mind.

7. Finally, have a last silent look at the picture. There should now be a photograph of this picture in the mind that stays for life.

How long should such a lesson take? About twenty to thirty minutes. Eve encourages teachers to remind the students about the actual size of the original work, perhaps by demonstrating the dimensions on the classroom wall. What a joy it is when, like our eighth graders, they get to see one of the originals in person.

How often should a class do a picture study? This will vary, but at our school we have developed the curriculum to include three artists per grade level, with at least four prints per artist. With a broad curriculum and so much to enjoy, we now require twelve to fifteen picture studies a year, usually led by the teacher, but sometimes a parent or one of our principals does the honor.

What about other areas of art? In our program, we have regular art classes taught by a trained art instructor, beginning at third grade. These classes help develop painting, drawing, sculpting, and the like and are valuable in helping students in their nature painting and illustrations for literature studies. The instructor's passion for beauty and creativity is contagious to the students.

However, art classes do not take the place of art appreciation through Picture Study. As Charlotte Mason wisely taught, training in styles and schools of painting and various techniques are important, but "the first and most important thing is to know the pictures themselves. As in a worthy book we leave the author to tell his own tale, so do we trust a picture to tell its tale through the medium the artist gave it."[69]

MUSIC APPRECIATION

By Bobby Scott

As with art appreciation, the taste for good music must be a vital part of a school's program beyond the teaching of music classes. Both have their place, but the regular classroom is where schools should train the spirit of the children. Like picture study, the spiritual aspect of music appreciation goes beyond an academic pursuit and lays the foundation on which music theory, composition, and performance builds. And like picture study, music appreciation does not take a teacher who is an accomplished musician.

As a bargain hunter, I am always looking for inexpensive compact discs. I am somewhat amazed at how many CDs found on the bargain racks are the works of the greatest composers of all time, usually performed by reputable orchestras. For those of us with limited school budgets, these selections are ideal in beginning to build a music library for our teachers. The idea to build such a legacy for children came to Charlotte Mason in 1897. She overheard one of her teachers exposing her own child to the best in music. Then "she realized that music might give joy and interest to the life of all, and she felt that just as children in the PNEU schools were given the best in literature and art, so they should have the greatest music as well."[70]

The importance of good music in our education far preceded Miss Mason's revelation, but she was instrumental in making it a consistent, planned practice in English schools. In 1997 I was in attendance at the morning assembly at the Rickmansworth PNEU school near London. Mrs. Sheila Marshall-Taylor, headmistress, presided as children presented poetry and other recitations written about astronomy with the great composer of *The Planets*, Gustav Holst, as their emphasis. His compositions were highlighted in all forms (grades) for the month. So for 100 years, since that original idea, the schools of Charlotte Mason have continued with this emphasis on music appreciation!

In our own school, I remember the joy I received as a parent when our teachers began this emphasis six years ago, and I saw my son recognize Vivaldi's music due to his classroom experience. I had never received this training as a child and still find myself far behind my children and students in this ability.

How can music be used as a tool to educate, using all styles of songs? Some simple, practical suggestions are:

• Select and play the music from the period of history of the student's study.

• During quiet times of reading or reflection play music that calms the soul, as David did for Saul.

• Select and play music from the time frame of the current literature study to enhance the reality of the story.

• Use music for square or folk dancing, preludes and postludes for drama events, poetry recitals to set a mood during lunchtime, and so on.

These suggestions recognize the power of music to set a mood, provide an atmosphere, and even enhance the ability to memorize facts. But music appreciation takes its greater form in studying the great composers. We recommend this general procedure:

1. Introduce the composer in a dramatic fashion by perhaps:

a. Playing his most moving or well-known piece and letting students try to identify it.

b. Having a parent or principal dress up as the composer and have the children ask questions to identify him.

c. Bring in a live musician to play one of his selections in the classroom.

2. Locate and place the composer's picture on the classroom timeline. Have books available for children to research his country (and locate it on the map), his lifestyle, his family, and ideas that influenced him.

3. Play (or replay if already introduced) a main selection and have the students talk about it. Students should listen to everyone's comments and not repeat them.

4. Play various selections from the composer throughout a longer time frame. If possible, make cassette tapes for children to listen to as they travel with their parents.

5. Have students discuss their favorite piece and why they enjoy it.

6. Look for outside resources such as concerts or musicians who could give students additional enjoyment.

Of course, the question then is asked, how many composers should students be exposed to and which do you choose? Our school only chooses to emphasize two to three composers at each grade level per year, while others select two to four composers every nine weeks, enjoyed by the school as a whole. Either way over an eight-year primary school education, students will hear works of many composers. This is all done in a low-key way with no examinations or pressure to recall specific pieces. The natural enjoyment of the music is the primary focus.

Finally, in regard to which composers to select, give attention to a wide variety of music and historical periods. Contemporary musicians should be chosen with caution, but certainly not totally eliminated. To produce only music of the past would be cutting off students from excellent works of this era. Talk with respected musicians and musical directors in your community for recommendations of current "good" music. It is better to have a few simple selections that children actually listen to than a library of dusty CDs. Great music will do its own work regardless of us, reaching down to the innermost being of the personhood of a child. We must let the student hear it.

BIBLE INSTRUCTION

By Bobby Scott

"The knowledge of God is the principal knowledge, and, therefore, their [students'] Bible lessons are their chief lessons,"[71] Charlotte Mason maintained. As a teacher and principal in Christian schools for almost thirty years and having taught many Bible classes, I can testify to strong differences of opinion among sincere educators in regard to the role of Bible teaching in Christian schools. The extremes go from very detailed, academic lessons that include all levels of theology to simple devotional-oriented mini-classes of fifteen to twenty minutes. There are points in the arguments for both, and it seems that Charlotte Mason had some wise instruction with regard to proper Bible lessons long before this controversy ever emerged. First, we will examine some guiding principles from Miss Mason and then present some suggestions as to how a school might practically work these out.

Before we jump in, a reminder is in order that we are not to confuse Bible instruction in schools with what Miss Mason called "the religious life of children." The habit of the knowledge of God is instilled in children first and foremost by their parents. As Miss Mason notes, "the child can read [whether] the things of God are more to his parents than any things of the world," and this more easily than in the life of his teacher.

The primary role of parents is to present the idea of God to the souls of their children. Like a bee who pollinates the flower, they wait for God to then touch their children's souls and produce life and fruit.[72] Our role in the school is to increase the child's knowledge of God primarily through the Word of God, not to supplant the home. Now to the principles with some current annotations:

1. The Bible should never be watered down into simple paraphrases; use the best translations.[73] We use the New International Version, but the New American Standard, New King James, New Revised Standard, and English Standard versions are also excellent.

2. Children are capable of dealing with the truth of the Scriptures.[74] Their fitness to apprehend the deep things of God is a fact, and perhaps nowhere does the idea that children must stay mired in the so-called "grammar stage" of rote learning do to them such a disservice as in Bible instruction.

3. The Bible itself as a book should be treated and handled respectfully.[75] This principle is a far cry from the way Bibles are thrown carelessly into church and school "lost item" bins by the hundreds in the United States.

4. The Old Testament and the Gospels should be handled in a pleasant and poetic way, enabling students to take delight in the stories and the life of our Lord.[76]

5. Great care must be taken not to present Christianity as moralism or the gospel as children "being good" or imitating all the character traits of Christ.[77] This approach is all too often used in Christian schools and denies the reality of living in a fallen world with total dependence on Christ. Students educated in moralism will often either reject the faith or become modern-day Pharisees.

6. The Bible must never be used as an instrument to punish children. For example, the teacher says: "Well, I am very concerned about the poor quality of class work I am receiving. I think the problem is laziness. You know

what the Bible says about being slothful, don't you? It says . . ." A continual diet of this type of rebuke does not teach children to develop a conscience sensitive to God's Word, but rather makes them see it as a tool to nag them. This approach can even create a dislike for God's Word.

There are several key aspects of knowing God that Mason encouraged us to include in all Bible instruction.

• *Knowing God as king.* Miss Mason described this as "passionate loyalty to our adorable Chief." This may be a difficult concept for American children who have been deprived of the concepts of devotion, loyalty, allegiance, and reverence for a monarch. Living books and the modeling of such an allegiance by their parents and teachers to their current authorities can help such children understand this attitude.

• *Knowing Jesus as Savior.* It is a constant challenge to help children grow both in their knowledge of the holiness of God and the depth of their own sin. Only with the proper grasp of these concepts, which is possible even for young children, can students increase daily in their understanding of the amazing provision of their Savior.

• *Knowing the fatherhood of God.* The tender nature of a loving Father whose love is not intermittent, can always be relied on, and is always present is critical in our culture today of absent or detached parenting. This concept is difficult for children in fatherless homes or for those with abusive fathers, but nothing is impossible with God. All children, regardless of their parentage, need to be constantly reminded from the Bible that they live, move, and have their being under His care.

• *Knowing the authority of God.* Never should their love for God as a heavenly Father be allowed to breed an irreverence for His authority or a lack of proper fear of Him. Indeed the Lord disciplines those He loves, and too often today our students have lost a proper respect for His Word and His authority in their lives. As Mr. Beaver was asked by the children regarding Aslan: "Is He safe?" "No," was the reply, "but He's good" (C. S. Lewis, *The Lion, the Witch and the Wardrobe*).

• *Knowing the indwelling of the Spirit.* This concept, Miss Mason emphasized, is actually more fit for children because their large faith does not stumble at the mystery of God's Spirit inhabiting the heart of a child. Again we are disturbed by those who teach that children are better left to "poll-parroting" words and phrases rather than discussing the ideas and truths that spring out of God's Word. Such a view can rob children of a spiritual life.

Considering these principles of Bible instruction in schools (which apply to homes and churches as well), we will look at some specific suggestions for classrooms today.

1. Young children from ages six to nine should read or have read to them simply the text of the Bible. No commentaries or embellished workbooks are needed or desirable. Charlotte Mason suggested that by the age of six, children should recite beautifully and perfectly three poems, three hymns, a parable, and a psalm. They should also narrate Bible stories. By the age of nine, children should have read for themselves the narrative portions of the Old Testament and two of the Gospels.

2. Reading the Bible to children should always be done reverently, carefully, and with expression. A segment of a few verses, a story, or a complete idea is enough. Then have children narrate as nearly as possible the words from the Bible. If students do the reading, the same atmosphere of attentiveness, reverence, and carefulness should apply.

3. After the narration, a discussion with the children should ensue. As with all "masterly inactivity," the teacher should direct the flow of the discussion but allow the students to apply the truths to themselves as they will.

4. The teacher's part is to read with enthusiasm, use illustrations, and share important knowledge that will enhance the understanding of the passages, but not in any manner that will inhibit the students' participation in the discussion.

5. Children are encouraged to form their own mental images of the scenes they read about or that are read to them, but illustrations of Bible events, particularly those by the great masters such as Rembrandt, can also bring enjoyment to the students as they see how others view the scenes. Using the picture study method of Eve Anderson (see section on picture study) will have benefit here.

6. Children from ages ten to eleven will benefit from this same general method but can be expected themselves to read more of the Bible, make maps, study pictures, do research, and go deeper into a text. Here they may go further academically, but we must be cautioned that reading the Bible itself must still take primary importance. Too much emphasis at this age on tests, grades, and homework will rob them of the life and joy of knowing God through His Word.

7. At ages twelve to fourteen, students can begin to look at doctrine, apologetics, and how to teach a Bible lesson themselves to younger children.

Lively, open, and real discussions of Bible truth, alleged contradictions, and difficult doctrines can truly enliven this group. Again reverence and care must be taken, but students should be allowed to ask the tough questions, and students should be directed to the real answers, remembering that "how do you think you might find the answer to that question?" is often better than the teacher simply giving the answer. We have found that a whole different person emerges from even skeptics as they are called upon to teach the little children. The more mature side of this age emerges in a most gratifying way.

8. Though textbooks and workbooks are not desirable, a sequenced plan of Bible content to be learned across the age levels is a necessary practice. There was a time when I permitted teachers to select their own areas of content, but it led to gaps and areas of repetition. The whole counsel of Scripture with deference to students' interests and needs should be implemented.

9. Bible memory and recitations are desirable at all age levels, about which Mason makes these practical suggestions:

• Begin at age six.

• Start with a few verses, repeated often in the classroom.

• Let the children recite the verses when they think they know them but not before.

• Build gradually on these verses until a whole idea or parable is memorized, always repeating the previous verses for reinforcement.

• Take this obvious point as my own suggestion: Make certain that students discuss and understand the passages they memorize. Memorizing with no understanding breeds discontent in both students and their parents.

10. A final thought concerns the contemporary practice of worship, singing, and prayer as a part of Bible instruction. As mentioned at the outset, some schools today would see these practices as the sole content of Bible classes, while others would eliminate these elements entirely as nonacademic. Other factors that enter in are the purpose of the school, what the administration will allow, and the time allotment. My view is that these expressions should flow out of the love for God that Bible instruction should bring. Whether these are a regular part of the classroom lesson, a morning assembly, or a special session is not important as long as children are not forced to participate and these elements do not usurp the time needed to study the Word of God. "Oh, teacher, let's sing another song!" can be a sincere desire to praise God or a deliberate attempt to delay the ensuing math lesson! Wise teachers will know the difference.

If indeed "the Bible lessons are their chief lessons," as Charlotte Mason stated, we must strongly battle the idea that any teacher can teach the Bible, with such lessons receiving the least of their attention. However, it does not behoove us to spend hours putting "bells and whistles" on our presentation of Bible instruction in order to entertain our students. We must carefully let the Word of God do what it will do in the lives of our students. We should not force it or use it for our own agendas. God will not let it return void in our children's lives.

FOREIGN LANGUAGES

By Jack Beckman

Charlotte Mason believed that the earlier children experienced foreign languages, the better. This idea held true if the teaching was oral only and if the teacher was fluent. She went so far as to say that the nursery was the proper place to begin languages and that the family should cultivate at least two.

In *Home Education*, she wrote that French should be acquired "as English is, not as a grammar, but as a living speech" (p. 300). She goes on to give this practical advice: "To train the ear to distinguish and the lips to produce the French vocabulary is a valuable part of the education of the senses, and one which can hardly be undertaken too soon."

Children should learn language, in this case French, when they are so young that difference in accent does not affect them. In the PNEU schools, French was the foreign language of choice, beginning in Form I (ages six to nine) with work in listening and speaking followed by narration. It was central to this activity, as with literature and other content areas, for the students to pay attention the first time the teacher read or spoke.

E. K. Manders, in *The Gateway to Charlotte Mason,* commented on French language instruction:

> [The students] should not see French words in print until they have learnt to say them as easily as if they were English. Whatever might have been her attitude to some modern mechanical aids to education, I feel sure that Charlotte Mason would have approved of the French records suggested in our programs, for as she truly says, language is learnt by the ear and not the eye. The classical method, with its dictionaries and its translations is not the best approach, though these have their value later on, when children are familiar with the spoken language.[78]

This movement from oral vocabulary and sentences to reading and writing is based upon the mastery of the spoken language initially. Then students will be able to read easy books in the lower forms around the age of nine. At this point French grammar is also added in gentle but deliberate fashion, using a good text for this purpose. Students at every level are required to listen and narrate the stories and sentences read or taught back to the teacher in French.

Children in the upper forms (nine to twelve) continue to have French read to them as sentences and paragraphs for the purpose of narrating. Students begin at this point to do some work in translating with the help of the teacher. The translation is then narrated and reread in French with narration. Students, after reading, will practice oral or written narration, first with short passages and then as they progress to several pages at a time. The act of narration is to give the students "some command of French phrases," fluency, and powers of expression. At this point, the students learn songs and act out certain stories and fables in French. The use of a text provides an entree into the grammar of the language—students read this and narrate as well.

Of course, all these suggestions can be applied to another more local foreign language such as Spanish. This approach does presuppose a native speaker or a teacher or parent fluent in the chosen language.

Latin was the second language on the PNEU syllabus. Charlotte Mason did not think this was a suitable subject for small children. We see no mention of it in *Home Education.* She believed that English language (grammar and expression) and literature should have precedence over the teaching of Latin. Latin literature and language took their place as aspects of the foreign language curriculum and not as primary subjects. The PNEU programs and curriculum schedules show that Latin was not introduced until Form II (ages nine to twelve).

The methods for teaching Latin are very similar to those for teaching French—the narration of a passage after the grammar, syntax, and style have been studied. Again E. K. Manders writes:

> The type of book set naturally increases in difficulty as the pupils advance in grammar, but, even at the earliest stages, nothing but good Latin is ever narrated. Thus the pupils acquire a good style and a knowledge of the structure of sentences. The narration usually follows the style of the original, and so for the children, Latin is a language and not merely grammar.

John Conant, in his book *The Education of American Teachers* (1963), well expresses the position languages take in the broad curriculum: " . . . unless a person has acquired something approaching mastery of one foreign language, he has missed an educational experience of the first degree."

PHYSICAL EDUCATION

By Bobby Scott

Though the importance of free play, exploration, and being outdoors is paramount in Charlotte Mason philosophy, the PNEU program included formal physical education drills as well. Indeed it was stated that such should be a "regular part of the child's daily life."[79] Such practice was taken for granted when Miss Mason described her schools' games, dancing, and exercise as "not exceptional" to those at other schools.[80]

What is exceptional is her insight into how education should view this area of physical training, even prophetic as to how a culture could deify the training of the body over the mind. Some of her ideas follow.

She saw that physical education must extend into the classroom where educators keep a watchful eye on the signs of nervous tension in students. In her words, "We are becoming a nervous, over-strained nation and though golf and cricket may do something for us, a watchful education, alert to arrest every symptom of nervous over-pressure would do much to secure for every child a fine physique and a high degree of staying power."[81]

A contemporary teacher, wise to this principle, will sense tension among her students and stop a lesson for a short trip to run around outside. Of course, when recess as well as drill is made a regular part of the student's schedule, the child's learning is enhanced, glassy stares are avoided, and fidgetiness is minimized.

Mason taught the biblical principle that children should see their health and physical education as a proper response to the authority of God in the government of their bodies. She likewise believed and taught the corresponding principle that physical education, though valuable, does not in itself sustain the mind or spirit.[82]

She recognized the importance of what she called *habitudes*, those half-physical and half-moral habits of life that make things as "easy to do as not."[83] The proper repetition of a skill in physical training can make it automatic, and Miss Mason believed that the same automation can occur in courtesy, cooperation, and kindness. In other words, those who can show self-discipline in games are more likely to do so in life.

She emphasized that in physical education as in all of life, moderation and plain common sense were to be operative. In stating, "[I]t is a grave question whether bodily exercise of any kind should be so frequent and so excessive as to leave us without mental or moral vigor in the intervals,"[84] she foresaw the extremes that some would go to in this area.

She also reminded us that the goal of physical education is self-discipline, so that coaching and supervision become less necessary as the students learn teamwork and sportsmanship as habits. For these to become habitual, they cannot be "practiced at school and relaxed at home."[85] This reminder cannot be overemphasized today.

Finally, Miss Mason utters a quite contemporary note by including heroes in physical education. She encouraged reading about Greek games and the "heroic impulse." She knew the value of an athletic role model, especially one who exemplified chastity, fortitude, courage, constancy, prudence, and temperance.[86] Unfortunately, parents and teachers must search diligently today to find such examples, but they do exist. From Eric Liddell to Jim Ryun to Gail Devers to John Smoltz, heroic athletes may still be found to inspire our children today.

HANDCRAFTS

By Maryellen St. Cyr

"[T]he human hand is a wonderful and exquisite instrument to be used in a hundred movements exacting delicacy, direction and force; every such movement is a cause of joy as it leads to the pleasure of execution and the triumph of success."[87]

I am reminded of this "exquisite instrument" in some of its first encounters of holding a crayon, tying a lace, and molding clay. I am also reminded of the "cause of joy" from these first movements to the varied exclamations of delight and the self-fulfillment in seeing what hand hath wrought.

This joy is not usually sustained past the primary years of schooling, for the child matures and puts away play. What has become of the work of his hands? His hands now hold pencil and pen to execute language, a ball to demonstrate skill, and a mouse to manipulate image. Real effort is required to train the young in the deft handling of tools and the practice of handicrafts. It was what Charlotte Mason was urging as she spoke of each child having a relationship with a vast number of things. "He practices various handicrafts that he may know the feel of wood, clay, leather and the joy of handling tools, that is, that he may establish a due relationship with materials."[88]

The practice of various handicrafts was very much part of the program of the PNEU. Children worked with their hands through paper folding, basket-making, chair caning, sewing and knitting, clay modeling, wood carving, and bent-iron work. They also tended gardens and participated in cooking as well as various other works of the hands. This work was to be accomplished during a set time and did not encroach upon their leisure time. Realistic expectations were set and kept. Projects were completed, demonstrating creativity and dexterity.

As with all of the practices of the PNEU, there were principles to bear in mind through the instruction and implementation of this relationship of the work of the hands. First, the children would not be "employed in making futilities such as pea and stick work, paper mats and the like." In other words, the work must not be accomplished in vain. It was not what we identify as macaroni-and-refrigerator art, but it involved hands touching varied mediums in expression of self. As always, it was "the book, the knowledge, the clay, the bird or blossom he thinks of, not his own place in the class or his own progress."[89] Handwork was to be appreciated and useful, following lines of form, order, and beauty.

Second, the children were to be "taught slowly and carefully what to do." They were to work in diverse mediums and gain familiarity with materials and tools. This goal was not accomplished in a single lesson but in single projects over the length of the twelve-week term.

Third, slipshod work was not allowed. No work was given a child that she could not execute perfectly. Immediately, the word *perfect* conjures up many a memory of dissatisfaction for any or all work attempted. This "perfect work" was not in the sense of flawlessness, but that which was attempted with both heart and hand. Today it seems more often than not that any attempt on the child's part is met with an exclamation of praise whether or not it meets the desired aim. It is not enough that the child has participated; she must also learn. Many a gentle teacher or mother has led a child to redo work that was carelessly executed whatever the reason (frailty, laziness, or misunderstanding) in a successful manner, allowing the child to grow, to learn.

Lastly, the children's work was to be kept well within their compass. It is important for the teacher to know the child's compass, not as it relates to the will but as it relates to the capabilities of a person. Young children of six can handle needle and thread, and girls as well as boys enjoy woodworking and handling tools.

In my work with children, I have seen the work of hands delicately stitch samplers, sew garments, mold Degas's ballerinas, build outdoor classrooms, and launch a canoe carefully crafted. Children and teacher alike achieved a sense of satisfaction in work attempted and accomplished in a manner that displayed both care and labor over a period of time. Individually and cooperatively, the inner person develops as hands are working, all the while demonstrating worthy work from able hands.

Sample of Student Work: *U.S. Constitution* ("Old Ironsides")

Broader Application of Charlotte Mason's Teaching Principles

By Susan Schaeffer Macaulay

SCHOOLS

The first most obvious use of this curriculum is in a school. The school may be tiny, one class with a range of ages in one room, or it may be quite large with a class and teacher for each age. Schools should be small enough so that children know the teachers, staff, and each other and so that each child is known by name by all the adults. As students aren't coming to have information poured into them, like into an empty pitcher, but to respond as persons, this optimum size will make a big difference. It is hard to have a family community when the school grows beyond a certain size.

If at all possible, there should be a pleasant outdoors area around the school, not a parking lot. Beauty and accessibility are important for a child to feel alive, to breathe, to be relaxed and receptive. Again if at all possible, light and air should come in through windows pleasantly placed in all the rooms.

Children should be able to be themselves, not what they "ought" to be. They should be in an atmosphere of loving concern. Can one love children in a job? Yes. One can appreciate them, serve their needs, laugh together, enjoy things together. Children need love.

Children need fairness. The reason Walt Disney films have been so wildly successful is because the "baddie" gets punished, good triumphs over evil. Yes, children are naturally attracted to God's character—love and justice, fairness.

Children need generous time to run about in the fresh air; time to skip; climb, and play; time to walk on cool grass barefoot; time to dig in the earth or wade in a stream.

They all need time for imaginative play—not organized games (though these have their place). In this age, many children are deprived of play at home. Perhaps they are driven in a car from home to classrooms. After school they are driven home. Maybe the parents are afraid to let them play outside in the neighborhood. So children sit and watch hours of videos and TV or play computer games rather than anything else. Children are arriving at school without having had experience with play that springs from their own imaginations.

Consequently, this type of play is a great, great need—dressing up, using "props" such as boxes to make forts, anything that can enrich the scene. People respond, "But the children don't want to play. They say they are bored."

These children need rehabilitation. One teacher packed away all the textbooks and workbooks in his inner-city classroom. Because his students were so troublesome that no one hoped much for them anymore, he was permitted to "waste" his time. Desks were pushed back; he brought in cushions and some traditional illustrated fairy-tale books. He told them they weren't going to do schoolwork for a few days (sighs of relief and curiosity). He had some favorite stories, and he'd read them one (more relief, nobody trying to get them to do more practice on the three R's they'd given up on). Soon these tough youngsters became fascinated. Such stories are robust, plenty in them. The children talked about the stories. The teacher had them act out the parts of the king, the beggar, the other characters in the stories. Suddenly he "remembered" a box of costumes. In great delight they dressed up and started strutting around, acting out various personalities. The long and the short of it was that he broke through their armor, regained their interest, and stirred their imaginations through the use of fairy tales. Art and music are other means of reaching a child's inner person. All these can be part of the child's own life, thoughts, feelings.

Speaking of the needs children bring to school, I must include two basic areas. One is that so many children come ill fed. They can be from inadequate homes, but often that is not the problem. Family mealtimes are disintegrating. People sometimes have to get their children up and out to school for long commutes. The child may not have been hungry in the rush or was offered unsuitable food. Schools are increasingly having to take over some of the family routines/roles if they are to serve the children in their care.

An idea some schools might consider is a breakfast table in the classroom— in fact, a "home corner." Here the children first gather with their teacher and start the day sitting down with attractively presented home-style food. Not only is the basic need of food insured, but the friendly group is a discipline, an educational experience—learning to pass milk, eating pleasantly, talking one at a time, listening to another person, having the teacher, like a parent, in charge of the table, clearing up. Yes, it is educational first in basic ways and then as the art of conversation grows, it is educational in a profound sense.

Soon classrooms will need not only such a dining corner, but also a comfortable couch and/or seating "family room" style, providing a restful, homelike area. Too many children watch television in their bedrooms until late and are not up to an entire morning of giving their full attention to anything! If they look exhausted, such provision could make a fundamental difference to them in their school life.

In some inner-city schools spare clean clothes must be available, and there may even be washing machines and dryers to help. Hot showers and a hot breakfast may transform an "unteachable" child.

Of course, most people using this curriculum do not need to worry about such measures. But all levels of society are expecting the school to do more and more. If we aspire to follow Charlotte Mason, we'll consider the whole child, not just his or her mind or any other fragment. We must take into account the emotions, which may be churning, making the body tense and weary. Maybe there are no regular home routines.

OUTREACH

Although many schools using this curriculum will have children coming to school who have had basic needs met, we must not, we may not, ignore the plight of all the others in our communities. The PNEU ideas and insights are just exactly what they need. Perhaps no one has built a successful relationship with them before, and/or perhaps the world around them is in a blur. Can their lives be reshaped? Simple measures such as homelike food, eating routines, personal warmth, caring attitudes, strong clarity about right and wrong—all these are excellent and will go far to accomplish that needed reshaping.

But we may not feed this undernourished child with the dull sawdust of dry facts. Especially this child needs *good books*, good stories, fun, laughter, beauty—things that are truly worthwhile. They will respond.

Marion Berry took such children into her home and garden to teach and introduce them to elements of a rich curriculum that seemed right for them.

> The last to clock in was Martin, the most difficult to handle, . . . a non-reader at twelve. He had been a boarder at a special school in London. . . . It was September, and we had our first session outside at my garden table. I found he could do the most beautiful Marion Richardson writing. Book III was about right for reading. His sudden exclamation, "Hi! Isn't my reading getting good?" was very gratifying. With intervals for orange drinks and mowing the lawn we stuck it out fairly well.
>
> The age-old folk lore in the Beacon readers had an appeal to all these backward readers, but I got the Ladybird *Pirates* book for him, and he was willing to battle through a page at a time after a "warming up" on Beacon III and then IV.
>
> He was very trying in all sorts of ways; dashing in without a word of greeting to flop in my armchair. . . . The breakthrough came with *The Hobyahs*. He suddenly announced he was going to read the whole story instead of the mandatory two pages.[1]

We need courageous people to serve today's real-life children, all of them. What could be better than to try to be creative in our response? There are many places and ways we can do this. Children have only one childhood— one time to play, to do games with friends, to become interested in areas presented in the rich spread of this curriculum.

Francis A. Schaeffer was a child with special learning needs in a public school. Although he didn't know it, the reason he never could spell was that he was dyslexic.[2] At home his parents had never opened any of the rich doors into life for him, and school seemed disappointing and barren. Happily, he'd had the Boy Scouts. That was his life. Thanks to them he'd come to love nature, a richness he'd enjoy all his life. He grew confident with activities such as camping, but school was plod, plod, plod. Then when he was twelve, he had a public school teacher who was different. She read out of some interesting books; they stirred his mind, fueled his imagination, woke him up. She also told him to go to a concert. He went, and it was as if life started for him that day.

Teachers! They give, serve, and open doors for children. They may or may not see the fruit of their work. But for such children as young

Schaeffer, if the teacher does not do this, perhaps no one will. If we cannot take over an entire school, or even a classroom, we could do something along the lines Marion Berry writes about—after-school activities in a homelike environment.

Could not a group or church see this as a community mission or service? Is this not a way to be salt and light just where we are? Why not provide such places?

Children need to belong to a stable group, following a steadying pattern. Homelike after-school centers could make a great contribution. These would need to be small and personal; the children have already spent a day in school. There should be a genuine welcome, someone to get to know the child, be a friend. Perhaps nobody has ever read one of these good books aloud to them. There are lots of possibilities for adapting a banquet of learning into a picnic or supper snack!

Many children need individual attention—children in hospitals or who are chronically ill or emotionally disturbed. This PNEU approach is ideal for one-on-one work. It is satisfying for both the teacher and the taught. Much of this curriculum could be used as a basis for such work. It is a wonderful thing to open doors and windows into worthwhile areas of rich enjoyment for children who have special difficulties. In fact, other problems can seem to shrink as the life of the mind and the whole self flourish. This approach also encourages expression of personal thoughts, reactions, and appreciation in words, discussions, drawing, and music.

HOME SCHOOLS

Once again many parents are choosing to educate their children at home rather than sending them to school. This can be the right choice for some, just as schools are the best for others. Certain factors are necessary to make home schooling a good provision for children. One is a clear, worthwhile curriculum guide.

Just as in a school, a well-thought-out curriculum makes sense. The one presented in this book has grown out of the professional experience of teachers and schools today and is based on long practice. It is a relief to have the fruit of many years of trial and error! More energy can then be put into actually teaching children rather than searching for fragments that will fit together, work with children, and also be worthwhile.[3]

It was the curriculum, the "programs" as they were called, that gave

Charlotte Mason's ideas life. After we know we should use living books, then we must ask, "Well, what are they? And what would a sequence look like?" Also the basic skills of literacy and numeracy must be mastered. It is not easy to get it all together.

Parents are well aware of the need for professional, experienced guidance. As this curriculum is the fruit of years of work in schools where children's minds and lives were growing, well nourished, and well educated, this guide will be a godsend to such parents. The curriculum was devised first for schools; hence parents will probably find they must adapt it. For instance, it is unlikely they can fit in everything. A curriculum like this gives them a basis from which to work.

One of the joys of teaching an individual child is that levels of work can be chosen specifically for him or her. The child can pursue areas of interest. A danger though is that such a child may only do what he or she tends to gravitate toward anyway! A curriculum should provide a well-rounded, balanced education. It should offer assistance in insuring that enough math, science, and writing/composition is done, as well as the reading of interesting books!

Some who have read Charlotte Mason think that in teaching their own children, they can apply her ideas according to personal whims. Finding out how powerfully a child learns and responds to literature, some make the mistake of believing that reading mostly enjoyable literary books will offer a complete education! Others are afraid of any textbook. They have the mistaken idea that every school subject should be "fun." Practicing the scales while learning to play the piano, learning new vocabulary when studying French, learning the times tables need not be fun at all. We must understand that "everything in life includes duty." But it is our job to balance duty and fun. Such "drills," if they don't last too long, become part of a routine. A curriculum can insure that we offer a balanced education to the child.

People who have to move from one area to another find that using a set curriculum for their child ensures continuity of learning. It gives both the teacher and the taught a confidence in the overall pattern of the work being done.

SMALL CHRISTIAN SCHOOLS

Parents have "voted with their feet" and removed children from mainstream schools to teach them themselves. This can work well. But it can also *not* work well. Like everything else in life, it depends. However, this trend has meant that there is a search for alternatives to large factory-like schools. Some parents need assistance from a school with some aspect or another of the educational process. Other parents think that it is good to teach their children during the early years but not later on. Yet others are enthusiastic about homeschooling, but the children really long to be part of a group, a school family. Some homeschooling families are finding they are getting burned out and need adjustments. Maybe homeschooling is making too many demands on the marriage or threatening someone's health.

Whatever the reasons, many will be looking for an alternative to the homeschool *and the public school.* Small Christian schools can be the answer. Smaller schools following this curriculum and Charlotte Mason's practical ideas can provide these children and their parents with "the best of both worlds." The ideas are workable on a small scale. In fact, one could argue that a really good Charlotte Mason atmosphere, discipline, and life could best be found either in one of the happily working homeschool classrooms or in a family-like small school. Both of these situations, especially if following such a curriculum, give the needed structure.

Small schools often have more resources than families in terms of excellent books, pictures, and other materials for a full life of the mind, heart, and soul. A smaller school unit offers more freedom to play, make crafts, or go out for walks. And in these smaller situations the atmosphere can also be lively and yet peaceful too. Children could thrive on it all. I pray they do.

CAMPS

Children in chaotic domestic situations or those in unattractive urban surroundings, children whose mischief is turning into vandalism and all too soon to petty crime, can have a life-changing experience through camps or longer residential schemes. Such programs should really last for a month or two, more if possible. Special programs, for instance, have taken "problem" older children or teenagers into wilderness areas for several months of community living. This can be such a contrast to their previous environment that the shock gives them something of a clean slate for new behavior patterns.

Children who feel powerful in an aggressive way under the glare of city lights may shrink to trembling timidity in the silence and dark of the deep countryside filled with unknown animal noises. A PNEU-educated student, taking a year off between the end of high school and university, was in charge of such a group of young thugs in a small outdoor center near a moor. What could she do with them? She took them out to explore, and their defenses dropped at the sight of a turbulent moorland stream. She showed them how to play Pooh Sticks,[4] and they were entranced. Here were these big, tough, even frightening guys rushing from side to side on the bridge to see whose stick bounced out first! Remembering childhood joys, she soon saw them *in* the stream, trousers rolled up, lugging rocks to make a dam.

These same "young punks" were picking wildflowers on the way home and asking what their names were. A new world! A question from one of them revealed that they had no idea what could be under the grass. The existence of soil came as a revelation. Upon arriving in the television-and-music-free simple farmhouse room, they gathered around while she gave them empty notebooks and put out colored pencils. Soon they were concentrating on drawing pictures of the flowers! What do we find? A friendly young person sharing her love of nature and going about it in an enthusiastic, refreshing, life-giving way. Such a group can also be introduced to an interesting book read aloud, chapter by chapter. It is fantastic when they become "hooked" by the material.

A number of years ago a young woman came to the L'Abri Fellowship branch where I was working in England. She heard my talks on Charlotte Mason before I wrote my book about her and before the Charlotte Mason books were reprinted. The girl enthusiastically returned to the city where she worked among people who had given up hope of having anything much out of life. She had thought hard about Charlotte Mason's ideas and as a result organized book packs to go on home "library visits." Her church supported her, if I remember correctly.

She'd visit a needy family and bring books to read with the children. Almost all mothers hope for better things for their children, and if they meet friendliness and a real relationship rather than condescension, people don't feel defensive about their situation. Of course, this can only work if the person coming in really *does* respect the family and can be entirely natural and confident. Anyway, they would chat, and the girl would read the storybooks to the children. The books were left until the next "library visit." Such a plan can have a profound effect on a child and family.

These families would also be taken on outings on a regular basis to beautiful places in the countryside outside the urban sprawl. They were introduced to the beauty of creation, which is awesome and can have a powerful effect.

This enterprising young woman went further. She organized summer residential camps in cabins in the great northern woods. In such imaginative ways the life-giving banquet can be spread for those with few advantages. Jesus Himself commended all efforts on behalf of the poor. In this case, the families were from inner-city situations where there is such need. But, of course, actual physical poverty is not the only problem. There is a poverty of the mind, a neglect of the heart—our society teems with lonely people. Many do not enjoy good relationships in stable families and communities, let alone relationships with great minds and ideas through books, art, music—or any enjoyment of nature. Even fewer thrive in a satisfying relationship with the Creator. In other words, these were totally empty, rootless lives. Poverty comes in many forms.

Residential camps and programs can use much from this life-giving curriculum. Care has to be taken not to turn the program into a school! However, listening to interesting books and telling, drawing, or acting out the stories is recreational. So are picture study, nature study, crafts, and simple play. But help with reading, writing, or math on a regular but not too extensive basis can be scheduled. Just as people long for satisfying food, so their minds enjoy feeding too. As always, genuine personal relationships are always a vital part of such teaching.

Camps or residential programs can also include scouting-type activities, sports, and teamwork on a practical project and shared chores. Such a program should include real work, one of the most health-giving ways a person develops self-esteem, maturity, and cooperation. There should also be leisure to "stop and stare" and for real conversations.

New patterns for life enrichment can be formed after supper in the gathering darkness. After meals served around tables where people learn the joys of sharing good food and conversation and washing dishes, what fun to enjoy a book read aloud chapter by chapter! What a new experience for so many!

Open campfires are a wonderful attraction, as are games in the dark for older youths. Evenings can be a fun time for games, competitions, skits, or music. And then they go to bed at a regular time. Ideally these campers will by that time be what we used to call "pooped." They are weary from fresh air and exercise, chores, fun and challenges, ready for a welcome rest. Although a program of several months can make a habit-changing impact, short periods of time can also be important. Always remember that "a little bit of help is a lot of help."

Excluded Children

In Britain right now, and probably in many other countries, there are more and more children whose behavior is such a problem that they are officially excluded from mainstream schools. For some, it seems that there is nothing between the school (where they've failed) and the detention center or even prison.

Here is another opportunity. These young persons badly need education in the most profound sense. The classroom model has failed, but in one industrial city a little, old red-brick, three-room primary school previously boarded up has come back to life to bring hope to some. A few interested persons had noticed a group of "derelict teenagers" congregating in a nearby playground during school hours. The observers gave their time to provide education on a one-to-one voluntary basis to these youngsters. The activity was popular; the kids felt befriended. Soon others came along, and it was possible to acquire the abandoned school. The school grew to have a "family" of around fifty students aged eleven to sixteen.

The atmosphere is relaxed. Children begin with nonthreatening art work or cooking. This art is displayed all around and makes an attractive, creative, and colorful environment. Soon students learn that being there isn't about passing or failing and that there are no class lessons they can disrupt. They are helped on an individual basis. The children gain confidence and self-respect and soon begin to see that they *can* learn. (Remember the PNEU motto: "I am, I can, I ought, I will.") They make progress and enjoy the new experience. The astounding thing is that eventually they do better than children in the city's mainstream schools. It can be done.

This curriculum could be ideal as a basis for such work. Children such as these need skills taught first, but also their minds need feeding. They need to forget themselves in entering the interesting, big world outside their own impoverished one.

Clubs

One or more areas in this curriculum could be offered as a "club." My husband and I, as well as some of our friends, have done this. Scheduled on a weekly basis after school, such gatherings allow both home- *and* school-educated children to mix and enjoy an area of life and learning together. Often these groups meet in the relaxing atmosphere of a home. However, sometimes larger facilities can be found for drama, bands, and other group activities. Clubs might meet at a minibus to travel to a hilltop or forest for a nature walk with a picnic lunch. Often the hour (or more) is given voluntarily by adults who want to share their joy in something, say literature, with the next generation. Other clubs employ someone expert in a field, and each child's parents contribute to cover the expense. We've done this for music/band, art, drama, and French clubs. Once when we organized such clubs, the local press reported it, resulting in several children with special needs being able to join too. An autistic child went swimming every week; a brain-damaged one enjoyed drama. Everyone benefited.

Another aspect that must be considered is that the children are not being pressured into this activity. They must choose to come. I've known children who were not enjoying school at all come alive with enthusiasm in an interesting literature group. One retired teacher has fired several generations of children with a love of Shakespeare.

In our busy society one could even have a "play club" where children would not be organized at all but would be able to gravitate to areas with various resources for play set out. Such a situation may be familiar in the nursery stage, but many older children don't have access at home to art and craft materials in one area or an attractive, quiet, and comfortable living room area with interesting books displayed. While some children flop down to relax in a corner, others are dressing up in a room with a full-length mirror and a rack of "costumes." They'll often go on to act out pretend situations.

Children love access to scrap pine, hammers, nails, and other tools. It would be ideal to have a few acres outside for play—with bushes to make camps under. A kitchen for real cooking is an attraction too. However, the location does *not* have to be ideal. It is wonderful to be able to provide such truly good things as space, order, and inviting materials both in and out of doors. But if there is no outdoors space, then an indoor hall imaginatively used is better than nothing. Once again the quality of adult relationships with the child or teenager is *the most vital factor.*

This relationship factor is why homelike routines such as eating together or sitting talking quietly one on one are such gifts to the young. Especially today. It is a gift to give them relationships with actual persons rather than unending televised images on a screen. It is a gift to remove the screens and provide real materials to use and play with. It is a gift to introduce thought through good books, art, and music. Enjoyment of nature—watching the wind blow trees, hearing birds sing, gazing carefully at ants—can generate a life's inner balance and peace.

Another home-based club that can and has been literally life-giving are children's Bible clubs. As these are in a home, children who would find the church atmosphere strange can relax and feel welcome. My parents, the Schaeffers, encouraged women in their church to have such clubs. This meant that in all kinds of city neighborhoods, local homes were opened "for the children's sake." All the degrees and high salaries in the world will mean nothing if the soul is not rooted into the ground of God's truth. The most "excellent education" is like a house being built. Unless it has foundations on the Rock that is Jesus Christ, the person has not entered the most vital relationship of all, getting to know God, His Word, and His works. Listening, trusting, and obeying God's Word brings life.[5]

It is good to have a smallish group, although I've taught weekly groups of up to thirty-five or so children who were enthusiastic about their "Elijah Club." (I always found this a more willing group than a Sunday school class. Club members had *chosen* to come.) We'd have a snack, sing the same repertoire of songs so that they would get to really know and enjoy them. Then using a tiny flannelgraph picture for each previous story in a series, they would tell back (very briefly) a sketch of each story. They could enjoy hearing an entire Gospel this way, a chapter at a time.

Other times we took a "bird's-eye" view of the Bible.[6] I would illustrate this either with flannelgraph or my own drawings. They would sit comfortably and quietly on the floor. The atmosphere was orderly but friendly. I'd try to time the story to match their attention span. Often they went to tables to draw a picture to illustrate the story afterwards. Many of these were children who knew little about God except that they had heard His name used as a swear word. They asked really thoughtful, interesting questions.

Sometimes we learned a few Bible verses or a psalm by heart for a few minutes each week. For memorizing the passage well, they got to stick a star on their cards. In the summer, if possible, they could come to an activity week where the mornings were a bit like a day camp. Once again we had large-group singing and teaching sessions, or if there were too many children, we held such sessions in their own age group. Then came a snack, followed by one activity chosen by the child for the week. Some chose a craft such as pottery, others swimming, and so on. One year they built a Saxon hut by the pond; another year they built a raft and sailed on the pond. Leaders shared their own interests and hobbies.

Children need to know God's Word. It is best taught by people who love and know children and don't talk down to them or at them. The adults should have a natural authority that is firm but friendly. They should themselves be sure of the truth of God's Word, know why they believe it is true, and enjoy trusting in God's love themselves. Ideally, they should have a gift to tell stories well to a large group or read it well with a small group. It is a wonderful, joyous privilege to have roots in life, to be in touch with God, and to enjoy forgiveness, goodness, *life*. These are the best things of all to share! Teaching children should not be a weary, churned-out business. We do it "for the children's sake." Jesus truly is "the way, the truth and *the life*."

Sample of Student Work: Allosaurus

PART
TWO

6

An Applied Philosophy

When Charlotte Mason continued her life's work in Ambleside, England, she envisioned an education that would transcend economic and social barriers by applying principles that would bring out the best in all children. The beliefs and values she wrote about extensively were transmitted into the daily routine of schooling. How one viewed the learner, the way to knowledge, and the role of the teacher affected the teaching and learning of each discipline, from handwriting to chemistry.

Today educators mostly concur with her expressed beliefs and yet operate within a framework of their own experience. An eclectic approach results in which one chooses from varied belief systems usually not in harmony with one another. For example, one may make a curricular choice dependent on a system that views the learner as an empty vessel, consequently separating information into manageable fragments but without overall coherence. Charlotte Mason's approach views the learner as a person, thereby introducing information richly clothed in literary language while at the same time expounding on skill development, including both the parts and the whole of learning. One is not forfeited for the other. This view offers the breadth and depth of learning that will meet the needs and diversity of individual learners.

Most children spend 14,000-plus hours housed in systems of educational thought that depend on the experience of teachers rather than on these tried and true principles described in Part One. At the outset, I must say that the principles of education as an atmosphere, a life, and a discipline are being applied in both private and public education by persons who know nothing of Charlotte Mason. Perhaps we all can look to a meaningful learning experience in our own lives when a coach, teacher, parent, counselor, or professor created an atmosphere where optimal learning took place. Our loss is that these practices were not widely experienced. They were limited to a class, a teacher, and a discipline rather than being readily available to us through our entire schooling. It was Miss Mason's vision that all children would have the opportunity to be educated according to these foundational principles every day and that students in turn would live full and free lives.

And it is here we begin. How can these principles be consistently applied as envisioned by Charlotte Mason in the classroom each day? The daily work of teaching and learning is built upon these foundational principles that are expressed through a curriculum. This prescribed course of study can take on variations from detailed plans and procedures, some that encompass minute-to-minute objectives, to others that lay out general overviews of instruction. As educators, we are tempted to stray from these foundational principles by looking for solutions that would constitute a solid education. And we most often look to the curriculum for this answer. Thus the curriculum or program, rather than the principles, takes on a governing role, defining the relationships that encompass the classroom.

For example, the teacher may take on a role of a behaviorist, using "carrots and sticks" to motivate students to learn multiplication, spelling, and geography rather than relying upon the child's innate desire for knowledge and power of mind to be the determining factor. When the curriculum takes supremacy, the idea that there is the "one best book or program" pushes educators to the marketplace seeking the latest manual, up-to-the-minute resources, the most highly reviewed text or book to be the answer to the dilemma of how best to educate. Thoughtful consideration and care should definitely be taken in choosing books and materials for the classroom, but not to the extent that they are the "be all and end all" for what constitutes a substantial education. We all at one time or another have been acquainted with a learning situation in which one of the best books was used, and an optimal learning experience did not result—because other factors were absent.

The "right curriculum" does not constitute a proper education. Charlotte Mason explicitly stated this in her books as she referred to learning as a relationship. This learning takes on manifold relationships—with self, others, God, authority, and the world. I think it is important to reiterate here that the curriculum is the means to the end—knowledge. It is not the end in itself. Many educators bring students into relationship with great works. Yet if the relationships as previously stated are not part of the learning process, the curriculum becomes the end. Charlotte Mason saw education not merely as information and the manipulation of facts and opinions, but rather the development of the whole person.

We have all been in relationship with persons, be it children or adults, whose knowledge of a particular discipline was superior. At the same time, however, it became apparent that the person was miseducated in that he or she lacked adequate skills in relating to self and others, as well as holding a limited view of life and living. Education involves the reciprocity of relationships. Advancement or progress in curriculum development is not necessarily in its innovation, as with technology, promising accelerated learning or higher achievement, but in its effectiveness in the outworking of a sound philosophy. Charlotte Mason warned her readers of looking to a system devised for the student, teacher, or parent and then locking into what it means for a child to be educated. Miss Mason spoke to this end in *Home Education*, pages 9-10:

> A system of education is an alluring fancy; more so, on some counts, than a method, because it is pledged to more definite calculable results. By means of a system certain developments may be brought about through the observance of given rules. Shorthand, dancing, how to pass examinations, how to become a good accountant, or a woman of society, may all be learned upon systems.
>
> System—the observing of rules until the habit of doing certain things, of behaving in certain ways, is confirmed, and, therefore, the art is acquired—is so successful in achieving precise results, that it is no wonder there should be endless attempts to straiten the whole field of education to the limits of a system.
>
> If a human being were a machine, education could do no more for him than to set him in action in prescribed ways, and the work of the educator would be simply to adopt a good working system or set of systems.
>
> But the educator has to deal with a self-acting, self-developing being, and his business is to guide, and assist in, the production of the latent good in that being, the dissipation of the latent evil, the preparation of the child to take his place in the world at his best, with every capacity for good that is in him developed into a power.
>
> Though system is highly useful as an instrument of education, a system of education is mischievous, as producing only mechanical action instead of the vital growth and movement of a living being.
>
> It is worthwhile to point out the differing characters of a system

and a method, because parents let themselves be run away with often enough by some plausible "system," the object of which is to produce development in one direction—of the muscles, of the memory, of the reasoning faculty—and to rest content, as if that single development were a complete all-round education. This easy satisfaction arises from the sluggishness of human nature, to which any difficult scheme is more agreeable than the constant watchfulness, the unforeseen action, called for when the whole of a child's existence is to be used as the means of his education. But who is sufficient for an education so comprehensive, so incessant? A parent may be willing to undergo any definite labors for his child's sake; but to always be catering to his behoof, always contriving that circumstances shall play upon him for his good, is part of a god and not of a man! A reasonable objection enough, if one looks upon education as an endless series of independent efforts, each to be thought out and acted out on the spur of the moment; but the fact is, that a few broad essential principles cover the whole field, and these once fully laid hold of, it is as easy and natural to act upon them as it is to act upon our knowledge of such facts as that fire burns and water flows.

When applied, this educational scheme would allow the child to grow in areas of intellectual and moral habit, flourish in a wide curriculum, and thereby develop conscience resulting in both character and conduct for living.

After reading Charlotte Mason's works, one desires to recreate this "educational scheme" for oneself and for the children. Some have moved in terms of this recreating to find all the books mentioned in her volumes or records, to purchase these, and thereby to have a more authentic chance of applying a "Charlotte Mason education." Upon visiting Olive Norton's school in England, I learned early on that the answer was not in the books as I zealously tried to gain information on titles and authors. She very wisely said, "Surely, you have good books in America!"

It is not the goal of the authors of this book to bring back a period in history, i.e., the Victorian, and imitate that manner of living and schooling in the twenty-first century. Nor are we keen on applying as a veneer some of the principles to an incompatible philosophy of education based on our own liking or the attractive nature of parts of the application. Rather, we hope to bring about a transformation in our own lives and in the lives of students as we look at education in the full scheme of things, i.e., the relationships of students with self, others, God, the world, and also the relationship of teachers with students, and teachers and students within the process of teaching and learning. It is here that Miss Mason was a pioneer in education, as she saw all of life within the context of relationships. She left for us a legacy of her work embodied in print and in the continuing rich lives of her students, all of which bear consideration. Now it rests with us to find the answer to so great a question: How is this education to be developed to be available to all of us?

Charlotte Mason Schools International and Ambleside School were established in 1999 with the hope of answering the above question for teachers, parents, and students. In the fall of 2000, educators came together in Fredericksburg, Texas, to launch a practicing school, demonstrating the principles of education espoused by Charlotte Mason. The following information was compiled and is being used in Ambleside School.

A CURRICULUM SCOPE

Looking at what is to be taught throughout the years of schooling can be an overwhelming task at times as we see examples of delayed and accelerated learning. These are two extremes to avoid. The attitude of not introducing a discipline of study until children show an interest allows children to limit themselves according to what they know, as well as to acquire a debilitating habit of acting according to feelings. By contrast, the accelerated approach looks at learning in the realm of conquest rather than as a natural affinity in relationship with the world.

The PNEU schools had a wide curriculum for all students, offering modes of disciplinary (skill-based) instruction as well as inspirational (content-based) instruction. These two forms of instruction were not exclusive of one another, for each discipline should be infused with inspiration, and each inspiration requires its consequent discipline. These modes were used in harmony with one another to enliven the means of how a child gets to knowledge, thereby providing a balance of effort and rest in a rigorous curriculum.

The materials chosen for the curriculum consist mainly of books, which Charlotte Mason would describe as living—that is, they are vital. They nourish the mind and allow it to do its work of assimilating information to gain knowledge. Some of these books are characterized as classics, standing the test of time. Others manifest beautiful language, universal themes, identifiable characters, intricate plots, or provide information in an interesting and inspirational way. Because time is limited in formal schooling, we must choose the best books available as these introduce children to the world of literary thought. Living in the twenty-first century, one has access to out-of-print books, books in the public domain, and books presently in print. We are resolved to use books in print, accommodating the broader community of schools and homeschools. When we do err, we err on being more selective to reach the mind of the student rather than following the trend or taste of the market.

The use of some twenty to thirty books within the school year acquaints students with thousands of pages each semester. The students read fewer books as opposed to many or the too many "snippets" offered in anthologies. The intent is that they read to know, for what benefit is it for a student to read and not know? Miss Mason thought it best that the student become well acquainted with three to four books in literature rather than read many and have no regard for the literature or the author.

A sampling of the areas of study and a brief description of the study are listed below according to elementary, middle, and upper grades. Noticeably, some areas of study are omitted from our program, i.e., physical education to name one. Presently, physical education is not a part of the formal school day. Time is set aside in each grade for play, but the direct work of training in sports and skills is left to after-school programs.

The curriculum coursework for Ambleside School provides:

• A wide and varied course of study.

• An alternating plan for both the development of skills and the mastery of content.

• An acquaintance with knowledge that is vital, fruitful, and interesting with its informing ideas.

• The use of books characterized as "the best thought of the best writers."

• The use of materials that aid in understanding and exploration without diluting the thought of the discipline.

COURSE OF STUDY

We endeavor that the students "should have relations of pleasure and intimacy established with as many possible of the interests proper to him; not learning a slight or incomplete smattering about this or that subject, but plunging into vital knowledge, with a great field before him which all his life he will not be able to fully explore." The courses of study vary between the grades, students' time at school, and the depth at which subjects are encountered. Below is a sampling of three courses of study in the lower, middle, and upper schools.

LOWER SCHOOL

Inspirational Subjects	Disciplinary Subjects
Bible	Arithmetic
Composer Study	Art
History Readings	Geography
Nature Study	Handwork
Picture Study	Handwriting
Poetry	Phonics/Reading Instruction
Read Aloud	Recitation
Tales and Fables /Myths and Legends	Singing

MIDDLE SCHOOL

Inspirational Subjects	Disciplinary Subjects
Bible	Art
Citizenship	Composition
Composer Study	Dictation
Literature	Foreign Language
Nature Study	Geography
Picture Study	Grammar
Poetry	Handwork
Read Aloud	Handwriting
Science	Mathematics
World History	Recitation
	Singing

UPPER SCHOOL

Inspirational Subjects	Disciplinary Subjects
Civilizations	Art
Composer Study	Composition
Literature	Foreign Language
Nature Study/Science Lab	Information Technology
Science	Mathematics
Spiritual Leadership	Singing

DESCRIPTIONS OF THE DISCIPLINES OF STUDY

Art: Formal instruction in technique and various mediums are introduced throughout the grades, providing experience, observation, and study.

Bible: Readings are selected from the Old and New Testaments as well as from Proverbs and Psalms, instructing in the knowledge of God and the knowledge of man.

Citizenship: Beginning in grade four, students read about the relationships of men and women as in relationship with self and others in choosing the good and refusing the evil, as well as their contributions of service to the city and the nation.

Composer Study: The students are acquainted with two classical composers and several of their works throughout the grades, cultivating taste and appreciation for classical music.

Composition: In the beginning years students are solely acquainted with oral composition in the form of narration. Narration is continued daily throughout the grades as a method of assimilating information. Written composition is begun in grade three with work in description and continues throughout the grades, resulting in formal research projects.

Dictation: Each week students copy beautifully written text, noting spelling, grammar, and punctuation from a classroom text or something studied. Later they are called upon to write a portion or the whole of what has been copied as it is dictated to them.

Foreign Language: Students are immersed in a language through a class taught mainly in this foreign tongue. The time is spent in imitation, repetition, dialogues, and writing.

Geography: Atlases are used throughout the days as a reference in areas of study; by this geography is naturally integrated into the curriculum. Geography is taught formally in grades five and six.

Grammar: In the early years students are introduced to the rules and regulations of our language by way of formal instruction. In the later years, instruction is based on addressing errors in usage.

Handwork: Each year students undertake two handwork projects taught by the classroom teacher or an artisan in the community.

Handwriting: In the early years students master manuscript writing and then are introduced to Spencerian writing, working out and practicing form, size, and style.

History: An introduction to history begins in grades one and two. Beginning in grade three, the history of the United States and the world is taught each year through the eighth grade. Students in the third grade begin with exploration for U.S. history and the history of Egypt and Greece for world history. Studies are continued in both of these histories throughout the grades, culminating with the twentieth century with both the United States and the world.

In the upper school, history is referred to as civilizations, insofar as this study reflects the geopolitical, religious, philosophical, and cultural influences as recorded through events, nations, and individuals. The four years are divided into studies from the beginning of recorded history through the present day. Original writings and a text are used to gain understanding of the part and whole of this period.

Literature: A variety of genres is selected each year, some to correlate with history and science and other classic works of literature.

Mathematics: Beginning with arithmetic, the art of computation is mastered in addition, subtraction, multiplication, and division in the elementary grades. The other branches consisting of algebra, geometry, trigonometry, and calculus are applied in the middle and upper schools.

Nature Study: Each student keeps a nature journal in which weekly entries are added to include drawings and descriptions. The students become acquainted with their natural surroundings as well as with species from two other classes of nature.

Phonics and Reading: In grades one and two, students go through a formal program of sight and sound correspondence to develop skills in pronunciation and spelling. Phonics rules are introduced and learned for application, not drill. Beginning readers are used to reinforce these developing skills.

Picture Study: Students are familiarized with two artists a year and four to six of their significant works. They also experience the style and technique of the artist through imitation of one of their works.

Poetry: Two poets and their works are introduced to the students each year. The students are given a volume of their works, and they memorize poems individually and corporately for personal enjoyment and formal recitation.

Read Aloud: The read-aloud program is designed with the intent of teacher and students growing relationally through the intimacy of a shared book. The teacher reads aloud while the students actively listen. Students respond by narrating passages read with ease and comprehension. Growth is not only evident in the work of the mind assimilating information and ideas, but in stirring the heart through imagination and vital action. It is our hope and desire to provide a storehouse of ideas and information through the books chosen for teachers and students alike as they acquaint themselves with that which is very much alive—living books.

Recitation: This time is used to rehearse passages and verses from Scripture, poetry, or history, which students are responsible for keeping in their hearts and minds.

Science: In grade three students are acquainted with animals and fossils through readings, drawings, and hands-on activities. Beginning in grade four through the middle grades, branches of physical, earth, and life sciences are taught each year. Through these varied branches, students are introduced to the principles of science, observation, and demonstration. In the upper grades, the sciences of biology, chemistry, physics, behavior, and technology are brought in more comprehensively.

Singing and Music: The students' voices and ears are trained individually and collectively. The harmonies and melodies of classical and folk music are introduced to the students through song, dance, and instrument. Choral groups perform at school and in the community.

Tales and Fables/Myths and Legends: In the early grades, tales and fables, as well as myths and legends, are chosen from history and various countries. These are read aloud to warm the imagination and instruct the conscience.

TIMETABLE

After you look at the course of study, the timetable will help you see how this coursework becomes a reality daily and weekly. Children in the early grades have a modified day with shorter lessons. The transition to longer days begins in grade three with three long days and two short days. Much is still accomplished in the morning hours, as class size is limited to fewer than twelve students in the early grades and twenty in the older grades. Each student participates actively in this broad curriculum alternating between inspirational and disciplinary subjects. Listed below are examples of timetables from both the lower and upper schools.

AMBLESIDE SCHOOL OF FREDERICKSBURG
LOWER SCHOOL (GRADE 3)

TIMETABLE

Time	Monday	Tuesday	Wednesday	Thursday	Friday
8:30–8:50	Old Testament	Old Testament	Chapel	Psalm/Proverb	New Testament
8:50–9:20	Arithmetic	Arithmetic		Arithmetic	Arithmetic
9:20–9:50	Literature	Literature	Literature	Literature	Literature
9:50–10:05	Handwriting	Composition	Handwriting	Recitation (Number) Poetry	Handwriting
10:05–10:20	Free Play	Free Play	Free Play	Free Play	Free Play
10:20–10:50	World History	American History	World History	American History	Book of Centuries
10:50–11:10	Grammar	Foreign Language	Grammar	Foreign Language	Composer Study
11:10–11:40	Science	Recitation (Bible) 11:10–11:20 Poetry 11:20–11:30	Science	Recitation (Bible) 11:10–11:20 Poetry 11:20–11:30	Science
11:40–12:10	Dictation	Read Aloud Myths and Legends (11:30–12:00)	Dictation	Read Aloud Myths and Legends (11:30–12:00)	Dictation
12:10–12:30	Geography	Dismissal (12:15)	Geography	Dismissal (12:15)	Geography
12:30–1:00	Lunch		Lunch		Lunch
1:00–1:45	Picture Study		Nature Study		Handwork
1:45–2:30	Music		Art		Physical Education
2:30–3:00	Read Aloud		Read Aloud		Read Aloud
3:15	Dismissal		Dismissal		Dismissal

AMBLESIDE SCHOOL OF FREDERICKSBURG
UPPER SCHOOL (GRADES 6-8)

TIMETABLE

Time	Monday	Tuesday	Wednesday	Thursday	Friday
8:30–9:00	Old Testament	Psalm/Proverb	Chapel	New Testament	New Testament
9:00–9:30	Literature	Literature	Literature	Literature	Literature
9:30–10:15	Science	Science	Science	Science	Science
10:15–11:15	Geography 10:15–11:00 Free Play 11:00–11:15	Music 10:15–11:00 Free Play 11:00–11:15	Art	Singing 10:15–10:30 Picture/ Composer Study 10:30–11:15	Geography 10:15–11:00 Free Play 11:00–11:15
11:15–12:00	World History	United States History	World History	United States History	Book of Centuries
12:00–12:15	Recitation (Bible)	Geography Drill	Free Play	Free Play	Recitation (Poetry)
12:15–1:00	7/8: Math 6: Grammar/ Composition	7/8: Math 6: Grammar/ Composition	7/8: Math 6: Nature Study	7/8: Math 6: Grammar/ Composition	7/8: Math 6: Grammar/ Composition
1:00–1:30	Lunch	Lunch	Lunch	Lunch	Lunch
1:30–2:15	7/8: Grammar/ Composition 6: Math	7/8: Grammar/ Composition 6: Math	7/8: Nature Study 6: Math	7/8: Grammar/ Composition 6: Math	7/8: Grammar/ Composition 6: Math
2:15–2:30	Handwriting	Dictation	Dictation	Read Aloud (Citizenship)	Dictation
2:30–3:00	Read Aloud	Read Aloud (Citizenship)	Nature Study	Handwork	Read Aloud
3:15	Dismissal	Dismissal	Dismissal	Dismissal	Dismissal

The following is an example of the curriculum coursework for grade three. Each teacher is given the coursework in this format along with other aids such as a teacher handbook, a sequence for each of the disciplinary subjects of grammar, composition, and mathematics, and writings that reflect the philosophy and practice of Ambleside.

AMBLESIDE SCHOOL OF FREDERICKSBURG
CURRICULUM COURSEWORK

GRADE 3

Inspirational Subjects	Disciplinary Subjects
Bible	Art
Composer Study	Composition
Literature	Dictation
Myths and Legends	Foreign Language
Nature Study	Geography
Picture Study	Grammar
Poetry	Handwork
Read Aloud	Handwriting
Science	Mathematics
Singing	Physical Education
United States History	Recitation
World History	

SYLLABUS

BIBLE

Semester	First	Second
Text	*The Bible* *The Dore Bible Illustrations* *Student Bible Atlas* *Halley's Bible Handbook*	*The Bible* *The Dore Bible Illustrations* *Student Bible Atlas* *Halley's Bible Handbook*
Coursework	Old Testament: Exodus New Testament: Luke Psalm 24–36	Old Testament: Exodus New Testament: Luke Psalm 37–50
Notes to Teacher	The work in this discipline should include reading the Bible, use of the atlas and the Bible handbook as well as memorization of Scripture (3-4 passages per semester).	
Philosophy of Teaching Bible	pp. 158-169 *(Philosophy of Education)* pp. 247-253 *(Home Education)* pp. 348-352 *(Home Education)* pp. 108-112 *(Parents and Children)*	
Example Bible Lesson	pp. 329-332 *(School Education)*	
Example of Narration	pp. 227-273 *(School Education)* p. 283 *(School Education)* p. 287 *(School Education)* pp. 294-295 *(School Education)*	
Example of Narration Questions	p. 308 *(School Education)* pp. 313-315 *(School Education)*	

COMPOSER STUDY

Semester	First	Second
Resources	*Brandenburg Concertos* *Organ Toccatas and Passacaglia* *Mr. Bach Comes to Call*	*Symphony no. 4* *Brahms Lullaby with Bird Songs*
Coursework	Johann Sebastian Bach	Johannes Brahms
Notes to Teacher	The work in this discipline should be deliberate in playing the composition upon arrival, during times of disciplinary work (handwriting, dictation, etc.) and at lunch. Compositions and their composers should be identified on the board for the student to see. Students will listen to the music of the composer for the purpose of enjoyment, recognition, and imitation.	
Philosophy of Teaching Composer Study	pp. 217-218 *(Philosophy of Education)* pp. 30-31, Book I *(Ourselves)*	

LITERATURE

Semester	First	Second
Text	*Little Maid of Old Connecticut* *Pilgrim Voices*	*Black Beauty* *Benjamin West and His Cat Grimalkin*
Notes to Teacher	The work in this discipline should include the mechanics of reading aloud, the elements of literature, informal analysis, and criticism.	
Philosophy of Teaching Literature	pp. 180-185 *(Philosophy of Education)*	
Example of Literature Lesson	pp. 340-341 *(School Education)*	
Example of Narration	pp. 292-294 *(School Education)* pp. 297-300 *(School Education)*	

MYTHS AND LEGENDS

Semester	First	Second
Text	*Tales of Ancient Egypt** *Tales of the Greek Heroes**	*The Trojan War and the Adventures of Odysseus** *Favorite North American Legends**
Notes to Teacher	The work in this discipline should include the reading and narration of the text, allowing the child to ". . . revel in such classic myths as we possess as a nation . . ." and to ". . . enrich the chambers of his House Beautiful with a thousand tableaux, pathetic and heroic, and should form in him, insensible, principles whereby he will hereafter judge of the behavior of nations, and will rule his own conduct as one of a nation."	
Example of Narration Questions	p. 273 *(School Education)* pp. 277-278 *(School Education)*	

*Tales from these books may be chosen selectively. It is not the purpose necessarily to read every tale, but rather to give the children a picture of the legends and myths of these ancient cultures.

NATURE STUDY

Semester	First	Second
Text	*Keeping a Nature Journal* *Handbook of Nature Study* *Appropriate field guides from the region*	*Keeping a Nature Journal* *Handbook of Nature Study* *Appropriate field guides from the region*
Coursework	Spiders, Trees, Wildflowers	
Notes to Teacher	The work in this discipline should include weekly field work, nature walks, and the keeping of a nature journal. This journal should include sketches (drybrush watercolor), descriptions, sightings, labels, and nature poetry.	
Philosophy of Teaching Nature Study	pp. 236-238 *(School Education)* pp. 42-72 *(Home Education)* p. 217 *(Philosophy of Education)*	
Example of Narration	p. 274 *(School Education)* pp. 278-280 *(School Education)*	

PICTURE STUDY

Semester	First	Second
Resources	*A Weekend with Renoir* *Renoir Painting Cards* *Renoir Paintings* *Flowers in a Vase* *Girl with a Hoop* *A Girl with a Watering Can* *Pont Neuf, Paris* *Oarsmen at Chatou* *Woman with a Guitar*	*Cezanne* *Flowers in a Rococo Vase* *House of Pere Lacroix* *Houses in Provence* *Still Life* *The Artist's Father* *Still Life with a Peppermint Bottle*
Coursework	Pierre-Auguste Renoir	Paul Cezanne
Notes to Teacher	The work in this discipline should include picture talks, one student reproduction per semester, and a brief biography of the artist.	
Philosophy of Teaching Picture Study	pp. 213-217 *(Philosophy of Education)* pp. 102-103, Book II *(Ourselves)*	
Example of Picture Study Lesson	pp. 309-311 *(Home Education)* pp. 353-355 *(School Education)*	

POETRY

Semester	First	Second
Text	*Poetry for Young People: Henry Wadsworth Longfellow Selected Poems*	*Old Possum's Book of Practical Cats*
Coursework	Henry Wadsworth Longfellow	T. S. Eliot
Notes to Teacher	The work in this discipline should include the daily reading and reciting of poetry as well as the memorization of 4-6 poems per semester.	
Philosophy of Teaching Study	pp. 222-226 *(Home Education)* p. 10, Book II *(Ourselves)*	

READ ALOUD

Semester	First	Second
Text	*The Railway Children* *A Little Princess*	*A Little Princess* *The Swiss Family Robinson* *Assigned Shakespeare play*
Notes to Teacher	The work in this discipline should be carried out daily with the teacher reading aloud and the students narrating what was read.	

SCIENCE

Semester	First	Second
Text	*Dinosaurs by Design* *Handbook of Nature Study*	*Handbook of Nature Study*
Coursework	HNS: pp. 214-253	HNS: pp. 254-293
Notes to Teacher	The work in this discipline should include the readings with one day per week designated for laboratory or observation work. A record of the student's work in this discipline is to be recorded in the student copybook with weekly compositions or narrations and illustrations.	
Philosophy of Teaching Science	pp. 218-223 *(Philosophy Education)*	
Example of Science Lesson	pp. 351-352 *(School Education)*	
Example of Narration	p. 285 *(School Education)* pp. 291-292 *(School Education)*	
Example of Narration Questions	p. 311 *(School Education)* pp. 325-327 *(School Education)*	

SINGING

Text	Various hymnals, songbooks, etc.
Notes to Teacher	The work in this discipline should consist of singing melodies from morning assembly, music class, history class, composer study, and foreign language when applicable.

UNITED STATES HISTORY

Semester	First	Second
Text	*The Age of Exploration* *First Voyage to America* *Atlas of United States History*	*The First Americans* *Atlas of United States History*
Notes to Teacher	The work in this discipline should include readings, dictations, and the geography of events and persons studied. A record of the student's work in this discipline is to be recorded in the Book of Centuries with weekly narrations and illustrations.	
Philosophy of Teaching History	pp. 169-180 *(Philosophy of Education)* pp. 36-38, Book I *(Ourselves)* pp. 279-295 *(Home Education)*	
Example of History Lesson	pp. 334-339 *(School Education)*	
Example of Narration	pp. 276-277 *(School Education)* pp. 281-282 *(School Education)* pp. 283-284 *(School Education)* pp. 287-290 *(School Education)* pp. 295-296 *(School Education)* pp. 298-299 *(School Education)*	
Example of Narration Questions	pp. 309-310 *(School Education)* pp. 320-322 *(School Education)*	

WORLD HISTORY

Semester	First	Second
Text	*The Pharaohs of Ancient Egypt* *Ancient Egyptian Art* *The Visual Dictionary of Buildings* *Historical Atlas of the World*	*The Story of the Greeks* *Ancient Greece* *The Visual Dictionary of Buildings* *Historical Atlas of the World*
Notes to Teacher	The work in this discipline should include readings, dictations, and the geography of events and persons studied. A record of the student's work in this discipline is to be recorded in the Book of Centuries with weekly narrations and illustration.	
Philosophy of Teaching History	pp. 169-180 *(Philosophy of Education)* pp. 36-38, Book I *(Ourselves)* pp. 279-295 *(Home Education)*	
Example of History Lesson	pp. 334-339 *(School Education)*	
Example of Narration	pp. 276-277 *(School Education)* pp. 281-282 *(School Education)* pp. 283-284 *(School Education)* pp. 287-290 *(School Education)* pp. 295-296 *(School Education)* pp. 298-299 *(School Education)*	
Example of Narration Questions	pp. 309-310 *(School Education)* pp. 320-322 *(School Education)*	

COMPOSITION

Coursework	Daily oral narration across the disciplines Grade 3: One daily written narration beginning second semester Grades 4-12: Two or three daily written narrations	
Notes to Teacher	The work in this discipline should allow the student to acquire language and learn how to use it. This usefulness will include content, vocabulary, a range of ideas, fluency and correctness developed through letter writing, answers to suitable questions (expository, explanation), verse making, description of scenes, incidents, persons, objects, analysis and synthesis, integrated through the knowledge obtained in various disciplines, experiences, and amusements.	
Example of Narration	pp. 312-313 *(School Education)* pp. 190-209 *(Philosophy of Education)*	
Example of Narration Questions	pp. 312-313 *(School Education)* p. 318 *(School Education)*	

DICTATION

Notes to Teacher	The work in this discipline should begin with one or two paragraphs carefully at one time, working up to a whole page by the middle of the second semester. These paragraphs are prepared early in the week, and the student is asked to write out the dictation later the same week. The dictation passages should be chosen from the books set in each semester from the disciplines of study, selecting those worthy of thought and language. Passages should be transcribed in the Transcription Journal (or Book of Centuries when applicable).
Example of Dictation Lesson	pp. 238-241 *(Home Education)*

GEOGRAPHY

Semester	First	Second
Text	*Answer Atlas* *Student Bible Atlas* *Atlas of United States History* *Historical Atlas of the World*	*Answer Atlas* *Student Bible Atlas* *Atlas of United States History* *Historical Atlas of the World*
Notes to Teacher	The atlases should be put to use every day during the teaching of all the subjects, bringing the child's attention not only to the locations of various places, but also basic geographic skills (cardinal directions, longitude, latitude, etc.).	
Philosophy of Teaching Geography	pp. 72-78 *(Home Education)* pp. 271-279 *(Home Education)* pp. 224-230 *(Philosophy of Education)*	
Example of Geography Lesson	pp. 347-351 *(School Education)*	
Example of Narration	pp. 274-275 *(School Education)* p. 282 *(School Education)* pp. 284-285 *(School Education)* pp. 290-291 *(School Education)*	
Example of Narration Questions	p. 310 *(School Education)* pp. 322-324 *(School Education)*	

GRAMMAR

Semester	First	Second
Test	*Simply Grammar*	*Simply Grammar*
Coursework	pp. 1-80	pp. 81-160
Notes to Teacher	The work in this discipline should include instruction beginning with the whole and moving then to the part. (". . . it is better that the child begin with the *sentence,* and not with the parts of speech; that is, that he should learn a little of what is called *analysis* of sentences before he learns to parse . . .") Using the text, the weaknesses of grammar that the children demonstrate in their compositions and written work will be addressed.	
Philosophy of Teaching Grammar	p. 296 *(Home Education)* pp. 209-211 *(Philosophy of Education)*	
Example of Grammar Lesson	pp. 342-343 *(School Education)* pp. 296-300 *(Home Education)*	
Example of Narration	pp. 296-297 *(School Education)*	
Example of Narration Questions	p. 310 *(School Education)* pp. 324-325 *(School Education)*	

HANDWORK

Semester	First	Second
Text	*336 Ten-Minute Quilt Blocks*	*Making and Decorating Your Own Paper*
Notes to Teacher	The work in this discipline should include one individual and one corporate project for each handicraft.	
Philosophy of Teaching Handwork	pp. 315-316 *(Home Education)*	

HANDWRITING

Semester	First	Second
Text	*Spencerian System of Practical Penmanship Book 2*	*Spencerian System of Practical Penmanship Book 3*
Notes to Teacher	The work in this discipline should include instruction in the aspects of beautiful writing; correct posture, proper hand position, correct formation of letters, etc. in order to train the hand to clearly communicate thought through the pen.	
Philosophy of Teaching Handwriting	p. 160 *(Home Education)* pp. 233-238 *(Home Education)* pp. 239-240 *(Home Education)*	

MATHEMATICS

Semester	First	Second
Text	*Mathematics Power Learning for Children Book 2*	*Mathematics Power Learning for Children Book 2*
	Mathematics Power Learning for Children Workbook 2	*Mathematics Power Learning for Children Workbook 2*
	Mathematics Power Learning for Children Workbook 2 Answer Key	*Mathematics Power Learning for Children Workbook 2 Answer Key*
	Mathematics Power Learning for Children Charts Book	*Mathematics Power Learning for Children Charts Book*
	A Most Incredibly Efficient Pathway Through Arithmetic Tape I of IV	*A Most Incredibly Efficient Pathway Through Arithmetic Tape I of IV*
	A Most Incredibly Efficient Pathway Through Arithmetic Tape II of IV	*A Most Incredibly Efficient Pathway Through Arithmetic Tape II of IV*
	Everyday Mathematics Teacher's Manual Volume A	*Everyday Mathematics Teacher's Manual Volume B*
	Everyday Mathematics Teacher's Reference Manual Grades K-3	*Everyday Mathematics Teacher's Reference Manual Grades K-3*
	Everyday Mathematics Journal 1	*Everyday Mathematics Journal 2*
Notes to Teacher	The work in this discipline should include student mastery of mathematical concepts through the use of demonstration, narration, and problem solving.	
Philosophy of Teaching Mathematics	pp. 230-233 *(Philosophy of Education)* pp. 253-264 *(Home Education)*	
Example of Narration Questions	p. 312 *(School Education)* pp. 317-318 *(School Education)* pp. 327-328 *(School Education)*	

RECITATION

Notes to Teacher	The work in this discipline should include the following:
	• 2 Psalms or Proverbs according to curriculum • an Old Testament passage (10-15 verses) • a New Testament passage (10-15 verses) • 6 poems from a book of verse • a history passage The recitation passages should be chosen from the books set in each semester from the disciplines of study, selecting those worthy of thought and language.
Philosophy of Teaching Recitation	pp. 222-226 *(Home Education)*

PLANNING LESSONS

As we look at preparing and planning lessons, it is worthy to bear in mind the difference between a process of education and a system of education. This lesson planning process was created with the educator in mind—that he/she would participate in "an applied philosophy of education" that considers the child as a person, knowledge as divine, and habits as life-giving tools acquired by training. The teachers at Ambleside Schools use the following lesson plan to organize their thinking and preparation for each of the disciplines.

Instructional Area	Discipline	Avenue	Ideas	Assimilation	Response

Instructional Area

Each instructional area listed on the timetable requires some deliberate thought and planning. As we are eager to apply a particular philosophy, we bear in mind these principles in relating to the student and the area of study.

Discipline

The function of parents and teachers is to help the child do what he lacks the power to compel himself to do. The persistent effort of training in habit becomes a habit in itself as educators begin the work of setting high expectations for relationships, whether in regard to habits of mind or moral habits. (See pages 135-168 in *Home Education*.) The educator looks at a particular area of study and clearly states the expectations in relating to both knowledge (attention, perfect execution, accuracy, etc.) and also the relationships with teacher and others (integrity, respect, courtesy, etc.). These expectations are stated and explained deliberately in the beginnings of courses and when there is a need for them to be addressed formally. Otherwise, they are enforced by the instructor's presence, with natural consequences for slipshod work and discourteous behaviors.

Avenue

The mind feeds upon ideas, and ideas are freely sown in books and things that are not predigested, prescribed, or diluted. Charlotte Mason terms these resources as "living" in that they provide nourishment for the mind, allowing it to grow, develop, and exercise, providing real and valuable knowledge. The question to the educator is, What direct avenue am I providing in this lesson to nourish the minds of my students? The direct avenue to knowledge includes text, music, pictures, maps, film, manipulative materials, and so on.

Ideas

The living books and living things provide a direct avenue into the mind of the student through the realm of ideas. These ideas are assimilated and understood in the mind of the student, informing the conscience. "A single idea may be a possession so precious in itself, so fruitful that the parent/teacher cannot fitly allow the child's selection of ideas to be a matter of chance; his lessons should furnish him with such ideas as shall make for his further education" (*Home Education*, page 174). It is necessary for the instructor to express a few ideas that might initially inform, but as the learning takes place, ideas will unfold and reproduce themselves in teacher and student alike. In the disciplines of literature, science, and history, ideas are readily seen. However, it is equally important that the instructional areas of mathematics, reading, and grammar bear ideas that would inspire and generate further thinking.

Assimilation

Let the child supply both the question and the answer through narration after a single reading or hearing. Narration allows the mind to formulate what happened first, what next, and then the idea that struck him is now supported by a context. In order to participate in thinking, discussion, and activities, the student must have a base of thought on the matter at hand. This thought is perceived and the meaning of it understood through the work of narration. Narration takes place after reading, seeing, and hearing. It is a retelling of sorts that is sometimes preceded by a direct question followed by a sequence of information and other times by a general retelling from start to finish of what was read, seen, or heard.

Response

It has been said that if one cannot write or speak about a matter, one does not know. In response to the work that has gone on before, the educator may aid understanding and further thought through discussion, recitation, or an activity that allows the student to be a producer of knowledge, not just a consumer. Not all lessons are followed by a response that includes tangible evidence of what was learned. Some are just followed by a response in which the mind and heart are at work, noticeably unseen!

ASSESSMENT AND EVALUATION OF STUDENTS' LEARNING

Students are expected to give attention and effort each school day. All students are active participants in the learning process and are called upon to narrate and discuss the readings, observations, activities, or lectures at hand throughout the day. They are also expected to produce their knowledge of a subject by way of written narrations, compositions, drawings, diagrams, maps, charts, and so on. This work is kept in student notebooks and copybooks, which are accessible to the parents at any time. Teachers are evaluating the students daily in areas of comprehension, skillfulness, habit development, and relationships. Knowing that learning consists of an orientation in both a process and a product, teachers are looking for individual student growth within the desired course expectations. Teachers communicate to the parents regarding their child(ren) in the following ways:

Parent/Teacher Conferences

Parent/teacher conferences are held twice a year to inform the parents concerning their child's progress or lack thereof in the varied relationships of knowledge, authority, peers, and self. Both parents are requested to attend these conferences and come with the intention of moving toward growth and building strategies in the areas in need of development.

Report Cards

Report cards are issued twice a year as a written record of the student's growth in his relationship with knowledge and his relationships with self and others. This is a narrative report, rather than one marked with numbers and letters.

Examinations

Examinations are given at the end of each semester over a week's time in the mornings. Students are dismissed at noon during this week so that teachers can read the examinations and remark on them. The exams, covering aspects of the semester's study in each subject, consist of broad questions in the inspirational subjects and more specific questioning as well as demonstration of specific skills in the disciplinary subjects. Younger students dictate their answers, which are scribed for them; older students write out their answers. Exams are evaluated and remarked upon. These results and the exams are returned to the parents and later filed in the student's permanent record.

AN EDUCATED CHILD

It is the hope of every teacher and every parent that the children who have been entrusted to them for a school year or for a lifetime would be characterized as educated. What must it mean for a child to be educated? The educational panoply is before us in the way of learning styles, whole language, standardized learning, unit studies, accelerated programs, hands-on learning, ability grouping, core curriculum, great books, and so on, almost amounting to every way in getting at what it means for a child "to know." And when he still does not know, there is yet another untapped resource to explore. For we are looking for a system we can "lock into" that will guarantee an educated child.

These ideas are devised into systems, which Charlotte Mason described as "a grain of knowledge in a gallon of warm diluent." She did not see the remedy in a devised system, but in a method of education. This method would allow the educator to have an end in mind and make step-by-step progress toward this end. Mason devised an educational philosophy built on the premise whereby a child will get knowledge and by knowledge grow and become more of a person. The product of this education should be:

• A person who displays the absence of self-consciousness, self-conceit, and vanity, who has an unconscious obedience to the necessity of putting duties before rights. (*School Education*, pp. 86-90, 103-112).

• A person who has a singleness of purpose and motives (*A Philosophy of Education*, pp. 128-137).

• A person who has absolute attention (*A Philosophy of Education*, pp. 72-79).

• A person who is a laborer and has absolute integrity in thoughtful, careful work (*School Education*, pp. 37-38).

• A person who is at home with a vast number of thoughts and things (*A Philosophy of Education*, pp. 31-32).

• A person who sees learning as a pursuit and a source of happiness for a lifetime (*School Education*, pp. 245-246).

• A person who develops new interests and finds enjoyment in mental, physical, spiritual, and aesthetic endeavors (*School Education*, pp. 79-83, 222-226).

• A person who displays an elevation in character and conducts himself or herself on principles guided by conscience (*Home Education*, pp. 329-352).

• A person who is more concerned with other people's rights and his or her own duties toward others than with the claims of self (*Parents and Children*, pp. 265, 287-290).

The education that provides for personhood in each individual is not one that relies upon systems and programs, but one that considers the full meaning of a child as a person and a child as a man or woman. Let us not forfeit fullness of life for ourselves or for the children by neglecting the natural desire and design of persons, considering this vast inheritance before us all.

Resources

Many of the books by or about Charlotte Mason are no longer available from their original publishers. However some have been republished and may be obtained from the sources listed here.

Books by Charlotte Mason
> The Original Home School Series
> *Home Education: Training/Educating Children Under 9*
> *Parents and Children: The Role of the Parent in the Education of the Child*
> *School Education: Developing a Curriculum*
> *Ourselves: Improving Character and Conscience*
> *Formation of Character: Shaping the Child's Personality*
> *A Philosophy of Education*
> (Order from Christian Book Distributors, www.christianbook.com or

phone 1-800-247-4784.)

Books about Charlotte Mason
> Essex Cholmondeley, *The Story of Charlotte Mason*
> (Currently available from Ambleside School, 106 S. Edison St.,

Fredericksburg, TX 78624, 830-990-9059 and from Child Light, P. O. Box 59, Petersfield, Hampshire GU32 3YL, England.)

Contact the authors at:
> Dr. Jack Beckman
> Department of Education
> Covenant College
> 14049 Scenic Highway
> Lookout Mountain, GA 30750

Bobby Scott
Perimeter School
9500 Medlock Bridge Road
Duluth, GA 30097
school@perimeter.org; www.childlightschools.org

Maryellen St. Cyr
Ambleside School of Fredericksburg
106 South Edison Street
Fredericksburg, TX 78624
Tel 830-990-9059; Fax 830-990-9065; www.amblesideschools.org

Notes

Preface

1. PNEU stands for Parents' National Education Union, formed by Charlotte Mason for the advancement of her teaching principles and practices. The object of the society was the study of the laws of education as they apply to the four aspects of education—the physical, mental, moral, and religious upbringing of children. Her immediate and lifelong work was always, in the first place, for parents and children. (Essex Cholmondeley, *The Story of Charlotte Mason* [London: J. M. Dent & Sons, 1960]. The book is currently available from Ambleside School, 106 S. Edison St., Fredericksburg, TX 78624, 830-990-9059, and from Child Light, P. O. Box 59, Petersfield, Hampshire GU32 3YL, England.

2. "Man" is used generically, representing all of mankind, i.e., man, woman, boy, and girl.

3. Charlotte Mason, *Home Education* (London: Kegan Paul, Trench, Trubner, 1896, 1930).

4. Charlotte Mason, *A Philosophy of Education* (London: J. M. Dent, 1954; Wheaton, Ill.: Tyndale House, 1989), 80.

Chapter One
The Value of Charlotte Mason's Work for Today

1. The book about the school is titled *Summerhill* by A. S. Neil.

2. *De rigueur*—roughly translated as the *only* way for something to take place, socially obligatory.

3. From her official obituary in *The Times* in 1955: "As private secretary to Miss Mason and secretary to the House of Education and to the Parents' Union School, she played a part second only to Miss Mason in building up the PNEU movement." From her friends: "How much more could we, who knew and loved her, add!"

4. From "Children Up to School Age and Beyond" by Elsie Kitching. Booklet published by the PNEU.

5. Elizabeth Raikes, *Dorothea Beale of Cheltenham* (London: Archibald Constable, 1908).

6. John 17:15-16.

7. "Give children such hold upon vital truths, and at the same time such an outlook upon current thought that they shall be landed on the safe side of the controversies of their day, open to truth in however new a light presented." From Charlotte Mason, *Parents and Children,* in Charlotte Mason's Original Homeschooling Series (Union, Maine: Charlotte Mason Research and Supply Co., 1993).

8. Robert Baden-Powell, *Aids to Scouting* (London: Gale & Polden Ltd., 1899). The book, written to provide training exercises in character and initiative for soldiers, came to Miss Mason's notice in 1905.

9. The "umbrella" school and organization for Charlotte Mason schools all over the world. It was from here, Low Nook, that the curriculum was constantly revised, updated with new books, and examinations prepared and sent out to pupils and external examiners. The staff also sent out the study programs to many hundreds of PNEU schools and home schools that used them around the globe. It was also where all the correspondence relating to children, parents, schools, and educational publishing was dealt with. The organization had carefully evolved under Miss Mason and Miss Kitching's clear guidance and was the forerunner of the PNEU office in London later on.

10. As I list qualities shared by children everywhere, of course there are children who suffer from emotional or learning difficulties and don't enjoy normal experiences. Speech doesn't come easily for one; another has limbs that don't respond to the brain, and so on. However, usually these are details; as *persons* our needs are the same.

11. From H. E. Marshall, *Our Island Story* (London, Edinburgh: TC and EC Jack,1909).

12. *The Children's Bible* (Tain, Rosshire, IV20 1TW Scotland: Christian Focus Publishing Ltd., Geanie's House, 1996).

13. *The Children's Story Bible* (Grand Rapids, Mich.: Eerdmans, 1989).

14. A most helpful book for adults is *True Heroism in a World of Celebrity Counterfeits* by Dick Keyes (Colorado Springs: NavPress, 1995).

15. Marion Berry, *I Buy a School* (London: Avon Books, 1996), 197.

CHAPTER TWO

THE CHILD IS A PERSON

1. Susan Schaeffer Macaulay, *For the Children's Sake* (Wheaton, Ill.: Crossway Books, 1984), 12-13.

2. Charlotte Mason, *A Philosophy of Education* (London: J. M. Dent, 1954; Wheaton, Ill.: Tyndale House, 1989), 14.
3. "A person is not built up from without but from within, that is, he is *living*, and all external educational appliances and activities which are intended to mould his character are decorative and not vital." Ibid., 23.
4. Charlotte Mason, *School Education* (London: Kegan Paul, Trench, Trubner & Co., 1929), 245.
5. Mason, *A Philosophy of Education*, 44.
6. Charlotte Mason, *Parents and Children* (Union, Maine: Charlotte Mason Research and Supply Co., 1993), 253.
7. Mason, *School Education*, 130.
8. Mason, *A Philosophy of Education*, 46.
9. Al Wolters in his book *Creation Regained* reminds the reader that the image of God in man and woman was not obliterated by the Fall, but was indeed broken. The child is now a broken image-bearer, pulled by the forces of sin and grace in all of life.
10. Mason, *School Education*, 146.
11. Maryellen St. Cyr is another of the major contributors to this book.
12. Mason, *A Philosophy of Education*, 238.
13. Ibid., 69.
14. Ibid., 71.
15. Ibid., 73-74.
16. Ibid., 74.
17. Ibid., 80.
18. Charlotte Mason, *Home Education* (London: Kegan Paul, Trench, Trubner, 1896, 1930), 330.

CHAPTER THREE
FOUR PILLARS OF EDUCATION

1. Charlotte Mason, *Parents and Children* (Union, Maine: Charlotte Mason Research and Supply Co., 1993), 32-33.
2. Ibid., 36. Appetency is a longing or desire for something (*Oxford English Dictionary*).
3. Ibid., 36-37.
4. Rosemary Sutcliff, *Blue Remembered Hills* (New York: Farrar Straus Giroux, 1983), 83-85.
5. Marion Berry, *I Buy a School* (London: Avon Books, 1996), 124.
6. Ibid., 148.

7. Mason, *Parents and Children*, 48.

8. Charlotte Mason, *Home Education Series*, Preface, Vol. 1 (Wheaton, Ill.: Tyndale House), 5.

9. Essex Cholmondeley, *The Story of Charlotte Mason* (London: J. M. Dent & Sons, 1960; Petersfield, Hants: Child Light).

10. Alfie Kohn, "The Big Score," *Newsweek*, September 6, 1999, 47.

11. Nancy Sizer, "Tests Are an Easy Way Out," *Newsweek*, September 6, 1999, 51.

12. Charlotte Mason, *Home Education* (London: Kegan Paul, Trench, Trubner, 1896, 1930), 176.

13. John K. Rosemond, *Affirmative Parenting*, Vol. 3, No. 6, 1999.

14. Mason, *Home Education*, 23.

15. Ibid., 42.

16. Ibid.

17. Ibid., 177.

18. Mason, *Home Education*, 12-16.

19. Ibid., 81.

20. Charlotte Mason, *A Philosophy of Education* (London: J. M. Dent, 1954; Wheaton, Ill.: Tyndale House, 1989), 96.

21. Ibid.

22. Ibid.

23. Mason, *Home Education*, 174.

24. Ibid., 177.

25. Ibid., 66-67.

26. Ibid., 67.

27. Charlotte Mason, *School Education* (London: Kegan Paul, Trench, Trubner & Co., 1929), 29.

28. Ibid.

29. Mason, *Home Education*, 98.

30. Ibid., 99.

31. Ibid., 330.

32. Ibid., 97, 106.

33. Mason, *School Education*, 120.

34. Mason, *Home Education*, 149-160.

35. Mason, *School Education*, 135.

36. Mason, *Home Education*, 160-168.

37. Mason, *School Education*, 101-112.

38. Ibid., 140-144.

39. Mason, *Home Education*, 132-133.
40. Ibid., 103.
41. Ibid., 123.
42. Ibid., 318.
43. Ibid., 100.
44. Ibid., 109.
45. Mason, *A Philosophy of Education*, 130.
46. Ibid., 131.
47. Ibid., 134.
48. Ibid., 136.
49. Mason, *Home Education*, 141.
50. Ibid., 330.
51. Mason, *School Education*, Preface.
52. Mason, *Home Education*, 173.
53. Mason, *A Philosophy of Education*.
54. Ibid., 23.
55. Mason, *School Education*, 95.
56. Mason, *A Philosophy of Education*, 18.
57. Ibid., 303.
58. Ibid., 109.
59. Cholmondeley, *Story of Charlotte Mason*, 156.
60. Mason, *A Philosophy of Education*, 20.
61. Renate Nummela Caine and Geoffrey Caine, *Making Connections: Teaching and the Human Brain* (Reading, Mass.: Addison-Wesley, 1991, 1994).
62. Ibid., 303; Mason, *Home Education*, 177.
63. Mason, *School Education*, 334-336.
64. Collier Schorr, *The Essential Norman Rockwell* (New York: Harry N. Abrams, 1999), 26.
65. Ibid., 55.
66. Mason, *A Philosophy of Education*, 239.
67. Susan Schaeffer Macaulay, *For the Children's Sake* (Wheaton, Ill.: Crossway Books, 1984), 87.
68. Mason, *Parents and Children*, 36.
69. Mason, *A Philosophy of Education*, 36.
70. Mason, *Parents and Children*, 131.
71. Schaeffer, *For the Children's Sake*, 83.

72. Cholmondeley, *Story of Charlotte Mason*, 102.

73. William Wordsworth, "The Prelude," in William Wordsworth, *The Complete Poetical Works* (London: Macmillan, 1888).

74. "Education as the Science of Relations," a paper by Charlotte Mason read to the Sixth Annual Conference of the PNEU, May 6-9, 1902, London. *The Parents' Review* 1902, 485-487.

75. Mason, *School Education*, 95.

76. Cholmondeley, *Story of Charlotte Mason*, 188.

77. Donovan Graham, "A Biblical Yardstick for Teaching" (Lookout Mountain, Ga.: Covenant College), unpublished.

78. Mason, *A Philosophy of Education*, 114.

79. Ibid., 117.

80. Mason, *School Education*, 161-162.

81. Mason, *A Philosophy of Education*, 62-63.

82. Mason, *School Education*, 65-66.

83. Cholmondeley, *Story of Charlotte Mason*, 199.

CHAPTER FOUR
DISTINCTIVES OF A CHARLOTTE MASON EDUCATION

1. Susan Schaeffer Macaulay, *For the Children's Sake* (Wheaton, Ill.: Crossway Books, 1984).

2. Charlotte Mason, *School Education* (London: Kegan Paul, Trench, Trubner & Co., 1929), 168.

3. Ibid., 263.

4. Charlotte Mason, *A Philosophy of Education* (London: J. M. Dent, 1954; Wheaton, Ill.: Tyndale House, 1989), 305.

5. See *Books Children Love* by Elizabeth Wilson (Wheaton, Ill.: Crossway Books, 2002).

6. Essex Cholmondeley, *The Story of Charlotte Mason* (London: J. M. Dent & Sons, 1960; Petersfield, Hants: Child Light).

7. Charlotte Mason, *Home Education* (London: Kegan Paul, Trench, Trubner, 1896, 1930), 231.

8. Cholmondeley, *Story of Charlotte Mason*.

9. Barry Sanders, *A Is for Ox: The Collapse of Literacy and the Rise of Violence in an Electronic Age* (New York: Vintage Books, 1994), 46.

10. Ibid.

11. Lynn K. Rhodes and Nancy L. Shanklin, *Windows into Literacy* (Portsmouth, N. H.: Heinemann, 1993).

12. Yetta M. Goodman, Dorothy J. Watson, Carolyn L. Burke, *Reading Miscue Inventory: Alternative Procedures* (New York: Doubleday, 1987), 37-59.

13. Parker J. Palmer, *The Courage to Teach: Exploring the Inner Landscape of a Teacher's Life* (San Francisco: Jossey Bass, 1998), 54.

14. H. W. Household, "Teaching Methods of Miss Mason," booklet, 1920s, 4.

15. Mason, *Home Education.*

16. Ibid.

17. Ibid.

18. Mason, *A Philosophy of Education.*

19. Mason, *Home Education*, 173.

20. Mason, *School Education*, 169.

21. Charlotte Mason, *Parents and Children* (Union, Maine: Charlotte Mason Research and Supply Co., 1993), 263.

22. Mason, *School Education*, 226.

23. Mason, *Home Education*, 215-216.

24. Ibid., 216.

25. Mason, *A Philosophy of Education*, 51.

26. Ibid., 260.

27. Ibid., 261.

28. Indicating those books, pieces of music, or things of acknowledged excellence that are outstanding and remarkable for a wider vision of humanity.

29. Mason, *A Philosophy of Education*, 271.

30. Mason, *Home Education*, 247.

31. Ibid.

32. Ibid.

33. Ibid., 297.

34. Mason, *A Philosophy of Education*, 10.

35. Mason, *Home Education*, 241.

36. Ibid., 242.

37. Ibid., 241.

38. Ibid., 241-242.

39. Mason, *A Philosophy of Education*, 192.

40. Ibid., 183.

41. Ibid., 209.

42. Mason, *School Education*, 130.

43. Charlotte Mason, *Ourselves: Improving Character and Conscience*, Part II (Wheaton, Ill., Tyndale House, 1989), 71.

44. Mason, *Home Education*, 223.

45. Mason, *Ourselves,* Part II, 71.

46. Mason, *A Philosophy of Education*, 274.

47. Ibid., 245.

48. Peggy O'Brien, "Doing Shakespeare," *English Journal*, Vol. 82, No. 4 (1993): 40-45.

49. Barbara Engen with Joy Campbell, *Elementary, My Dear Shakespeare,* (Salt Lake City: Market Master Books, 1988).

50. Mason, *A Philosophy of Education*, 183.

51. Shakespeare, *The Merchant of Venice*, I.ii.12.

52. Shakespeare, *The Winter's Tale*, I.ii.258.

53. Shakespeare, *Richard II*, II.iii.15.

54. Mason, *A Philosophy of Education*, 178.

55. Macaulay, *For the Children's Sake*, 108.

56. Mason, *A Philosophy of Education*, 295.

57. Ibid., 231.

58. Mason, *Home Education*, 254.

59. Mason, *A Philosophy of Education*, 157.

60. Mason, *School Education*, 237-238.

61. Mason, *A Philosophy of Education*, 223.

62. Ibid., 256.

63. Mason, *School Education*, 237.

64. Mason, *A Philosophy of Education*, 40.

65. Ibid., 222-223.

66. Ibid., 238-239.

67. Ibid., 214.

68. Ibid.

69. Ibid., 216.

70. Ibid., 217.

71. Mason, *Home Education*, 251.

72. Ibid., 343.

73. Ibid., 249.

74. Ibid., 248.

75. Ibid., 252.

76. Mason, *A Philosophy of Education*, 165.

77. Mason, *Home Education*, 347.

78. E. K. Manders, *The Gateway to Charlotte Mason* (London: Parents' National Educational Union, c. 1930s), 20.
79. Mason, *Home Education*, 315.
80. Mason, *A Philosophy of Education*, 253.
81. Ibid., 48.
82. 1 Timothy 4:8; Mason, *A Philosophy of Education*, 72, 255.
83. Mason, *School Education*, 105-107.
84. Ibid.
85. Ibid.
86. Ibid., 112.
87. Mason, *A Philosophy of Education*, 328.
88. Ibid., 31.
89. Ibid.

Chapter Five
Broader Application of Charlotte Mason's Teaching Principles

1. Marion Berry, *I Buy a School* (London: Avon Books, 1996).
2. Francis A. Schaeffer—the theologian, philosopher, and writer—was Susan Schaeffer Macaulay's father.
3. This curriculum contrasts with the easy-to-read type of "educational package" so available today. These are to be avoided.
4. Each person gathers a few sticks. All go to the same side of a bridge, and each drops one stick into the water—all at the same time. Then they rush to the other side to see which stick emerges first.
5. Jesus said, "I am the way, the truth and the life."
6. Material covered in this activity can be found in *Christianity Is Jewish* by Edith Schaeffer. This concept can be expanded with the biblical stories told chronologically.

Index